Alfred Heales

The History of Tanridge Priory, Surrey

And Some Account of the Canons Regular of the Order of St. Augustine, Commonly

Called the Austin Canons

Alfred Heales

The History of Tanridge Priory, Surrey
And Some Account of the Canons Regular of the Order of St. Augustine, Commonly Called the Austin Canons

ISBN/EAN: 9783337326197

Printed in Europe, USA, Canada, Australia, Japan

Cover: Foto ©ninafisch / pixelio.de

More available books at **www.hansebooks.com**

THE HISTORY

OF

TANRIDGE PRIORY,

SURREY;

AND SOME ACCOUNT OF THE

Canons Regular of the Order of St. Augustine,

COMMONLY CALLED

THE AUSTIN CANONS.

BY

Major ALFRED HEALES,

F.S.A., F.R.S.L., Hon. F.R.I.B.A.

LONDON:
PRINTED BY ROWORTH & CO. LIMITED,
NEWTON STREET, HIGH HOLBORN.
1885.

PREFACE.

On the occasion of a visit by the Surrey Archæological Society to Tanridge, the Council asked me to supply some account of the Priory: subsequent research was necessary in order to present the subject in a complete form for the purpose of publication; then occurred the suggestion that some account of the Inhabitants of the Priory would be desirable as a supplement; that led to notes respecting the Austin Canons, who (like other monastic bodies) have been very much neglected by English writers; and so a ten-minutes' Paper expanded into the present Work.

A. H.

Streatham;
October, 1885.

LIST OF AUTHORITIES AND WORKS

QUOTED FROM OR DIRECTLY REFERRED TO.

Manuscript.

Assize Rolls; Surrey, 43 Henry III, M $\left\{\frac{6}{1}\right\}$ 5.

Augmentation Office; Deeds of Sale of Fee-Farm Rents.
,,   Miscellaneous Books, No. 105.
,,   ,,   No. 244.
,,   ,,   No. 406.

Bodleian Library; Laud MS. 723.
British Museum; Additional MS. 2044.
,,   ,,   6167.
,,   ,,   6168.
,,   ,,   6169.

Cotton MS.; *Cleopatra*, C. VII.
,,   ,,   C. IX.
,,   *Tiberius*, III.
,,   *Vespasian*, D. I.
,,   ,,   F. IX.

Harleian MS.; 1777.
,,   4785.
,,   4786.

Inquisition *ad quod damnum*, 24 Edw. III; Surrey, No. 21.
,,   *post mortem*, 12 Edw. I; No. 49.
,,   ,,   28 Edw. I; No. 69.

Ministers' Accounts, 28 & 29 Henry VIII; Surrey, No. 108.

Patent Roll; 13 Edward I, m. 16.
     ,,   30 Edward I, m. 3.
     ,,   25 Edward III, m. 12.
Pedes finium; 10 Henry III, Surrey, No. 74.
     ,,   19   ,,   ,,   No. 181.
     ,,   47   ,,   ,,   Case 2, No. 177.
     ,,   49   ,,   ,,   ,,   ,,

Winchester Diocesan Register; *Asser.*
          ,,   ,,   *Fox.*
          ,,   ,,   *Langton.*
          ,,   ,,   *Orleton.*
          ,,   ,,   *Stratford.*
          ,,   ,,   *Wayneflete.*
          ,,   ,,   *Wodelok.*
          ,,   ,,   *Wykeham.*

Printed Works.

ACTS OF PARLIAMENT:—27 Henry VIII, cap. 27; cap. 28.

BERINGTON; *Literary History of Middle Ages.*
BIRCH & JENNER; *Illuminations in British Museum.*
BRAYLEY; *History of Surrey.*

Calendar of Letters and Papers, temp. Henry VIII. (Record Off. Publ.)
CASSAN; *Lives of Bishops of Winchester.*
Constitutions of Pope Clement V. (Basle Ed., 1476.)
COX, J. C.; *How to write History of Parish.*
CUTTS; *Turning Points of English Church History.*

DIXON; *History of Church of England from Abolition of Roman Jurisdiction.*
DUCANGE; *Glossarium.*
DUGDALE; *Monasticon Anglicanum.*

FOSBROOKE; *British Monachism.*
FOSS; *Judges of England.*
FOX; *English Monks and Monasteries.*

LIST OF AUTHORITIES AND WORKS.

GODWIN; *Handbook of Archæology.*

HALLIWELL-PHILLIPS; *Archæological Dictionary.*

JAMESON; *Legends of the Monastic Orders.*

LYNDWODE; *Provinciale.*

MAITLAND; *Dark Ages.*
MANNING & BRAY; *History of Surrey.*
MIGNE; *Patrologiæ cursus;* S. Augustin.

Originalia, 30 Edward I. (Record Off. Ed.)

Piers Plowman's Crede. (Early English Text Society.)

Surrey Archæological Society; *Collections,* Vol. III.
Surtees Society; *Priory of Hexham,* Vol. I.

TANNER; *Notitia Monastica.*
Taxation by Pope Nicholas IX. (Record Off. Ed.)
TAYLOR, ISAAC; *Transmission of Ancient Books.*

WALCOTT; *Church and Conventual Arrangement.*
WEAVER; *Funeral Monuments.*
WILKINS; *Concilia.*

TANRIDGE PRIORY,

AND

THE AUSTIN CANONS.

By Major ALFRED HEALES, f.s.a., f.r.s.l., hon. a.r.i.b.a.

ON commencing the study of local topography one looks first to the work of the old County Historian, especially in Surrey where we possess a book of high eminence on account of the vast research by its authors, which becomes fully manifest only to the comparatively few archæologists who themselves enter on such researches; but very generally some additional facts remain to be gleaned. In the case of Tanridge Priory, the history given by Manning and Bray is limited to half a folio page, with the addition of a list of Priors. Their notes from the Winchester Diocesan Registers are full and careful, but further and fuller information, chiefly obtained from other sources, was still obtainable and will aid in furnishing the reader with what may fairly be termed the first attempt at a history of the Priory.

It seemed to the Writer that it would supply a desirable sequence to the history of the Priory if he gave some account of those who dwelt there, how they lived and occupied themselves, and by what rules they were bound; and more especially, because so very little is generally known respecting monastic life in England that the subject is practically a new one: there exists no special history of any of the Monastic Orders in this country, and there seems to have been little written by other authors than Dugdale and Fosbroke, whose works are rather of a general than a special nature.

In the limited space which is here fairly available for the purpose, it would have been absurd to attempt to give any general history of the Order, but the endeavour has been rather to contribute some notes towards a subject which one may hope will some day receive a merited attention.

Only five years ago, it was remarked by an archæologist of much research and learning,[1] that the English Abbeys or Priories whose history can be said to be exhaustively written, could certainly be counted on the fingers of both hands; a round dozen would cover them now.

In the following pages, the names of places and persons are spelt as they are spelt in the document therein referred to, and the dates of the years are given as commencing on the first day of January; thus, instead of printing 12th March, 1308-9, it is put according to modern reckoning, 1309. At the end will be found an Appendix of original documents, selected from the rest on account of their importance, or as illustrative of the forms used in such cases.

It may also be noted that the authorities here given were directly referred to; in the case of any being taken through the medium of Manning and Bray the fact is so stated.

OF THE PRIORY.

THE Charitable Institution known by the name of Tanridge Priory (now commonly spelt Tandridge, with the supplemental *d* interpolated) was not originally monastic. The earliest existing record, which dates probably not very long after the foundation, speaks of it as the Hospital of St. James, in the Ville of Tanregge, with 3 priests, in perpetuity there serving God, and Confraters of the said Hospital.[2]

The nature of the institution was more nearly what we understand by the modern French "Hospice"—an asylum, or refuge, for the poor and needy—a home for those in want or sickness, served by the devotion of its staff, as distinguished from an Act of Parliament, Godless, workhouse where the object, but too generally, is a

---

[1] J. Chas. Cox, *How to write the History of a Parish.*

[2] In these preliminary remarks, it seems unnecessary to note the authorities which are fully referred to in the subsequent pages.

provision in the most stinted way against actual physical starvation: it was for the support and maintenance of the sick and poor, and wayfarers needing refuge.

Whether in consequence of the insufficiency for the purpose, of the funds provided, or from what other cause, and how or under what authority, there is no means of knowing, but the fact is clear that, within little more than a quarter and certainly less than half of a century after the foundation, the Hospital of St. James became a Priory of Canons Regular of the Order of St. Augustine, which Canons were commonly, for brevity's sake, called Austin Canons. In certain legal proceedings in 1306 it is spoken of as Collegiate,[1] and so in 1309;[2] in 1461 it is called the Priory of St. James, Tanrigge.[3]

The subsequent history of the Establishment, so far as it is practicable to be traced, will be seen by the present account deduced from the various and scattered records now existing: but a few of the more noteworthy points may be indicated as a preface.

The property of the House given at the time of its foundation, sometime about the year 1200, received occasional accretions, but apparently not to any very large extent, for we find that at the time of the Dissolution of Monasteries, between three and three and a-half centuries afterwards, the income was still quite moderate, though sufficing for the maintenance of the five Canons of the House: it does not appear that the number ever exceeded five. In 1263, an arrangement was made under which they bound themselves to provide a Chaplain, being one of their number, to celebrate daily for the benefit of a contributor and his family: and, nearly a century later, in 1351, a further gift was made to the House towards the support of a Canon-Chaplain to celebrate Divine Service daily for the Souls of all faithful departed, for ever.

Perhaps it was in consequence of the limited number of Canons (which, assuming five to have been usual,

---

[1] Winchester Register, *Wodelok*, fol. 40 v.
[2] Ibid., fols. 101 v and 110.
[3] Winchester Register, *Wayneflete*, I, fol. 68*.

would upon the decease of the Prior have left but four, who, unless unanimous, were therefore not unlikely to be evenly balanced in votes), but it repeatedly happened that, when there occurred a vacancy of the Head of the Priory, the Chapter of the House demitted to the Bishop their right of election, and requested him to undertake the duty of appointment to the vacancy, for that turn. On other occasions, whether from want of skill and care in fulfilling the formalities legally requisite, or whether from any desire on the part of the Diocesan to gradually acquire a permanent right of nomination one cannot tell; but the circumstance repeatedly did happen that when the election of a new Prior came before the Bishop for confirmation, he pronounced that the election was void for informality, and himself made the appointment; though, perhaps as a matter of policy, he appointed the individual who had been, as he stated, invalidly elected. And such appointments frequently turned out ill, as in the cases of John Hansard, who was, or became, incompetent to perform his office, and Philip de Wokingham, whose neglect and desertion of his office ultimately led to his deprivation. No other or more grave charges were at any time made against any Prior or member of the House: this should be borne in mind.

The Priory appears to have gone on its way steadily and quietly, as it should have done, without drawing upon itself any special attention; when called upon to appear in General Chapter it gave a proxy to some other Prior, and so appeared by its representative: the Prior was sometimes summoned to attend and take part in the Convocation of the Diocese.

Ultimately the Priory was suppressed, under the Act for the robbery and destruction of Religious Houses having an income under £200 per annum,[1] which was so easily passed that it almost immediately led to the robbery and destruction of all the others; and the property which had been during many centuries devoted by men of religious mind for Divine Service and

[1] Act 27 Henry VIII, cap. 28.

religious purposes, was in a few years squandered by the monarch upon his profligate pleasures.

The actual date of the foundation of the Priory is not known, but we can by a comparison of records and facts fix the period approximately. In a Deed dated the 17th June 1217,[1] Odo de Dammartin is referred to as the Founder, but not as being then deceased. The fragmentary pedigree of the Dammartin family[2] given by Manning and Bray[3] (from records to which they refer), states that Odo, son of William de Dammartin, lived in the reigns of Henry II (1154 to 1189) and Richard I (1189 to 1199)—dates which give a range of very nearly half a century; but it appears from another source that he was living at least as late as 1218. One of the witnesses to the next-mentioned Deed was living in 1198, while the Deed itself is, from internal evidence, prior to the Deed which we have placed after, and which was certainly executed between 1210 and 1222. We may therefore reasonably assume the date of foundation, as a matter of probability, to have been somewhere about the year 1200.[4]

The earliest existing record, as so frequently happened in early documents, has no date; it contains a grant for endowment of the Hospital of St. James in Tanregge, and the priests or confraters there serving God; and is evidently subsequent to the Deed of Foundation.[5] It runs to the following effect:—

To all Sons of Holy Mother Church to whom the

---

[1] Cartulary of Merton Priory: Cotton MS. *Cleopatra*, C. vii, fol. 86, referred to *post*.

[2] The family probably took its name from a place named Dammartin, now represented by a village about 35 miles N.E. from Paris.

[3] Manning and Bray, *History of Surrey*, II, p. 324.

[4] Odo de Dammartin was one of the witnesses to the endowment of Newark Priory (Dugdale, VI, p. 383), which Manning and Bray show was prior to 1204. (Manning and Bray, III, p. 110.)

[5] Referred to in Tanner's *Notitia Monastica*, and printed in Dugdale's *Monasticon*, VI, p. 604, from a MS. which he mentions as formerly in possession of Sir William Howard. I venture to reprint it in order to make my work complete in itself, so far as lies in my power. (Vide *Appendix*, I.)

present writing may come, Odo de Dammartin, son of William de Dammartin, Health. Be it known to you all that I have given and granted, and by this my present charter have confirmed, for the health of the souls of myself and my wife and my children, and for the souls of my father and mother, and my predecessors and successors, to God and the Hospital of St. James in the Ville of Tanregge, and three priests in perpetuity, there serving God, and Confraters of the said Hospital; all my land at Warlinggeham, in pure and perpetual alms, for the support and maintenance of the sick and poor, and wayfarers needing a refuge; together with a windmill, with all its pertinents without restriction; in crofts, pictlakes,[1] woods, plain, meadows, pastures, cornlands, ways, waters, marshes, hedges, enclosures, in common pastures, and in all liberties; To have and to hold entirely, peaceably, and free from all service and secular exaction due from me to the heirs of William de Hammes,[2] viz. xx shillings sterling and 2 gilt shoes of the price of six pence, or the sum of six pence annually, at two terms, that is to say, at Easter ten shillings and the shoes, and at the feast of St. Michael ten shillings, without fraud; and saving service so much as pertains to the fourth part of a knight's fee; for all services and demands. And I and my heirs are bound to defend and warrant the aforesaid land and gift and confirmation against all men and all women.[3] These being Witnesses — Ralph, Chaplain of Rigate; Henry, Chaplain; Hamon de Turbeville; Ralph Pimpe; Luke de Laundecote; Peter de Perefricht; William de Danmartin; Graland and Baldric, brothers; Peter de

---

[1] *Pictlakes*: evidently the same as *Pightell*, or *Pightle*; any small enclosed piece of land. (Halliwell.)

[2] William de Hamme obtained from the Abbey of Chertsey the grant of their Manor of Hamme, to him and his heirs for ever, at a rental of 20s. per annum. *Chertsey Leiger* (Manning and Bray, III, p. 214).

[3] This will be noted as an illustration of the well-known fact that women's rights in respect to land were far more extensive than they have become in more recent times.

Thaleuurthe; Ralph de Turneham; Ralph, parcarius; John Bolle; Nicholas de la Dene; and many others.

Another gift was made by the same liberal donor, a copy of which is also printed by Dugdale, and is to the following effect:—

Know all men present and future, that I, Odo de Dammartin, son of William de Dammartin, have, for my soul's health, given to God and the Hospital of St. James at Tanregge, all my relics and 2 silver cups to make a chalice and the vestments and all books and all other things of my chapel. Moreover, I have given to the aforesaid Hospital ix oxen, and one bull, and a sow and farrow, which are at Suevic (Southwark), reckoned at the value of xii oxen; which I have allotted to the said Hospital to be taken from the best of the oxen of my land. And that this my gift may be valid and assured I have confirmed it by my present Charter and seal. These being Witnesses:—Robert, Chaplain; William, Chaplain; Thomas de Wllst, Prior of Merton; Ralph Dean;[1] and many others.[2]

Thomas de Wllst was installed as Prior of Merton on the 11th November, 1218, and died previous to 12th September, 1222, on which day Letters Patent for the election of his successor were granted, and we are thereby enabled to fix the date very closely.

The document, previously referred to, in which Odo is spoken of as the Founder, is a Charter granted by Walter, Prior of Merton, the predecessor of Thomas, and is therefore necessarily antecedent to the last-mentioned Charter, and possibly to the first; but, perhaps, more probably coming between the two. It is dated the 17th June, 1217; and runs to the following effect:—

WALTER, prior of Merton and the Convent of the same place, to all the faithful of Christ who shall inspect these present letters, send greeting in the Lord. Be it known

---

[1] A Ralph de Dene is mentioned in a Fine, 7 Henry II, 1161; and on his inheritance, 10 Richard I, 1199. (Manning and Bray, II, 228.)

[2] Dugdale, *Monasticon*, VI, p. 604. (Vide *Appendix*, II.)

unto you all, that moved by the impulse of Divine piety, we have received and admitted, specially, into the fraternity of our house of Merton, Sir Odo de Dammartin the founder, and all the brothers and sisters, and all the benefactors of the Hospital of St. James of Tanridge; so that they shall have a share and mutual participation with ourselves, in all the prayers, alms-deeds, fastings, vigils, disciplines; in the celebration of Masses, in the ordinances and observances of religion, and in all other good acts and benefits, which are or shall be done in our House and in all our Religious Houses, for ever. In testimony of this fraternity we have caused our seal to be appended to the present writing. Farewell. Given in the year of our Lord 1217, on the 15th Kalend of July.[1]

The next record is that of a Charter executed by Odo, son of Odo de Danmertin, presumably after his father's death; whereby, for the health of his soul and the souls of his father and mother and ancestors and successors, he gave to God and the Hospital of St. James of Tanregge and the Brothers there serving God, a half-acre of land called "le Brome" in the Ville of Chepsted, which Alfrid "Soxere" held of him; together with the houses thereon: and he warranted it, &c. Witnessed by William de Danmertin, Robert Burnerd, Ralph de Pip^r., Robert son of Pagan, William de St. John, Peter de Talewrth, Adam de Talewrth, Eustace de Wlkest, William de Novatra, and many others. The MS. (which is an early collection of such matters) gives a drawing of the seal and counterseal to this Charter. Odo is represented on horseback, in chain mail, with a long sword and small heater-shaped seal bearing 2 fesses and a chief vair: legend, "Sigill: —d—Martin." The seal is circular. On the smaller counterseal is a shield bearing, vairy of 5, and on a chief a label of 3 points extending across the shield: legend "S. Evdonis de Danmartin" interrupted in 4 places by a leopard's head.[2]

---

[1] Cotton MS. *Cleopatra*, C. vii, fol. 86; No. 177. (Vide *Appendix*, III.)

[2] British Museum, Add. MS. 2044, fol. 114. (*Appendix*, IV.)

The next document is a final Concord or agreement made in the King's Court at Westminster, between the Prior of Tanridge and others, in the octave of the Purification of B. Mary, in the 10th year of King Henry III (1226), at Westminster, before Martin de Patershill,[1] Thomas de Muleton,[2] Thomas de Heiden,[3] Robert de Lexinton,[4] and Warin son of John,[5] Justices, and others of the King's faithful subjects there present: between John de Wauton, by Thomas de Grava on his behalf, and Alice, wife of the said John, by William de Kingestun on her behalf; and on the other part Thomas,[6] Prior of Tenrugg: concerning four score acres of wood with pertinents in Tenrugge about which was a suit between them in the said Court. It was agreed that the said John and Alice should give up and quit claim for themselves and the heirs of Alice, to the said Prior and his successors and the Church of Tenrugge, all right and claim which they had in the said four-score acres of wood with pertinents in perpetuity. And in consideration the Prior, for himself and his

[1] Martin de Pateshull was, in the year 1217, appointed by King Henry III to be a Justice, and thenceforward was remarkable amongst his colleagues for his singular activity: he was appointed to be Archdeacon of York in 1226, and Dean of St. Paul's two years later, but died 14th November, 1229. (Foss, *Judges of England*.)

[2] Thomas de Muleton was a member of a Lincolnshire family, and was Sheriff for that county during three years: he got into difficulties twice with King John during his troubled reign, but became Justice and Chief Justice under King Henry III, and died about 1240. (Foss.)

[3] Thomas de Heyden, called "Clericus noster" in Letters Patent, 4 John (1203). He acted as a Justiciar from the 3rd to 11th Henry III. (Foss.)

[4] Robert de Lexinton, a cleric, was a person of eminence, and acted as a Justice from 1220 till 1243, and died in 1250. He undertook the defence of various military posts, and enjoyed much royal favour. (Foss.)

[5] Warin, son of Fitz-Joel, is mentioned as one of the Justices Itinerant in 1224 and 1225. (Foss.)

[6] The name of Thomas as Prior at this date has not previously been recorded: the first Prior whose name is given by Dugdale, or Manning and Bray, is Walter who was installed in 1306, eighty years later.

successors, gave up to the said John and Alice and her heirs in perpetuity, the right to which the Prior was entitled by grant of Odo Danmartin the Elder, of mast[1] for 30 hogs in their wood, and also the right of chase with 13 dogs and 6 harriers or greyhounds, in the warren thereof, to which the Prior was entitled by gift of Odo Danmartin the younger.[2]

A final Concord was made in the King's Court at Bermundsey, in the quindena of St. Michael in the 19th year of King Henry III (1235), before William of York,[3] William de Insula,[4] Ralph of Norwich,[5] and Hugh de Playz,[6] Justices Itinerant: between Gillebert Oisel and Richalda his wife, plaintiffs, and Adam,[7] Prior of Tenrigge, defendant, concerning 16 acres of land with pertinents in Tenrigge. Whereon a Post Mortem Assize was held in the said Court. The said Gillebert and Richalda acknowledged the said land and pertinents to belong to the Prior and his Church of Tenrigge. And for this acknowledgment, fine, and concord, the Prior granted to them 9 acres of land with pertinents, namely those 9 acres of land which Robert de Shortehal lately held: To hold to them and the heirs of the said Richalda, of the Prior and his successors and the said Church in perpetuity, at an annual rental of 12 pence at the feast of St. Michael, for all service and demand. And moreover the Prior gave them half a mark of silver.[8]

---

[1] *Mast*, fruit of beech and oak trees.

[2] Pedes finium; 10 Henry III; Surrey, No. 74. (*Appendix*, V.) Unfortunately neither of the grants here referred-to are extant.

[3] William of York was Bishop of Salisbury; Justice Itinerant from 1227 to 1251, in which year he died, and was buried in his own cathedral. (Foss.)

[4] William de Insula obtained a good position under King John, and became a Justice Itinerant in 1224, and continued as such for nine years. (Foss.)

[5] Ralph of Norwich rendered considerable service to King John in Ireland; was a Justice of the Bench from 1230 to 1234. (Foss.)

[6] Not mentioned by Foss.

[7] This is the first time in which the name of Adam as Prior of Tanridge has appeared in print.

[8] Pedes finium, 19 Henry III; Surrey, No. 181. (*Appendix*, VI.)

By the Assize Rolls for the County, in the 43rd year of King Henry III (1258 and 1259), it appears that a trial took place upon a complaint that the Prior had enclosed a certain public pond in Warlingham where the people of the place had been accustomed to water their cattle, to the manifest injury of all. Which being proved, the Sheriff ordered the removal of the enclosure in sight of the Jury. And the Prior, who was present, was condemned for the transgression.[1]

In 1262-3 a final Concord was made in the King's Court at Geldeford, in the 15 days after St. Hilary in the 47th year of King Henry III. Before Martin de Littilbyry,[2] Walter de Bersted,[3] Geoffrey de Leukenore,[4] and Richard de Hemington, Justices Itinerant.[5] Between Humphrey,[6] Prior of Tanrigge, plaintiff, and Thomas de Warblington, defendant; concerning a messuage, 14 acres of land, and 12 acres of pasture, with pertinents in Tannerigge. And upon the suit before the Court the said Thomas acknowledged the tenements and pertinents to belong to the Prior and his church; that they should have them, of his gift, to hold to the Prior and his successors and church, of the said Thomas and his heirs, in free, pure, and perpetual alms, in perpetuity; and he warranted it accordingly, and free from all secular service and demand, against all men. And moreover the said Thomas, in addition, granted for himself and his heirs, to the Prior and his successors and church, a yearly payment of 20 shillings by equal

---

[1] Assize Rolls, Surrey; 43 Henry III, M $\left\{\frac{6}{1}\right\}$ 5, m. 5 d.

[2] Martin de Littilbyry or Littlebere, held an Assize in Kent in 1247 and became a Justiciar in 1261, and continued till 1272. (Foss.)

[3] Walter de Berstede was Sheriff of Kent in 1257: in 1262 Constable of Dover Castle and Custos of Cinque Ports: Justiciar from 1262 to 1266. (Foss.)

[4] Geoffrey de Leuknore was Justice Itinerant, &c. from 1255 to 1276. (Foss.)

[5] Richard de Hemington was a Justiciar from 1263 till 1270. (Foss.)

[6] The present is the first occasion in which the name of Humphrey, as Prior, is recorded.

half-yearly instalments, viz., at the feast of the Nativity of St. John the Baptist, and at the Lord's Nativity: with power, in the case of default in payment, to distrain upon all the cattle[1] of the said Thomas and his heirs, which might be found on or in their lands and tenements in the Manor of Tenrigge, for full payment of all arrears. And the Prior undertook, for himself and his successors and church, to provide a Chaplain, being one of their Canons, who should every day celebrate in their church, at the Altar of B. Mary, for the souls of the said Thomas and his predecessors and heirs.[2]

In the 10th year of King Edward I, 20th November, 1281 to 1282, the King, by writ addressed to the Barons of the Exchequer, acquitted the Prior (to whom the manor had been given *temp.* Richard I) of the 15th due on account of their Manor of Westhall, in Warlingham, which had been granted on lease by John Hansard, late Prior,[3] to Charles, Parson of Collesdon (who was thus accepted as the responsible person).[4]

On the 28th January, 1283–4, being the 12th year of Edward the 1st, King of England, Lord of Ireland, and Duke of Aquitaine, there was issued a writ to the Sheriff of the County of Surrey commanding him to enquire by Jury whether it would be to the detriment of the King or others, if he granted to his beloved in Christ the Prior and Convent of Tanregg, permission to receive in perpetuity as a gift from William de Aegstede (Oxted) one carucate of land with its pertinents, situate at Aegstede, and in the fee of Roland de Aegstede; by the King himself, at Holodenlyn. The

---

[1] *Catalla,* apparently here used for cattle, not chattels = goods.
[2] Pedes finium, 47 Henry III; Surrey, case 2, No. 177. (*Appendix,* VII.)
[3] John Hansard was Prior on 2nd April, 1324, to 4th September, 1335.
[4] Manning and Bray, II, p. 429: no authority for either of these statements is printed; but considering the general exactness with which the references in this work are specified, and the immense research given to its materials, we may (even in the study of archæology, in which every material fact ought to be vouched by a direct reference to the original authority) accept it as a fact.

Inquisition found that there would be no injury to the King or others, Roland and his heirs performing the due and accustomed service.¹

Thereupon a charter was executed by Roland de Okested (Oksted, or Aegstede), who, for himself and his heirs, granted and confirmed to the Prior and Convent of Tenregg, with the King's grace and of the gift of William de Okstede, admission to the lands and tenements, in his fee, in the ville of Okstede, to hold of him and his heirs and assigns, but subject to the performance of all due and accustomed service; as in a chirograph between them fully appeared. In witness he set his seal on the Thursday after the feast of St. Edmund the Confessor, in the King's 13th year.² The Letters Patent, or Licence in Mortmain, were granted by the King on the 7th June following.³

In the year 1291, when the taxation of Pope Nicholas IX was compiled, the Prior of Tanridge held property in Tanrugg and Warlingham which was assessed at the annual value of £2 : 6s. 8d., upon which the tithe was 4s. 8d.⁴

Not very long afterwards we find that the Archbishop of Canterbury was stopping at Tanridge, whence, on the 14th March 1296-7, he issued a mandate

---

¹ Eschaets 12 Edw. I, No. xlix. (Brit. Mus., Add. MS. 6168, fols. 26 and 27.)

² *Inquisition post mortem*, 12 Edw. I, No. 49. (*Appendix*, VIII.) The Charter is attached to the above Inquisition. The particular date intended is not certain. The decease of St. Edmund the Confessor is commemorated on the 20th November, on which day the regnal year commenced; the Thursday before the 20th Nov., in the King's 13th year, would be the 16th November; but if the reference be to the feast of the Translation (the 9th June), the date would, as seems most probable, be the 7th June, which was the same day as that on which the Licence in Mortmain was granted: though, as a general supposition, it would seem unlikely that all requisites were not obtained long before the completion of the formalities attending the grant of Letters Patent; and if so, the earlier date must be assigned.

In the British Museum, Add. MS. 6168, fols. 26 and 27, being extracts from the Eschaets, the reference is given 12 Edw. I, No. xlix.

³ Patent Roll, 13th Edward I, m. 16.

⁴ Taxation by Pope Nicholas IX; Record Off. Ed., p. 206.

(dated 2nd Ide of March), addressed to the Official for Surrey, directing him to cite the Clergy of certain Deaneries to appear before him in Carshalton Church, but for what purpose is not stated.[1]

By authority of a Writ dated the 16th November, 1299 (27th Edward I), an Inquisition *ad quod damnum* was held, and the Jury found that it would not be to the damage of the King or others if Licence were granted to Henry de Guldeford to give to the Prior and Convent of Tenrugge the advowson of the Church of Croweherst to hold to them and their successors in perpetuity. Also that the said Advowson, together with 5 acres of land in Croweherst formerly belonged to Adam de Chiveningge and Robert de Stanegrave who enfeoffed the said Henry de Guldeford thereof. And it was found that the said 5 acres of land, together with the said Advowson, were held of Reginald de Chelesham free of any service; and that the said Church was worth yearly, in all issues, One hundred shillings.[2]

The next step was the payment of a fine to the King for his Licence, and we accordingly find the record in the 30th year of the King's reign (1301 and 1302) of the payment of £10 for the purpose.[3]

And after the lapse of a further time the Licence in Mortmain was granted, in 1302, enabling Henry de Guldeford to grant to the Priory the Advowson of Crawehurst (Crowhurst). The Patent recites the Statute forbidding the entry into possession by Religious of any fee so that it would fall into mortmain, except with licence from the King and the capital lord of the fee from whom it was held by fine. But that, notwithstanding, the King had, upon application of the Prior through the venerable Father, Walter, Bishop of Coventry and Lychfeld, the King's Treasurer, granted to Henry de Guldeford permission to give and assign the Advowson of the Church of Crawehurst to the said Prior and

---

[1] Merton Cartulary, fol. Clij, *v.* (No. 356.)
[2] With *Inquisitions post mortem*, 28 Edward I, Surrey, No. 69.
[3] Originalia, 30 Edward I, rot. 13 (Record Office Ed.).

Convent to have and hold to him and his successors in perpetuity; and to the said Prior and Convent that they might receive and have and hold the same accordingly. Desiring that neither the said Henry nor his heirs nor the said Prior and Convent nor their successors should be molested on account of the said Statute. But saving to the capital Lords of the fee their due and accustomed service for the same. Given by the King, at Westminster, the 14th November.[1]

The legal proceedings leading to the appointment, on the 4th June 1306, of Walter de Pedeleshurst to be Prior, are of considerable interest, as showing the extreme care and systematic manner in which such matters were transacted, even in a Monastery such as this where the number of Canons seems never to have exceeded five. From the records in the Bishop's Register we learn what was done.

The Canons in Chapter having (no doubt after the usual Congé d'èslire) elected Walter de Pedeleshurst (described as a Canon of the Collegiate Church of Tanrugge) to be their Prior, their Proctor, Brother Thomas de Woldham, one of the Canons, appeared before the Bishop at his Manor of Merewelle on the kalend of June, viz., the third juridical day after the feast of the Holy Trinity (3rd June), 1306, and exhibited their Proxy under Seal; the Elect being also personally present. Then was read a Certificate of the Archdeacon of Surrey to the effect that citation, with due publication thereof, of all opposers to appear in canonical form at this time and place, had been made: and the proceedings were adjourned till the morrow. At that time the Elect and Proctor appeared personally as before, and no one appeared in opposition, though waited for a sufficient time; whereupon an order was made precluding them from opposition. The proceedings were then adjourned till the first juridical day after the feast of St. Barnabas the Apostle (11th June), at the latest, to proceed with the business.

[1] Patent Roll, 30 Edward I, m. 3. (*Appendix*, IX.)

Which day being come, the Elect and the Proctor of the Chapter again appeared before the Bishop, and the matter being propounded by John de Tyccheseye, and the various instruments read, and two Witnesses produced (viz., Brothers Thomas de Woldham and John de la Pende, both Canons of the said Church), being sworn and examined, and the Decree and other instruments relating to the Election being carefully examined, the Bishop found the said Election to be in manywise defective, and, putting his words by the mouth of Master Peter de Grunvull, his Official, made his Decree to the following effect:—

It appeared by the instruments touching the election, that the same was evidently defective, although the probable fitness of the person was shown; and he declared it to be void for informality, and that in consequence thereof the right to fill the vacancy devolved upon him; and at a further sitting of the Court on the same day, in the Chapel at Merewelle, he, by his pontifical authority, preferred the said Brother Walter de Pedeleshurst to the Priory, desiring to suit the Priory with him rather than with any other person.

This Sentence was followed by a Decree in the usual form for the induction and installation of the new Prior, dated at Merewell on the ides of June (13 June), 1306, and the second year of the Bishop's consecration. On the same day, Letters were formally addressed to Thomas de Woldham (who is here mentioned as the Precentor of the Priory) and the Convent, announcing the appointment and enjoining obedience according to the Rules of the Order: this also was dated at Merewelle.[1]

The Bishop, by virtue of his office and duty, made a Pastoral Visitation of the Convent on the Thursday after the feast of St. Edmund the King and Confessor, the 21st November, 1308: and a month later made an Ordinance concerning matters to be reformed, which, as will be seen by the following abstract of the document, in fact, simply required a careful observance of certain

---

[1] Diocesan Register, *Wodelok*, fols. 40 *v.* to 41 *v.*

of the Rules of the Order which we may assume were not sufficiently rigidly observed, though, it will be noted, he made no direct complaint of laxity: so far, therefore, the document presents a strong testimonial to the good conduct of the House, for had there been any serious cause for blame it must necessarily have formed the ground and basis of matters to be reformed, especially as it had no further publicity.

The Bishop's Ordinance is directed to the Prior or his deputy, and the Convent: referring to the recent Visitation, he states that various things were found needful of correction, as appeared in the following orders:—

In the first place he ordered, enacted, and commanded that Divine Service both by day and night be celebrated with fit ceremony every day, with Masses such as, whether by writing or by oath, they were bound to celebrate for benefactors, viz., one Mass of St. Mary, by note; and another by note, which is called the High Mass, to the observance of which they were bound by the Rule; and any one absent without reasonable cause and without special licence of the Prior should be subject to a fast on bread and water.

Also, following the footsteps of Othobon, Legate of the Apostolic See to England, it was directed that the Canons professed and in priest's orders, frequently confess to the Prior or some other of the Order with his licence, and celebrate Divine Service in places appointed for the purpose and hitherto usual. Also that a Sub-prior be unanimously appointed according to ancient custom. That silence be carefully observed amongst them in times and places in accordance with their Rules; and the outer door be closed at due hours, and kept closed. He ordered that no one in any way presume to go out of the premises without licence of the Prior, nor that the Sub-prior himself, as accustomed amongst the Brothers, should give licence of exit without just and reasonable cause; and that then the person going out should have a fit companion provided for him by the Prior; and that he should return without any delay beyond the time fixed. That none of the Brothers be engaged in such matters as he chose, but in such as might be most useful.

The Bishop prohibited the Canons from wearing clothing different from and unfit for their Order, and directed that they should only wear such as the Rules, and propriety of Religion, required; and with the provision that all wore a uniform habit. They were not to have curtains round their beds in the dormitory, but each, lying alone, might be seen by any one passing.

He ordered that the infirm Brothers be visited according to their wants and to the Rules, and their needs be supplied by brotherly kindness, and in due and accustomed benevolence, more in future than usual hitherto. He further prohibited the Brothers from sitting at table with unfit secular persons, or eating either with domestics or external persons, or waiting till after the refection of the Brothers, or taking food in other places. Also the taking of food or drink after bed-time, or being in the refectory or elsewhere without reasonable cause, except in the usual and accustomed hours. Also he ordered that none of them hold converse with any suspected woman, or one who might be suspected, whether secular or religious, or in any manner going to the house of such person, lest from this cause a public scandal be raised. He specially commanded that twice in the year, in grand Chapter, and before the Brothers (according to the requirements of the Holy Fathers), the Prior and Cellarer should render a full account of their administration, and strive to their utmost therein for the welfare of the Monastery. And that, according to ancient custom hitherto in use amongst them, and to the rule of the Order, there be provided food and drink, clothing and other necessaries, according to the means of their church; and that if anything be unlawfully alienated, it be recalled to the best of their power, and that the more important matters of business be under the seal of the House and by common assent; and that their woods be not cut down, nor trees disposed of without their unanimous consent, and except for express and reasonable cause, approved by the majority.

These Injunctions he sent under his patent seal, affecting them and every of them jointly and severally, and to be diligently and faithfully observed in future by virtue of their obedience; and he directed the same to be read in full chapter 4 times a year, viz., on the first Sunday in Advent, on Mid-lent Sunday, on the feast of the Ascension, and within the Octave of the Nativity of Blessed Mary the Virgin, fully, distinctly, openly and publicly, lest any one pretend ignorance of them.

Given at Essher, 13th kalend of December (20th December), in the above-mentioned year of our Lord, and of his own consecration the fourth.[1]

On the 26th December, 1308, the Bishop addressed letters to the Prior or his deputy notifying that he had issued a Commission to Brother Laurence of Gloucester, Professor of Sacred Theology, and Brother Adam of Salisbury, Monk of St. Swithin, Winchester, in his (the Bishop's) place, and with power of canonical coercion, to enquire as to things which in his late Visitation he had found requiring correction; and commanding the Brothers by virtue of their obedience to amend all those things relating to the state of the House which he had enjoined, both as to temporalities and spiritualties.

Dated at Farnham, the 7th kalend of December (25th November), 1308.[2]

The Visitation was accordingly held on the morning of the 5th ferial day after the feast of St. Andrew (6th December, 1308), in the Chapter House of the Priory, in presence of the Prior and Cellarer and the whole Convent. In the first place, the Decree of the Bishop and the various Articles contained therein were carefully explained. Secondly, the Canons were asked for a Certificate of an account required by the Mandate on a given day. And as they had not certified, judgment on account of that disobedience was reserved to the Bishop.

---

[1] Diocesan Register, *Wodelok*, fols. 148 *v.* to 149 *v.* (Appendix, X.)
[2] Ibid, fol. 97 *v.* (Appendix, XI.)

Thirdly, it was enquired whether the Cellarer had rendered an account, and it appeared that, from the time of the foundation of the House to the present time, neither the present Cellarer nor any other had ever rendered any account. So that he did not know the value of the House, nor the amount of annual rents or proceeds from the Grange, nor the amount of seed yearly sown of any kind of grain, nor the proceeds of the corn, nor the quantity of corn to be provided yearly, nor grain for making beer, nor the supplies to the household: nor, indeed, did the Prior, Cellarer, or any one else know how much was necessary. Fourthly, they caused the Cellarer to render an account before the Prior and Convent, and beginning from the first year of his administration, which was found to contain so many omissions and untruths as would take many days to go through: therefore a new one, commencing at the last year of his administration and for one year, was made by Simon de Schirford as a pattern for future accounts. Fifthly, the said Adam with William de Schire, Canon, their Bailiff, by order of the said Laurence, inspected part of the woods and noted which of the old oaks there might, without loss to the House, be sold for a value of 20 marcs, for the purchase of corn and payment of debts. In the sixth place, because their secular officers were heavily taxed, a schedule of their future charge was adjoined to the present return. Seventhly, it was appointed that the Bishop be supervisor of extrinsic things, and Sir William de Schire receiver of all things within the Priory, as contained in a Schedule, and the state of the House and the order for account appearing in a marginal schedule. Eighthly, all those things about which discord existed were reduced to concord by the said Laurence. Ninthly, he enjoined them to enter in their Martyrology the Bishop's Statutes and Ordinances; and dismissed them in peace; and wrote to Sir Robert de Strangave to permit Sir William de Schyr to rest in the House.[1]

---

[1] Diocesan Register, *Wodelok*, fol. 96 *v.* (Appendix, XII.) Of what other Priory William de Schyr was a Canon, and Sir Robert de Strangave Prior, does not appear.

The Bishop's Commissary also issued an exhortation to the Brethren to avoid contention and strife, but rather to bear contumely from any of the Confraters and let the offender be corrected by the Prior, or other acting for him, in the presence of all the others in chapter; and if on the third reproof he did not amend, he be punished by withholding his ration, and if the fault be repeated the penalty be increased until he amended. But this order was not intended to inhibit the Prior or other from correcting any delinquent Brother, only observing moderation in all things. Also he ordered that the Brother to whom was committed the charge of kitchen expenses, should render a full account of his administration every week. Also that the secular officers in charge of granges and granary, and those appointed to take care of the live stock, should be bound to render accounts on oath of their administration and receipts and outlay, and account faithfully for the proceeds from the animals; which account they should be bound to furnish to the Prior or Brother in charge of the temporalia. All the premises he ordered to be strictly observed, and to be recited with the Bishop's Decree before them all in chapter, four times a year. Given at Tanrugg on the day of St. Andrew the Apostle (30th November), 1308.[1]

On the vacancy in the office of Prior occurring by the resignation of Brother Walter, admitted as of force by the Bishop in his Chapel at Essher on the 4th Ide of March (12th March), 1309, the latter at the same time and place issued a Licence to the Brethren and College of Tanrugg to harmoniously elect, in fear of God and observance of the laws of the Order, a new Prior to fill the vacancy.[2]

About the latter part of the month of February following, the Bishop issued a similar Commission for Visitation as to certain things relating to his recent Visitation, addressed to Master Philip de Bartoñ, Arch-

---

[1] Diocesan Register, *Wodelok*, fol. 96 v. (Appendix, XIII.)
[2] Ibid., fol. 104.

deacon of Surrey,[1] and Laurence of Gloucester, Monk of St. Peter's, Professor of Sacred Theology; noting that their censures should be solemnly observed.[2]

Apparently, the Cellarer did not take heed to the Ordinances of the Bishop, for, on the 4th February 1309 following, the Bishop issued Letters to the House to the effect that for various reasons seen at the Visitation he had removed Brother Henry from the Office of Cellarer and supervisor of extrinsic affairs as assistant to Brother William de Shyre, who for the benefit of the Monastery had been appointed to be Receiver. He therefore commanded the Prior and Convent by virtue of their obedience not to permit the said Brother Henry, thus removed from the administration of the temporalities, to interfere therewith, or to leave the bounds of the Monastery until further orders; and to substitute the said William de Shyre in the office of Cellarer. This seemed an arbitrary interference with the Monastery, since William de Shyre was an outsider. The Bishop further directed them to appoint Brother John de Gotham, or some one else of the College fit for the purpose, to be joined with the said William in looking after affairs within the limits of the Priory and in assisting him with advice in the administration of the Church. Dated at Merewell, 2nd none of February (4th February), A.D. 1309, and of his consecration the 4th.[3]

The Bishop's next proceeding was no doubt, under the circumstances, a very wise one: having deprived Henry de Pecham (for such we find was his surname) of his office of Cellarer, he banished him to another House of the same Order at Newark. But he went beyond banishment, for in the Letters which the Bishop addressed to the Prior and Convent of Newark, after reciting that he had for due and lawful reasons touching the honour of religion and the good of his soul, removed

---

[1] Archdeacon of Surrey from about 1300 till his death about 1320. (Cassan, *Lives of the Bishops of Winchester*, I, p. 90.) The name, as written, is probably an abbreviation of the name Philip of Bath.

[2] Diocesan Register, *Wodelok*, fol. 103 v.

[3] Ibid., fol. 101 v. (Appendix, XV.)

the said Henry from Tanrugg; they were commanded to receive him favourably whilst he should dwell with them, and to provide him with a room and necessaries at the cost of the former Priory; but that he should not be permitted to leave the place, or hold intercourse with secular persons, except with the special leave of the Prior or Sub-prior, and should be looked after by two of the Brothers of mature age and honest conversation, to whose charge he should be specially deputed. These directions to continue in force until further orders. Dated at Essher, the 4th of the ides of March, 1308 (10th March, 1309).[1]

A few days later, viz., on the 24th March, 1309, the Bishop gave directions to the Prior and Convent of Newark as to the treatment of the offender, viz., that he was to be kept in solitary confinement, and to fast every Friday on bread, beer, and soup, and on other days to content himself with the same with the addition of one dish for his ration; not to leave his room except for unavoidable or reasonable cause, nor be permitted to celebrate the Divine Office, nor to talk with any person whether secular or religious, except in the presence of his keeper or some other of them. For this the Prior and Chapter of Tanrugg were to pay twelve pence per week. Obedience to these orders was most particularly enjoined. Given at Newark, the 9th kalend of April (24th March), 1308.[2]

After two months the Bishop relaxed the severity of the punishment, and sent letters to the Prior of Newark to the effect that, as the offender had borne his sentence patiently and with humility, he should be released from imprisonment and be permitted to accompany the Convent in choir, dormitory, refectory, and other places within the walls under the care of a guardian to be appointed for the purpose; but on no account to be permitted to leave the Monastery. Dated at High Clere, 6th kal. of June (27th May), 1309.[3]

[1] Diocesan Register, *Wodelok,* fol. 103 *v.* (Appendix, XVI.)
[2] Ibid., fol. 105 *v.* (Appendix, XVII.)
[3] Ibid., fol. 108. (Appendix, XVIII.)

This was followed, two months later, by Letters from the Bishop, addressed to the Prior and Convent of Newark, reciting that the punishment of Henry de Pecham had been borne patiently, with all humility and great contrition, and his amendment was manifest; in consequence of which his punishment had been relaxed; and directing them to permit him to return freely to Tanrugg, to which Monastery authority had been granted to receive him. And the Bishop further mentioned that he had forwarded letters to that Monastery to pay them 12 pence for every week that the culprit had been resident at their House. Dated at Essher, the 17th kal. of August (16th July), 1309.[1]

On the same date as the letters above mentioned, Letters were addressed to the Prior and Convent of Tanrugg; reciting that the Bishop had at his late Visitation thought proper to remove the offender to Newark for punishment and ordered that a payment of 12 pence per week should be made on that account: that at the instance of the Prior and Convent of Newark, and their testimony to the contrition and devoutness with which the punishment had been borne, he had relaxed its infliction, and now ordered the Priory of Tanridge to receive the said Brother Henry back to their cloister, but that he should not be permitted to interfere in either their intrinsic or extrinsic affairs.[2]

Presumably in the month of May or June, 1309, but the date is not stated, the Bishop sent Letters to Newark stating his intention to prefer Thomas of St. Alban to the Priory of Tanrugg—the preferment to which fell to him for this turn, but which could not be done unless by their special licence: he asked and required of them to absolve the said Thomas from his obedience to them, and to grant him their Letters Patent to that effect and to permit his transfer to Tanrugg.[3]

This was followed by Letters (not dated, but appa-

---

[1] Diocesan Register, *Wodelok*, fol. 112. (Appendix, XIX.)
[2] Ibid. (Appendix, XX.)
[3] Ibid., fol. 108 v. (Appendix, XXI.)

rently early in June) addressed to the said Thomas of St. Alban, reciting that the Priory of Newark had, with the consent of the Chapter, and in legal form, released him from all subjection and obedience to that Monastery, and granted him special licence by Letters Patent to pass to Tanrugge; and that he, the Bishop, to whom the preferment fell for this turn, had preferred him to the Priorate of the latter Monastery; and commanding him to attend on the Tuesday following, at Essher, to do and receive in the premises according to rule.[1]

On the 17th June the Bishop proceeded to the next step, and issued letters addressed to the Precentor and Convent of the Collegiate Church of Tanrugg, reciting the vacancy caused by the resignation of Brother Walter de Hetfeld, late Prior, and that they had by unanimous consent and assent submitted to his ordination, and that he, with the concurrent assent of their patron, should provide a fit Prior to dwell there; whereby the right fully devolved upon him, and he had accordingly preferred Brother Thomas de St. Alban, Canon of the Monastery of Newark, to be Prior. And he enjoined and commanded them by virtue of their obedience to attend to and obey him as their Prior, as taught and required by the Rules of the Order, and the observance of which he would enforce. Given at Essher, the 15th kal. of July (17th June).[2]

The same day the Bishop directed Letters to the Archdeacon of Surrey, reciting the appointment, and that the same had been made with submission and consent of the Canons; and commanding him to induct the said Thomas de St. Alban into corporal possession of the Priory, and instal him according to custom.[3]

In the 4th year of King Edward II (1310 or 1311) the King's Eschaetor for the County of Surrey held an Inquisition with reference to the statement that the Prior of Tanregge had appropriated to himself and his

[1] Diocesan Register, *Wodelok*, fol. 109 v. (Appendix, XXII.)
[2] Ibid, fol. 110.
[3] Ibid.

House 5 acres of land with pertinents in Okestede of the gift and grant of Henry atte Donne, of Warlingham, a Brother of the said House in the time of the King, the father of the present King (*i.e. temp.* Edward I), and after the publication of the Statute of Lands and Tenements in Mortmain, without obtaining the royal licence. The Jurors found that the said Prior held the said 5 acres of land as parcel of a carucate of land granted in the time of the said King (Edward I) when an Inquisition was held by his Eschaetor.[1] Some further difficulty about this property arose a few years later.

We next come to some records respecting the Priors.

Another Visitation of the Monastery was made by Master Laurence of Gloucester, Monk, Professor of Sacred Theology, with the Bishop's Official, when they found that the Priory, through the incapacity and negligence of the Prior, was in such a state of collapse that they could scarcely get on or recover: whereupon the Bishop, on the 22nd November, 1312, directed them to depute Sir Charles, Rector of the Church of Colesdon, a provident and discreet man, to be coadjutor of the Prior; that without his advice and assent nothing should be done in relation to the administration of the temporalities; that he should daily eat with the Brothers in the refectory and sleep in the dormitory, and look after things except spiritualities. Also that Brother John de Pende, a concanon, should be the deputy Cellarer, acting in all things with the advice and assent of the said Sir Charles. Providing that the Common Seal should be carefully kept under triple keys, one of which to remain in the care of the Prior, another with the Rector, and the third with the Sub-prior. The Bishop in accordance with this arrangement made by his Commissary commanded them, by virtue of obedience, to carefully observe these things, and all things which the said Sir Charles, in his ministration respecting the temporalities, might determine; and desiring that neither he nor they, without the approval

---

[1] Inquisition *ad quod damnum*, 4 Edw. II, No. 6. (Add. MS. 6168, fol. 233.)

of the Bishop, should proceed to make any alienation. He commanded that the Prior (to whom he interdicted the use of any seal) should be content with one only servant. The present Letters he directed to remain in the care of the said Sir Charles. Dated at Suthwerk, the 10th kal. of December (22nd November), 1312, and of his consecration the 8th.[1]

Upon the Priory becoming vacant by the death of Henry de Pecham, the Bishop, on the 16th kalend of April, 1323 (17th March), issued a Decree addressed to the Official of the Archdeacon of Surrey, reciting that John Hansard, a Concanon of the House, had been (as alleged) canonically elected, upon licence of the patron sought and granted. That the Bishop intended to proceed to the examination of the election, on the 5th juridical day after the feast of the Annunciation of Blessed Mary, in the Conventual Church of Suthewerk, and further to proceed as incumbent upon him therein. He therefore commanded the Official to cite or cause to be cited peremptorily all opposers in special (if any), and all others in general, to appear at that time and place before him (the Bishop), or his Commissary, and state their objections against the person elected or the form of election; and at that time or by prorogation the business would be continued. Dated at Suthewerk.[2]

Accordingly, on the Wednesday after the feast of the Annunciation, being the 30th March, in the Conventual Church of Suthewerk, the Bishop proceeded with the business of the Election of Brother John Hansard, elected by the Precentor and Concanons to fill the vacancy. The certificate by the Archdeacon of Surrey of the publication of the Citation was read, and the petition of the Precentor and Concanons, by their Proctor lawfully constituted, praying the Bishop to proceed with the business, as also their election pursuant to letters, from the patron of the House, giving licence to elect; and proclamation was made at the door of

---

[1] Diocesan Register, *Wodelok*, fol. 175. (Appendix, XXIII.)
[2] Diocesan Register, *Stratford*, fol. 3. (*Appendix*, XXIV.)

the Church that any one desiring to object to the person elected or to the form of election should appear and propound his objection; and, none appearing, the Bishop appointed the following Saturday to proceed in the matter. On which day and place the said Proctor and Elect appeared, and no objection was made; and all submitted entirely to the Bishop's decision. But the Bishop held that the election and form of election was in many respects null and altogether invalid, wherefore the duty of providing the Church with a Prior devolved upon him, *pleno jure*, for this turn; and he made an appointment for the Elect and the Proctor of the House to attend at the same place on the Monday following, to do and receive in the matter as justice might require.

Afterwards, on the Monday, at the sitting of the Court, the Bishop preferred the said Brother John Hansard to the Priory, by a formal Decree, and committed to him its administration as well in spiritualties as in temporalties; and on 2nd April issued a mandate, addressed to the Official of the Archdeacon of Surrey for the induction, and also letters to the Precentor and Concanons announcing the appointment and enjoining obedience as required by the Rules of the Order.[1]

These forms are highly interesting, for we find that the various steps required to be taken, and the extreme care with which the election, confirmation, and induction of a Prior, however small the Priory might be, were conducted, and with the same care and legal precision, and the exact forms and even formulary as were customary upon the election, confirmation, and installation of a Bishop; and here it may be noted that, though monastic institutions under ecclesiastical sanction and control do not now subsist in the English Church, yet, in reference to the Episcopate, the same forms are systematically observed at the present day, and the very wording of the various documents (merely translated into English) are still used as they have come down to us, and have been in use during eight hundred or a thousand years.

---

[1] Diocesan Register, *Stratford*, fol. 3. (*Appendix*, XXV.)

The question as to the acquisition by grant of Land at Okestede without Licence in Mortmain, again cropped up. Upon an Inquisition *ad quod damnum*, held in the 19th year of King Edward II (1325 or 1326), the Jury said that the King's Eschaetor for the County of Surrey had legally found, upon a certain Inquisition held before himself, *ex officio suo*, that the Prior of Tanrugge had appropriated to himself and his House, 5 acres of land, with their pertinents, in Okstede, of the gift and grant of Henry att Donne of Warlyngham, made to the House in the time of the King, the father of the present King, subsequent to the publication of the enacted Statute of Lands and Tenements in Mortmain, without obtaining Licence of the King. But they said that the said Prior was seized of the said 5 acres of land, as parcel of a carucate, from the time of their gift and assignment until the Eschaetor took the same into the King's hands by virtue of the said Inquisition.[1] This is just the same property with respect to which Inquisitions had been held in the same King's 4th year and in the time of his predecessor, showing the uncertainty prevalent in such matters.

The appointment of John Hansard as Prior seems to have been an unfortunate one, for although no fault was charged against him, he appears to have become quite incapable of the due rule and management of the House, whether from the effect of age or else from lack of the requisite ability; and the Bishop, in consequence either of an appeal to him, or, at all events, from information received, caused Letters to be addressed on a day occurring between the 25th March and the 25th June, 1330 (the precise date of which is left blank in the record but apparently was the 31st May[2]), to Sir Laurence de Rustynton, wherein he recited that he had lately visited the

---

[1] Inquisition *ad quod damnum*, 19 Edward II, No. 6. (Brit. Mus., Add. MS. 6167, fol. 415.) (*Appendix*, XXVII.)

[2] Diocesan Register, *Stratford*, fol. 51. The entry says: "Daī apud Essh'e, ij° kīn (blank), anno Dñi milłio CCC^{mo} t'cesimo, et cons̄ n̄re vij°:" the 7th year of his consecration ended on 25th June. He was at Esher on 2nd kalend of June 1330. (*Appendix*, XXVI.)

Prior and Brothers of the House, and for certain lawful causes had interdicted the Prior from administration of the goods of the House until he (the Bishop) should issue further directions. The Bishop now deputed Sir Laurence to be Co-adjutor to the said Prior, directing that without his counsel and assent neither the Prior nor anyone else should in any way meddle in the goods of the House; and committed to him until further order the care and administration of the said goods. Given at Essh'e ij kal. (blank) 1330, and of his consecration the 7th.

At the same time and place Letters were written to the Prior, informing him of the appointment of the Co-adjutor.[1]

The incapacity of Prior John Hansard, however, became still more pronounced and led to a Canonical Visitation of the House by the Bishop, on the 4th September, 1335, when the Prior, on account of bodily weakness and personal incapacity, freely resigned his rule; whereupon his cession being admitted and canonically accepted, the Canons placed the vacant appointment in the hands of the Bishop, to fill up. The Bishop appointed Brother Philip de Wokingham, of the Monastery of Newerk, a professed Canon of the same Order, and in priest's orders, a prudent and discreet man, and very circumspect in temporal and spiritual matters; the licence of the Prior of Newerk being first obtained. A Decree to that effect was accordingly made in the presence of Master John Lowe, Professor of Civil Law; Henry de London, Rector of the Church of Withihame, in the Diocese of Chichester; and William de Alresford and John de Beautre, Notaries Public by Apostolic authority.[2]

Perhaps it was through the incapacity of John Hansard, but at all events during his incumbency, the Manor of Westhall, in Warlingham, given to the Priory at some antecedent period, was granted on lease, to Charles, Parson of Collesdon, whereby the Priory was,

---

[1] Diocesan Register, *Stratford*, fol. 51. (*Appendix*, XXVI.)
[2] Diocesan Register, *Orleton*, I, fol. 26 v. (*Appendix*, XXVIII.)

it would appear, deprived for the time of any benefit from it; for we find (as stated by Manning and Bray) that the King, by writ to the Exchequer, did quit the Priory of Tandridge of the 15th due on account of the Manor.[1]

The appointment of Philip de Wokingham to be Prior, proved unfortunate; instead of striving to remedy the mischiefs which the incapacity of his predecessor had necessarily caused to the House, he deserted his flock and went no one knew whither; and, it must be presumed, they needed him and applied to the Bishop for aid; since we find that, on the 17th January, 1341, a Decree was issued by the Ordinary, addressed to the Official or Commissary General directing him to cite the Prior, and admonish him to residence, under pain of the law. The decree is prefaced by a note of the duty of prelates to rule the Lord's churches and feed his flock, and use all diligence to preserve them by the laws and powers of the church from inroads of the ravenous wolf; it sets forth that he (the Bishop) had received a serious complaint from the Canons of the Priory that Brother Philip, their Prior, had absented himself (*se fraudulenter absentavit*) and for no little time deserted them without due licence, or reasonable or honest cause, and resided in unknown places. Lest, therefore, from dereliction of governance of the church, its discipline and straight rule should be shipwrecked (*quod absit*), he strictly enjoined and commanded his Commissary, by virtue of his obedience, to enquire after the Prior in places where he was believed to be likely to be found, and, if possible, personally serve him with this Citation and Monition; otherwise by his Proctor if he should have appointed any in the said church, and among his family and friends publicly; and admonish him to return to his church and cure, within the time fixed by

---

[1] Manning and Bray, Vol. II, p. 429. The date stated is the 10th Edward I (1282), which is clearly an error, as the writ refers to John Hansard as the late Prior: he held the office from 1325 to 1335. Probably it should be the 10th year of King Edward III (not 1st), 1336 or 1337. The authors give no reference to the authority for their statement.

the ecclesiastical canons, and diligently rule the same. And further, that the Official should certify by his Letters Patent to the Bishop the reception of the Citation within 5 days of its receipt. Dated at Esshere the 17th day of the month of January, 1340-1, and the 8th of the Bishop's translation.[1]

This Citation was followed on the 28th July by another, addressed to the Official, in which the former document was recited, and then the fact that the Prior had been diligently sought, but in vain, and that he had left no proctor in the church, and that the Decree had been thrice published amongst his family and friends, calling upon him to return within the time limited by the canons, and diligently rule, which he had neglected to do, as appeared by Letters certificatory. In such default, the Bishop now directed that the Prior should be peremptorily cited to appear before him or his Commissary in Winchester Cathedral on the 7th juridical day after the feast of the Exaltation of the Holy Cross, and show reasonable cause, if he had any, why he should not be deprived, and further to do and receive as under canonical sanction the business might require. The day of the receipt of this Citation to be duly certified at the said time and place. Given at Farnham the 28th July, 1341, and the 8th year of the Bishop's translation.[2]

The Citations having proved ineffectual, the Bishop issued a Commission to his Official to proceed with the Deprivation, in which was recited that the original Citation had been served in the church on the 21st January, then on the 8th March, and finally on the 29th June; without effect. The Bishop therefore committed to his Official his authority, for this occasion, for the deprivation. Dated at Waltham, 22nd September, 1341.[3]

The Sentence is dated two days later, viz.: on the 6th kalend of October. It recites the complaint made, the

---

[1] Diocesan Register, *Orleton*, I, fol. 108. (*Appendix*, XXIX.)
[2] Ibid. (*Appendix*, XXX.)
[3] Ibid., fol. 108 v. (*Appendix*, XXXI.)

Monition to the absent Prior, and its triple publication in default of any other practicable form of service, and the peremptory Citation and non-appearance, and the final adjournment to this day, when in default of appearance he was pronounced contumacious; and in pain of such contumacy, and duly weighing the said circumstances, the Bishop pronounced by Definitive Sentence that the said Philip be amoved and deprived of his church; and decreed that those to whom the election of a future Prior belonged might proceed to an election. Given by the Official of the Diocese in the Consistorial Place in Winchester on the 6th kalend of October (26th September) in the year of our Lord 1341, the tenth of the Indiction, and the seventh year of the pontificate of Pope Benedict the 12th. There being present the discreet men Messieurs John de Enham and John de Ware, advocates in the said Consistory, and Messieurs Roger Bryan and Roger Scolys by apostolic authority notaries public &c.; and witnesses &c.[1]

The great formality and precision with which the whole proceeding was carried out will be specially noted, as well as the great care with which the final decree was delivered and attested, and the several forms in which the date is specified after the custom usual only in matters of more than ordinarily grave importance.

The Convent thereupon proceeded to fill up the vacancy by the election of the religious man, brother John de Merstham, a Canon of their Church; and on the Monday being the day after the feast of St. Martin (*i.e.* on the 12th November), before John de Wolveleye, the Commissary of the Bishop, specially deputed in this matter, and in the parish church of Farnham (under the direction of Adam de Wambergh, Official of Winchester and Commissary General), all persons desiring to object to the election, either by reason of form or the person elected, having been cited and called and none appearing or opposing, any future opposition was declared to be excluded. The Decree of Election and 5 other letters

---

[1] Diocesan Register, *Orleton*, I, fol. 108 *v*. (*Appendix*, XXXII.)

under seal of the Convent being exhibited by their Proctor lawfully constituted, there were produced two witnesses to the full facts of the Election, viz. Brother John de Sontynge, Canon of the Church, and Sir William, Chaplain of the parish church of Tanrugge, who being admitted as witnesses were sworn and examined; and the business was adjourned to the following day in the Chapel of Farnham Castle, there to do and receive as unto right and justice might appertain in the premises. On which day and place the Elect and the Proctor attended before the Commissary General, and the Petition and all other documents relating to the election being read and considered, the Commissary proceeded to a Final Decree in the name of the Bishop, reciting the election to the vacancy and pronouncing that all the requisites for the election of a fit person had been fulfilled and canonically celebrated; and (the Grace of the Holy Spirit having been invoked) he confirmed the election, fully committing to the Elect the cure and administration of the said Church; and the Canticle *Te Deum laudamus* being solemnly sung, and all other things accustomed in such cases being performed, the elected Brother John made the accustomed acknowledgment of obedience to the Bishop.[1]

This formal Decree was followed by Letters from the Bishop to Brother John de Merstham, the new Prior, reciting the vacancy by the deprivation of Brother Philip de Wokyngham, late Prior, and the subsequent election; and confirming the Elect in the Priory, and fully committing to him the pastoral cure and administration thereof, with firm hope that, by Divine Grace, the Priory might through his faithful ministry increase in prosperity. Dated at Farnham the 13th November in the year of our Lord 1341, and in the eighth of the Bishop's translation.[2]

The series of documents was completed by a Commission addressed by the Bishop to the Prior of Reigate

---

[1] Diocesan Register, *Orleton*, I, fol. 109. (*Appendix*, XXXIV.)
[2] Ibid., fol. 109 v. (*Appendix*, XXXV.)

and perpetual vicar of the parish church of Walkenestede. It recites that Master William Inge, Archdeacon of Surrey *de facto* and not *de jure*, being under the greater excommunication for notorious excesses, defaults, and offences, and so publicly pronounced in this and the adjoining dioceses; he therefore directed the Commissioners to instal the said Brother John de Merstham in the Choir and place in the Chapter hitherto assigned to the priors. Dated at Farnham the 13th November above mentioned.[1]

Archdeacon William Inge, who was thus superseded, became Archdeacon of Surrey in 1327, but before long came into collision with the Bishop—from whose fault does not appear; and thenceforth was engaged in constant litigation with him and his successor. The Archdeacon was suspended in 1332, for non-appearance to a Citation in a suit respecting a Vicarage, and in 1334 was excommunicated, but the sentence was over-ruled by the Archbishop, on appeal; in the following year he was again excommunicated, and his appeal to the Archbishop was unsuccessful: towards the end of the year 1339, we find him still under excommunication.[2]

Upon an Inquisition on the death of Hugh le Despenser, who died in the year 1350,[3] respecting all knights' fees, &c., held by him of the King *in capite*, and taken at Croydon, it was found that three knights' fees in Chelsham and Warlingham, which were held in domain of the said Hugh, by Andrew Pendrell, John Redmigersh, and the Prior of Tanrugge, were of the value, from all sources, of Ten pounds per annum. The shares of the several occupants are not stated.[4]

On the 13th February, 1351-2, an Inquisition upon the death of John de Warlynham was held, and the Jurors found that the Manor of Tanrugge was charged from old time with an annual payment to the Prior of

---

[1] Diocesan Register, *Orleton*, I, fol. 109 *v*. (Appendix, XXXVI.)
[2] Ibid., fols. 23 *v* and 81.
[3] Manning and Bray, II, p. 123.
[4] Inquis. *post mortem*, Hugh le Despenser. (Add. MS. 6169, fol 157.)

Tanridge of xx*s*. viij*d*. payable at the feasts of Easter and St. Michael, by equal portions, as appeared by a fine levied in the Curia Regis. And they found that the perquisitions of the Court there were worth xij*d*. per annum. And that John de Warkyngton (? Warlyngham) died on the xiij day of February, &c. And they found that John Warblynton (? Warlyngham),[1] son of the said John deceased, was the next heir, and of the age of 6 years.[2]

An Inquisition was held at Croydon on the 14th April, 1351 (25th Edward III), when it was found that it would not be to the damage of the King or others if Licence were granted to Walter de Mestham, Parson of the Church of Lymenesfeld to grant to the Prior and Convent of Tanrigge two messuages, one hundred and forty[3] acres of land, 14 acres of meadow, 13 acres of wood, and two shillings and eight pence rents in Tanrigge and Wolkenstede; to hold to them and their successors in perpetuity, towards the support of a Canon-Chaplain to celebrate Divine Service daily for the souls of all faithful departed, for ever. It was also found that all the said tenements were held of John Forester of Wolkenestede by the service of Twenty-four shillings per annum, for all service, and payments of 3s. 4d. to the Prior of Merton, and 3s. 4d. to Katherine, Widow of John de St. John of Nagham. Further, that John Forester, Robert de Stangrave, and the heir of Hugh le Despencer were mesne lords between the King and the said Walter. And that the messuages, lands, meadow, and wood, were worth 10s. per annum beyond the rent resolute, and no more.[4]

Consequent upon this finding, Letters Patent were on the 3rd May following granted by the King, in

---

[1] The variations of spelling of the name are presumably clerical errors.

[2] Inquisition, 25 Edward III, No. 54. (Brit. Mus., Add. MS. 6167, fol. 416.) (*Appendix*, XXXIII.)

[3] This would appear to be a clerical error for one hundred and four score, which is the quantity stated in the Patent.

[4] Inquisition *ad quod damnum*, 24 Edward III, Surrey, No. 21.

consideration of a fine of 40s. The quantity of "land" is definitely stated as 180 acres, and the celebration of Divine Service is specified as to be performed in the Priory.[1]

Upon the resignation of Prior John de Merstham in 1380, Richard French was elected as his successor, but, on the 8th May following, a Commission to enquire into the regularity of the election was issued:[2] however, he died while holding the office, on 9th December, 1403,[3] and was succeeded on 14th March following by William Sonderesh, though the Bishop again declared the election void, but himself appointed the elected person to the office.[3]

There is an account of the Rents payable to the Priory at the Feasts of St. Michael, the Lord's Nativity, Easter, and St. John, in the 9th year of King Henry IV. His reign began on the 30th of September, so that it is not clear whether, as probably was the case, it was intended to express Michaelmas in his 8th year, and the other feasts in his 9th year, viz. A.D. 1407-8; but whether the date was that year or the next matters little. The account was taken at "Le Barwe" in the parish of Oxstede, and refers to manorial rents and heriots and reliefs when they might happen. They refer also to the Manor of Berstede; and state the amounts receivable at the Manorial Court at Okstede, which (apparently) included St. Peter's pence there (2 pence halfpenny) and amounted to thirty-six shillings and nine pence, with the addition of 12 pence fees of Court. Out of this gross receipt was a payment to the Abbot of Battle of 12 pence for the half-year from Michaelmas to Easter.

Also various returns of rents and payments on account of property at Tanrugge, amongst which may be noted a Collection for the Pope of 3s. 6d., for St. Peter's pence 1d., and in aid of the Sheriff of the County 4d.; at Wolkstede, Chepstede, and the Court of Chelsham, all in

---

[1] Patent Roll, 25 Edward III, p. 1, m. 12.
[2] Diocesan Register, *Wykeham*, II, pt. 3, fol. 186 *v*.
[3] Ibid., I, fol. 344 *v*.

Surrey; Holyndene, Chydyngstone, and Edenbridge in Kent; Long Sutton in Hampshire; Hertfyld, including a small payment to the Warden of Pevensey Castle, and the Court of Wythyhamme, &c., in Sussex. And Rents at le Berwe in the parish of Oxstede (where part of a rental included 4 men's labour every autumn, presumably at a bederipe), at Berstede, Tanrugg, Wolkested, Worlingham, and Herfeld, in Surrey, Sondressche in Kent; subject to a rent of 10s. per annum payable on a lease granted by the Prior of Merton (for meadows called Mertonemede and Mertonefeld); and some other holdings: the payments to the lord of Henedene pursuant to a Placitum, were 3d. and 1 cock and 1 hen or 5d., and for another croft 9d. and 1 cock or 3d.[1]

Among the Harleian Manuscripts, there is an early transcript of a Rental of the Priory, dated 1431 and 9th Henry VI, and stated to be, at the time of making the copy, in custody of Richard Bostocke of Tanridge, gent.

The amounts are arranged in 4 columns, so as to show at a glance what is receivable each quarter of the year. The following is, briefly, the list:—

> John Stoket for lands called Pecies, late of William at Pire, paying thence to Lord, beside a heriot, and suit of Court *a tribus septim⁸ in tres Sept* a quarterly rent of ix^d.
>
> John at Hethe for lands called le Gore, late of John Whynn, late William at Hethe, with returns at same terms, and suit of Court, heriot and relief and homage, and quarterly rent vij^d. ob.
>
> Thomas Wilkin, land late Richard Wilkin, late Elie Aaron, with suit of Court, heriot, and as may happen, and quarterly iij^d.
>
> Henry at Mille, tenement called Smythes, late Benedick la Seni, suit of Court, heriot, &c., and quarterly vi^d.
>
> John Chawre, Senr., land called Techele, &c., and quarterly ij^d. ob.
>
> Richard at Yard, Senr., tenement called Fortes, late Walter Melwards, in alternate quarters ij^d and j^d.

---

[1] I am indebted to Granville Leveson Gower, Esq., F.S.A., for the loan of a copy of this Rental, but, unfortunately, the reference to the original in the Record Office is lost.

Richard Cowper, 2 tenements called Gardyners and Braces, late held by William Northampton, quarterly vj^d. ob.

John Crowhurste, Junr., tenement called Skynners, late held by Robert Stonehurste, quarterly iiij^d. ob.

John Crowhurste, Senr., tenement called Sawnders, late held by William Pire, quarterly iij^d.

Edmund Mathewe, tenement called Combers, late held by Stephen Mathew &c., quarterly iij^d.

Richard a Yard, Senr., holds parcel of that tenement, per annum j^d.

Same Richard, 3 tenements called Pawles, Bugles and Carbonell, late held by Richard Mowsherste, quarterly v^d.

Lawrence Clerke, field of land containing 3½ acres late held by Richard Cowper, next Moultredens, quarterly vj^d.

Same Lawrence Clerke, tenement called Eliotts, late held by Richard Yerde, Senr., quarterly iij^d.

John Champyn, tenement called Howewots, late held by John Lysinae, half yearly j^d.

John Pakke, tenement called Oteweyes, late held by William Butcher (Note in margin—*In manus Dñi*), quarterly ij^d.

Richard at Berne, tenement called picards, late held by Richard Cowper, half-yearly j^d.

A footnote in another hand, is subjoined, that

This rentall above recited was made by the Pryor then of Tanridge, and in the same rentall is also contained the other rents of the aforesaid farm rents then belonging to said Pryor.[1]

In 1452 the Bishop granted to William Wiltshire, a Canon Regular of the Priory, Letters Testimonial to the effect that, although one Walter Lathum had affirmed to the contrary in a Suit in Court, he the said William was in the year of our Lord 1441 and of King Henry VI the 19th, duly professed of the Order of St. Augustine in this Priory, and under obedience to Brother John Fremyngham at that time Prior; and from that time till the date of the present letters continuously, regularly,

---

[1] Rental of the manor :—Harleian MS. 4785, fol. 1. The same MS. contains rentals of the manor of Bursted, otherwise Oxsted, for the year 4 Henry VIII, April 1512 to 1513, amounting to xxiiijs. vd.; and another dated 18th December, 20 Elizabeth, when the receipts were xixs. ix$d$.

and laudably remained, and was so held and notoriously reputed. In witness of which things the Bishop set his seal at his Manor of Essher, on the 4th July, 1452, and of his consecration the 5th.[1]

Thenceforward, for a long period, no event appears on record beyond the documents connected with the succession of Priors, who were elected, confirmed, and inducted (as mentioned in the subsequent list of Priors), and who held rule over the House; these were John Fremyngham, who was Prior in 1452. John Hamond, who resigned about 1458.[2] John Graunesden, whose election was confirmed by the Bishop on 15th May, 1458, and in whose time the House seems to have been in serious financial difficulties, for we find that on the 14th October, 1461, a Sequestration was granted by the Bishop to Nicholas Assheton, Justice of the King's Common Bench, John Hamond, a canon regular of the Priory of St. James, Tanrigge, and William Gaynsford and John Elynbrigge, literates (two well-known Surrey names); in which he recites that after an enquiry, made under his authority, by his Chancellor Master William Darsset, Doctor of Laws, he, on account of the waste of goods of the Priory, committed to them the sequestration and care of the fruits, returns, and pervenients thereof. Given at his palace of Wolveseye, under seal, the 14th October, 1461, and of his consecration the 15th.[3] This Prior resigned in 1463.[4] John Odierne was appointed by the Bishop to be Sub-prior,[4] and died in 1464.[5] William West, who was appointed by the Bishop, 22nd December, 1464,[5] and resigned 1467.[6] John Kyrton, elected 16th April, 1467, resigned in 1469, whereupon the usual Sequestration was granted, on the 10th April, 1469, to Master Hugh Heghstale,

---

[1] Diocesan Register, *Wayneflete*, I, fol. 15* v. (Appendix, XXXVII.)
[2] Ibid., I, fol. 90 v.
[3] Ibid., I, fol. 68*.
[4] Ibid., fol. 108 v.
[5] Ibid., fol. 135 v.
[6] Ibid., fol. 154.

Rector of Blechyngle,[1] and Brother Robert Haysant, a Canon of the Order.[2] Robert Mitchell, the next Prior, was cited to attend in Convocation in 1470 and in 1472, and again in 1474;[3] and so, in 1478, was William, his successor,[4] and in 1495, Robert, the next Prior after him.[5]

On the 9th July, 1499, John Barnarde, describing himself as Canon and President of the Chapter, addressed Letters to the Bishop, in which he stated as follows:—Consequent upon the voluntary resignation of Sir Robert Michell, late Prior,[6] the Members of the House conventually and capitularly assembled on this day, at the hour of 9. in the forenoon, in the Chapter House, and the Canons John Barnarde (himself) as President, Bartholomew Alleyn, William Danne, and William Elmeden, having a voice in the election of Prior, and being the only persons by Law or custom in any way entitled to vote; and they appointed the 11th hour of the same day for the purpose of the election. At which hour the Mass of the Holy Ghost was solemnly sung in their Church, and the bells were rung for them to assemble in Chapter. They then having assembled in the Chapter House, invoked the Grace of the Holy Ghost by devoutly singing the hymn, "Veni Creator Spiritus." The President made the usual admonition and protestation, and the "Quia propter" constitution of the General Council was read and explained. Having consulted together they resolved to proceed *per viam compromissi*, and nominated their Ordinary, the Bishop, as their compromissary to elect some person to be their Prior; and they humbly petitioned the Bishop to accept

---

[1] Hugh de Heghstale was instituted Rector of Bletchingly, 19th April, 1451, and died in 1476. (M. and B., II, p. 315.)
[2] Diocesan Register, *Wayneflete*, I, pt. 2, fol. 96*. (*Appendix*, XXXVIII.)
[3] Diocesan Register, *Wayneflete*, II, fols. 142, 150 *v*, and 156 *v*.
[4] Diocesan Register, *Langton*, fol. 15 *v*, at foot.
[5] Ibid., fol. 56 *v*.
[6] Robert Michell was appointed by the Bishop on the 13th July, 1499, to be Prior of Reigate, but did not long hold that appointment, for on the 19th November following he was elected Prior of St. Mary Overy.

the burthen of such election. This document was given under their Common Seal, in Chapter, and attested by Simon Watson, Clerk, of the Diocese of York, Notary Public; in the presence of Masters John May, Bachelor in Degrees, Perpetual Vicar of the parish church of Ledered (Leatherhead), and John Richardson of the Diocese of Carlisle, Notary Public.

The Bishop on receipt of this document accepted the position, and nominated Sir Robert Wodd, a Canon Regular, to be Prior.[1]

Robert Wodd, or Wode, did not long hold the appointment, for in July following, being less than a twelvemonth, he was nominated by the Bishop to be Prior of the Priory of St. Denis, near Southampton;[2] and on the 9th July, 1500, John Barnarde, Bartholomew Alyn and William Danne, Canons, addressed a letter to the Rev^d. Father and Lord, the Lord Thomas, by Divine Permission Bishop of Winchester, their most singular lord (domino nostro singulari), to the effect that the Priory, being now vacant by the free resignation of Sir Robert Wode, late Prior, made to the Bishop, and by him accepted, they empowered the Bishop to nominate a Prior for them, they renouncing for this turn all their right and power of election. Given under their Common Seal at their Chapter House on this day.[3]

On the 11th August following, the Bishop, having accepted the submission, nominated to the Office Sir John Forster, a Canon Regular of the Order. Dated at Merewell.[3] Robert Mitchell seems to have returned, for we find him mentioned on the Court Rolls from 1521 to 1524:[4] he resigned on 24th February, 1524, and was succeeded on 21st February, 1525, by John Lyngfeld, the last Prior.[5]

Among the Harleian Manuscripts is a little volume of post-octavo size, containing a collection of forms of legal

---

[1] Diocesan Register, *Langton*, fols. 51 and 52.
[2] Ibid., fol. 54.
[3] Diocesan Register, *Langton*, fol. 55.
[4] Harleian MS. 4785.
[5] Diocesan Register, *Fox*, V, fol. 95.

documents, or Formulare, dating towards the latter part of the 15th century, amongst which is the form of a Corredy granted by John, Prior of Tanridge, and the Convent of the same. The number of Priors named John is curious: there were four successively within a few years in the middle of the 15th century, viz: John Fremyngham, who died in 1441; John Hamond, who resigned in 1460 and was succeeded by John Graunesden, who resigned in 1463; his successor John Odierne, Prior or Sub-prior, died in 1464, and John Kyrton, who was elected in 1467, resigned in 1469. The grant might have been made by either of these, but more probably by John Forster, who was nominated to be Prior on the 11th August, 1500, which would fairly coincide with the probable date of the Manuscript in which the form is preserved. A corredy was a grant in the nature of a provision for life made by a corporate body to some individual, presumably for an adequate valuable consideration, but the nature or value of the consideration is not usually stated. Such grants were very frequently made by monastic houses, and generally no doubt to their ultimate advantage, but in many cases so improvidently that various monasteries became, for the time at least, seriously impoverished: in fact, corredies were by no means an unimportant item in monastic affairs. But as it might seem to be somewhat wandering from the present limited subject if we went further into details upon this point, we limit ourselves to the document before us, which furnishes a fair example of a corredy.

The Prior and Convent by this Indenture made by the unanimous assent and consent of all the Chapter of the House gave and granted for certain considerations (not specified in this formulare) and confirmed to A. B., esquire, the following corredy. Food and drink for himself at the Prior's table, as that of a Canon, with accustomed service and attendance, and allowance for one servant; a room, and a smaller room, and a latrine, all situated within the precincts of the Priory, in the part called "le ffermery;" and there to be always entertained; and to be provided with a supply of underwood for firing delivered at the door; one loaf of conventual white bread, a quart of beer, and 2 candles of twelve to the pound, for use in his rooms, or elsewhere as he pleased; together with a daily supply from the orchards and gardens of the Priory; and, at will, free entrance and exit without impediment. The Priory moreover undertook to maintain and repair the said rooms at their expense, and to keep up the corredy during the life of the said A. B., under penalty of twenty pence, with power to him and his heirs to enter and distrain for the same.[1] In fact board and lodging for life, for so much down.

Early copies of various Court Rolls are preserved, chiefly of the Manors of Breysted or Bersted,[2] in Oxted, but as they relate only to parts of the property of the Priory, and moreover run to a very considerable length, it would not seem worth while to give them much space here; but they may be enumerated as follows:—

    1502, Michaelmas (18 Henry VII), Court Rolls of John ffoster, Prior of Tanregg, of the tenants of Breysted.
    1503, May 8 (18 Henry VII), relating to Breysted.
    1505, May 8 (20 Henry VII), relating to Garston.
    1507, June 7 (22 Henry VII), Tanrigg.
    1507, Decr. 7 (23 Henry VII), Bersted and Tanrigg.
    1508, May 16 (23 Henry VII), Bersted and Tenrigg.
    1512 or 1513 (4 Henry VIII), relating to Bursted otherwise Oxsted; giving a total rental of xxiiijs. vd.
    1521, Feb. 28 (12 Henry VIII), Robert Michell, Prior of Tanrigg, relating to Bersted.
    1521, Novr. 12 (13 Henry VIII), Bersted.
    1524, May 19 (16 Henry VIII), Bersted.
    1525, June 8 (17 Henry VIII), Court Rolls of John Lyngfeild, Prior of Tanrigg, relating to Bersted.
    1526, Oct. 22 (18 Henry VIII), Bersted.
    1527, Novr. 8 (19 Henry VIII), Bersted.
    1529, April 13 (20 Henry VIII), Bersted.
    1529, Oct. 11 (21 Henry VIII), Bersted.

The MS. also gives the rental of Bersted on 18th December, 1577 (20 Elizabeth), amounting to xixs. ixd.

---

[1] Harleian MS. 1777, fol. 43.
[2] Harleian MS. 4785, fols. 3 to 16.

In 1522 (14 Henry VIII), an Order was made for an annual grant by the Spiritualty for the King's personal expenses in France for the recovery of the Crown of the same, and the list of contributors was headed by the Lord Legate with £4,000, followed by the Archbishop of Canterbury with £1,000. We find that Tanrigge was put down for £20 (the same as Reigate), which would indicate that its property was assumed to bring in a fairly good amount of revenue.[1]

It appears to have been customary to let various parts of the Property on lease; no example of such a document seems to be now extant, and indeed the chances against the preservation of a long-expired Lease are very great under any circumstances, but especially in such a complete disturbance of legal ownership as took place at the Dissolution of Monasteries. But we find noted in the Ministers' Accounts[2] the following Leases granted within the period of a few years, from which the usual practice of the House may be assumed:—

> On the 21st Sept^r., 1516, the Priory granted a lease of the Rectory of Crowhurst, with all its pertinents, to John Gaynesford and Edward Lee, Clerk, for the term of the life of the said John Gaynesford, at a rent of £2 : 13s. 4d. per annum.
>
> 1521, Feb. 27. Lease of the Manor of Sentie, in the parish of Hartfelde, Sussex, to John Haywarde, for 16 years at a rent of £4.
>
> 1522, June 28. The Manor of Godstone, and all lands, tenements, meadows, and pastures in the parish of Blechinglye to William Barbour, for 31 years at £4 : 6s. 8d. per annum.
>
> 1523, Sept. 16. Sowthelonds, in Tanridge, and 5 cows, to George Topsell, for 4 years, at £3 : 16s. 8d.
>
> 1527, March 26. Land called Thomlyn's Londs, in Oxstedd, to Henry Cowper, for 21 years, at a rent of £2 : 10s. 0d.
>
> 1531, March 20. Tenement called Botelers, in the parish of Tanridge, to Richard Topsell, for 21 years, from Michaelmas 1531, at a rent of £4.
>
> On the same day, a lease of lands called Chamberlonds, Scott's Croft, Myllfelde, Harteslonde, and Downlonds, in Tanridge, to Alice Huntley, for 40 years, at a rent of £2 : 10s. 0d.

---

[1] Record Office, *Calendar of Letters and Papers, temp.* Henry VIII (edited by Brewer); Vol. III, p. 1048.

[2] Ministers' Accounts, 28 and 29 Henry VIII, Surrey, No. 108 (Augmentation Office).

On 12th August following: Moiety of Rectory of Godstone to Robert Darby, for 7 years, at £3 : 11s. 8d.

1534, Oct. 31. Manor of Rokesnest, to Thomas Banco, for 21 years from Michaelmas following, at £9 : 6s. 8d.

1535, Oct. 26. Two tenements and certain lands and closes in Oxstede, to Thomas Aleyne, for 30 years, at £3 : 16s. 8d.

There were also the following Leases about the same period, but of which the precise dates are wanting:—

Land called Studmerhill in Tanrygge, let to John Squyer at 2s.

Land called Dirgefelde, let to John Holmann at 5s. 8d.

Twenty acres of land, called Le Olde Parke, to John Lyntonne, at 4s.

Lands called Conny Pytches, Downe Londe, and Ovesnet, to William Dyxon, at 7s.

Lands called Lullinge, and Goodweye Londs, to John Pope, at 45s. 4d.

A tenement and 14 acres of land at Barowe with 12 acres of pasture, called Robyns Grove and Multrydene, to Richard Holman, at 35s. 8d.

A tenement and certain lands called Bakers, let to John Marten, at 28s.

Rents of land, tenements and cottages at Godstone, let to William Barbour, as Farmer, at 16s. 8d.

Rent of a field called Priorsfelde, at Godstone, let to William Harlyng, at 6s. 8d.

Farm of certain lands called Brownes, at Chepstede, in tenure of Richard Cadingtonne, at 15s.

A Tenement, with all lands, meadows, feedings and pastures, at Westhall in Warlyngham, to William Comporte, for 26 years, at £4 : 13s. 4d.

The Prior was summoned to attend a Meeting of Convocation in the year 1529,[1] which tends to show that his House at that time was not unimportant.

In the 27th year of King Henry VIII, 15th April, 1535-6, was passed the Act for the Suppression of all Monasteries which had not lands worth above £200 per annum, whereby after reciting the (asserted) daily use and commission commonly in such little and small Abbeys, Priories, and other Religious Houses of Monks, Canons, and Nuns, where the congregation of such Religious Persons was under 12 in number, "to the High Dis-

---

[1] Record Office, *Calendar of Letters and Papers, temp.* Henry VIII (Edited by Brewer); Vol. IV, p. 2697.

pleasure of Almighty God, and Slander of good religion, and to the great infamy of the King's Highness and the Realm;" and with the object that the inhabitants should be compelled to live in one of the greater Monasteries; it was enacted "That His Majesty shall have and enjoy "to him and his Heirs for ever, all and singular such "Monasteries, Priories, and other Religious Houses of "Monks, Canons, and Nuns, of what kinds of Diversities "of Habits Rules or Order soever they be called or "named, which have not in Lands, Tenements, Rents, "Tithes, Portions, and other Hereditaments, above the "clear yearly value of Two Hundred Pounds;" together with their lands granted (on lease) within a twelvemonth previously, and all and singular their Manors, Lands, Tenements, Rents, Services, Reversions, Tithes, Pensions, Portions, Churches, Chapels, Advowsons, Patronages, Rights, Entries, Conditions, and all other Hereditaments to them or any of them, appertaining or belonging (every kind of property, in fact, which could be suggested), to have and to hold *unto the King's Majesty*, and his heirs and assigns for ever, to do and use therewith his and their own wills, to the *pleasure of Almighty God* and to the Honour and Profit of this Realm. The Act orders that the King shall have all Monasteries, Abbies, and Priories, which at any time within one year next before the making of this Act had been given and granted to His Majesty by any Abbot, Prior, Abbess, or Prioress, under their convent seal, or that had otherwise been suppressed or dissolved; showing that the process had already commenced, without even the semblance of right which was then conferred.[1]

It would be difficult to suggest a much better *non sequitur* than the reasons given for the confiscation, or a more impudently dishonest pretence for sacrilege.

At what exact date sacrilegious hands were laid upon

---

[1] Statutes at Large; 27 Henry VIII, cap. 28. The Court of Augmentations which Parliament established at the same time, but by another Act (cap. 27), was in fact a Commission, with special and extensive powers for dealing with the income and disposing of the property itself and handing over the proceeds to the King.

the Priory does not appear, but it was evidently very soon after the passing of the Royal Robbery Act, for the earliest Ministers' Account, being for the year from Michaelmas 1536 (the King's 28th year) to Michaelmas in the following year, refers to a former account not now in existence. The formal surrender, if any, is not extant.

Upon the Suppression thus effected, a Pension was granted to John Lyngfeld, the last Prior, who had held the Office for some time. The King desiring to provide a reasonable annual pension or suitable promotion for him *ad victum et exhibitionem suam* and for his better support: therefore with the advice and consent of the Chancellor and the counsel of the Court of Augmentations of Revenue of the Crown, gave and granted to the said John an Annuity or annual pension of £14 sterling, to have and receive to him, or his assigns, from the feast of the Annunciation of B. Mary the Virgin last past, for the term of his life, or until he should be presented by the King to one or more ecclesiastical benefices, or other suitable promotion, of the same clear value; such pension to be paid by the King's Receiver of such Revenues, by equal payments on the feasts of St. Michael and the Annunciation of B. Mary the Virgin. This order is signed by Richard Ryche, and dated at Westminster, 2nd July, 28th Henry VIII (1536).[1]

Evidently, at a date very shortly after the Dissolution, an account of the revenue of the House was prepared, by which it appears that the total gross receipts amounted to four score and six pounds, seven shillings, and tenpence half-penny; upon which the charges and payments amounted to £7 : 10s. 11¾d.; so that there remained a net income of £78 : 16s. 10¾d., besides something from the Priory of Esborne, the account of which was wanting.[2]

Very soon after the date of the Account, the King, not content with the vast revenue which he had obtained from the confiscated income of Monastic property, pro-

---

[1] Augmentation Office, Miscellaneous Books, 244, No. 127. (*Appendix*, XL.)

[2] Augmentation Office, Miscellaneous Books, 406, p. 49.

ceeded to sell the property itself, in order to raise money for his profligate expenditure.

On the 2nd January, 1537–8, he granted to John Rede, son and heir of William Rede, late of Weybridge in the County of Surrey, Esquire, deceased, All the House and Site of the late Monastery or Priory, suppressed and dissolved by authority of Parliament; and all the Church and Bell-tower, and Cemetry: together with all messuages, houses, edifices, barns, stables, granges, dovecotes, mills, kitchen gardens, orchards, gardens, waters, ponds, vivaria, land and soil, as well within as without, and nigh and adjoining the site limits, circuit, bound and precinct. And also all the domains and Manors of Tanrigge, Oxsted, Garston in Blechinglye, and Westhall in Warlingham, with their men and entire pertinents, in the County of Surrey. And also the Manor of Sentye, in Hertsfelde, with its members and pertinents in the County of Sussex, whether parcel of the late Monastery or belonging or pertaining thereto. As also the Rectories and Vicarages of the parish churches of Tanrigge, Crowherste, and Wawensted[1] otherwise Godstone, with their men, and all pertinents, in the County of Surrey; together with their Vicarages and everything in any way belonging to them; and all and all manner of messuages, houses, edifices, barns, lands, glebes, pensions, portions, tithes, oblations, fruits, pervenients, profits, and emoluments whatsoever of the said Rectories of Tanrigge, Crowhurste, Wolkensted otherwise Godstone, or otherwise belonging or pertaining thereto. Also all other domains and manors, and all and singular messuages, tofts, mills, gardens, cottages, lands, tenements, meadows, pastures, moors, marshes, fields, brueria, underwoods, revenues, returns, services, rents of fees, rents, annuities and returns, and rents of tenements and leases, customs, villans and their offspring, knights' fees, wards, maritages, eschaets, reliefs, heriots, Courts leet, view of frankpledge, and all matters which pertain or belong to view

---

[1] Also spelt Wolkensted, Walkinsted, and Walkamstede.

of frank-pledge, assize, assize of bread, and services; goods and chattels, waviats and goods and chattels of outlaws and fugitive felons and of all convicts and felons de se, and deodands; waters, ponds, running streams, wardmote, common fisheries, turbary, and other liberties, jurisdictions, franchises; rectories, privileges, vicarages, advowsons, donations, nominations, presentations and rights of patronage of churches and vicarages, chaplains, chantries, hospitals and other ecclesiastical benefices whatsoever, pensions, portions, annuities, all kind of tithes, oblations, fruits, pervenients, obventions, commodities and all other the King's (so called) possessions, interests, and hereditaments whatsoever, both spiritual and temporal, whether general or special, and by whatever name called, taxed, known, or reputed, situated lying or being in villes, meadows, bounds, parishes, or hundreds of Tanrigge, Oxsted, Crowhurste, Wawensted otherwise Godstone, Blechinglye, Warlingham, and Chepsted, or elsewhere in Surrey; in the parish or hamlet of Hertfeld, Sussex; the ville or parish of Chedingstone, Kent; the hamlet or parish of Longesutton, Hants; and elsewhere in the Kingdom of England and Wales or the Marches. As fully and entirely as John Lyngfelde, late Prior, and his predecessors on the 4th February in the King's 27th year, or previously, when monasteries were dissolved by Parliament begun at London 3rd November in his 21st year and adjourned to Westminster with divers prorogations till 4th February in his 27th year.[1] Which lands and possessions were of the clear annual value of £69 : 8s. 0½d. To hold to him and his male heirs, of the King and his heirs and successors, *in capite*, by military service, viz., the 20th part of a knight's fee, and the annual payment of £18 : 10s. 0½d. in the name of an annual tithe, according to the decision of the Court of Augmentation of the Revenues of the Crown; from Michaelmas (last ?)

---

[1] The Act 27 Henry VIII, cap. 28, gave to the King all monasteries (with their property of all kinds) which had not lands producing a rental of above £200 per annum : it refers to suppressions having already taken place.

for all services, return, exactions, and demands whatsoever.

The Patent gave, in default of heirs male of the Grantee, a remainder to Henry Rede, brother of the said John Rede, and his heirs male; with remainder to Anthony Rede, son of the said William Rede and his heirs male; and in default to Thomas the brother of Anthony; and, failing him and his heirs, to the said John and his heirs and assigns for ever.

And the Grant was warranted against all persons, and free from all returns, fees, annuities, concessions, incumbrances, and all other charges, except as above mentioned, and also excepting an annual payment of 37s. 4d. in respect of certain lands and tenements in Oxsted, to the Lord of Borowghe and his heirs of his Manor of Oxsted; and free from a return of 14s. per annum to Nicholas Carewe, Knt., and his heirs, payable to his Manor of Bletchinglegh, and from 3s. 4d. payable to the Prior of Merton, and 17s. 6d. to the Archdeacon of Surrey for Procurations, and 12d. to the Abbat of Battle, and 13s. 4d. to John Skynner, Gentleman, for life (payable at the Court of the said Prior), and 40s. for fee to Henry Compord (receiver of the late Priory) for his life; and except £12 per annum payable to 2 Chaplains for their stipends as Chaplains[1] of the Churches of Crowhurste and Tanrigge.

And also all profits arising from such grants; from the feast of the Annunciation of B. V. Mary last past. Free from any account.

And it was further granted that he should have Letters Patent under the Great Seal of England, without fee to the great or small Hanaper of the Chancellor.

Given at Westminster on the 2nd January in his 29th year by the King with the authority of Parliament.[2]

No doubt there was great difficulty in ascertaining the full particulars of the properties of the vast number of Monastic foundations, which were seized by the authority of the King, with the assent of a Parliament composed

---

[1] Vicars.   [2] Harleian MS. 4786.

of persons who were some of them subservient to the despotic and ruthless tyrant who ruled the British nation, many venal, but probably not a few culpable only from deficiency of moral courage to do that which they felt right. In some cases, it may fairly be presumed, there were Abbots, or Priors, or minor officials, within whose province the knowledge was contained, who, from whatever motive, furnished very full particulars from which the Commissioners appointed by the Crown to form " the Court of Augmentations of the Revenue of the Crown," in other words, to collect, get in, and manage the property and spoil of the Abbeys, Priories, Chantries, Free Chapels, and similar endowments given freely for the purposes of Divine Worship and works of religion and charity, but now sacrilegiously diverted from the service of God to profligate, heartless prodigalities.[1]

In the present case there arose a difficulty, of no great importance, but illustrative of the abundant difficulties which thus occurred, and which had to be overcome, if overcome at all, by means of influence, moral or otherwise.

John Rede thus, "by waie of purchas and eschaunge," obtained Letters Patent under the Great Seal dated 2nd January (1537–8), 29th Henry VIII, with a clause of exoneration whereby he was discharged of payment of a certain rent thereon, or else promised recompence from the King's Majesty for the same, as by the said Letters Patent; and he had also obtained an Indenture, bearing date the 27th January in the same year, made by the King, of the one part, and the said John Rede and Sir Thomas Cromwell, Knt., guardian of the said Thomas Rede during his minority, of the other part, and it appearing that a rent-charge of 23s. 1d. was payable out of the tenement and lands called Seynt Tie (being parcel of the possessions of the Priory in the

---

[1] It is a noteworthy fact that while for every other English monarch, no matter what were his or her faults, failings, weaknesses, or incapacities, apologists have been found, no one has yet attempted to palliate those of King Henry VIII.

County of Surrey), to the Provost and Scholars of Kynge's Colledge in Cambridge, as belonging to the Manor of Withyham in the County of Sussex. The Court therefore declared that the said John Rede ought to be discharged of the said rent or else to have recompence from the King for the same: and it plainly appeared the said rent had not been paid to the said Provost and Scholars since the time of making the said Letters Patent, though the same was chargeable on the said tenement and lands called Seint Tie; but that the said John Rede ought to be exonerated therefrom. Therefore the Chancellor and General Surveyors of the Court of Augmentations and Revenues of the King's Majesty's Crown, on the 4th June, in the 3rd year of King Edward VI (by the grace of God Kynge of England, Fraunce, and Ireland, Defendour of the Faith, and of the Churche of England and also of Ireland, in earth the supreme hedd), ordered that the said Provost and Scholars and their successors and farmers should have and enjoy the said yearly rent of 23s. 1d., to be payable from the said tenement and lands, together with all arrearages of the same due to them since the making of the said Letters Patent, and be paid by the owners and possessors of the said tenement and lands without any let or denial. And, in consideration thereof and because the said John Rede was deceased, it was ordered and decreed by the said Chancellor and General Surveyors that the heirs male of the said John Rede and other issue (as in the Letters Patent) that he and they should have from the King the said sum yearly, by the hands of the General Receiver of the said Court, being of the King's money and revenues remaining in his hands at the feast of St. Michael the Archaungell yearly; together with the arrearages of the same 23s. 1d. due since the making of the said Letters Patent.[1]

From the Ministers' Accounts we learn what were the possessions of the dissolved Priory and their value. The Accounts are stated to be an Account of all Bailiffs,

---

[1] Augmentation Office, Miscellaneous Books, No. 105, fol. 72 b.

Farmers, and other Ministers of King Henry VIII, from all and singular domains, manors, villages, possessions, and Monastic and Priorie hereditaments in Surrey belonging or in any way pertaining to the Priory lately suppressed and dissolved by authority of Parliament, existing in the hands of the King; viz., from the feast of St. Michael the Archangel in the 28th year of the said King, till the same day in the year following, being one entire year[1] (Michaelmas, 1536, to Michaelmas, 1537). In the case of Tanridge the Account was rendered by Francis Mores, Bailiff and Collector of rents there during such time; and, briefly, runs to the following effect:

The Accountant stated that there were no arrears as shown in the preceding account.[2]

In Tanryg there were the following rents:—

Lands called Turneys Lands held by Henry Torner by rental made and renewed by the Seneschal on 20 October, 28 Henry VIII, at per ann.	ijs. ijd.
Harwards Lands[3] held by Robert Heyward at	ijs. jd. ob.
Luxfords Lands, held by Christopher Luxford at	vjd.
Hethe Lands held by William Hethe at	xvjd.
Comport's Lands[4] held by John Comport at...	xxd.
Plawes' Holding, held by John Plawe at	xviijd.
Standfords, held by Edmund Standford at	ixd.
Studmerhill, in the tenure of John Squyer by indenture, at	ijs.
Dirgefelde, in the tenure of John Holmann by indenture, at	vs. ivd.
Le Olde Parke, 20 acres, in the tenure of John Lyntonne, by indenture, at	iiijs.
Conny Pytches Downe Londe and Ovesnet, in the tenure of William Dyxon, by indenture	vijs.
Lullinge and Goodweye Londs, in tenure of John Pope, by indenture, at	xlvs. iiijd.

Annual charges on the following property in Oxstedd:

Welbeck Croft, freehold of Maurice Wolbeck	ijs.
Ball's Londs, freehold of Robert Genys	iijs.

---

[1] Ministers' Accounts, 28 and 29 Henry VIII, Surrey, No. 108. (*Appendix*, XLI.)
[2] No earlier account can now be found.
[3] This may be the property called Howewots in the Rental of 1431.
[4] Possibly that called Combers in the rental of 1431.

Le Londs, freehold of John a Lee	iijs. viijd.
Cowpers, tenement, garden, and 1 acre of land, freehold of Henry Cowper	viijd.
Crowhurst, land, freehold of same	xviijd.
Holmes Land, freehold of Thomas Holmdenne ...	ijs. vjd.
Cokes land, freehold of Richard Coke	xijd.
Alynslonde, freehold of Thomas Aleyne	xijd.
Brokyslonde, freehold of John Boke	viijd.
Avys, freehold land of William Smythe	ijs. vjd.
Pyrres, freehold land of John Ownsted	iijs.
Barowe; rent of tenement and 14 acres of land, and at Robyns Grove and Multrydonne, 13 acres of pasture let to Richard Holman, by Indenture	xxxvs. viijd.
Bakers; tenement and certain land let to John Marten, by Indenture	xxviijs.

Rents of divers tenements at Holm in Oxsted:—

Prestfelde, lands let to John Loke, at will	xxxs.
Tenement in which John Foster lately lived ...	vijs.
Phelipps, at Barowe; tenement in which William Grene lately lived	xiijs. iiijd.

Charges on property and rent in Godstone:—

Charged on certain lands, tenements and cottages there, by William Barbour, of Godstone, lessee by Indenture	xvis. viijd.
Priorsfelde; field let to William Harlyng by Indenture	vjs. viijd.

Rent of certain lands in Chepstede:—

Brownes; land in occupation of Richard Cadingtonne, by Indenture	xvs.

Charge on property in Edenbrydge, Kent:—

Alchornes; freehold tenement of Andrew Cole ...	ijs.

Charge on property in Chyddington, Kent:—

Charge	vijs. xd.

Charge on property in Long Sutton, Hants:—

Chobhammes; freehold lands of Thomas Byflete ...	xijs.
Perquisition of Court there: no profits, Court not being held in consequence of nothing happening (by oath of Accountant).	

Sale of Wood:—

No profits arising from sale of wood or underwood,
none being sold this year.
Total ... ... xiij*l*. viij*s*. xj*d*. ob.

Against these receipts were the following payments:—

Dnō Borowgh, from lands in Oxstede, as allowed, for one entire year to Michaelmas, in the King's 29th year (1537) ... ... xxxvj*s*. iiij*d*.
Nicholas Carewe, knight, for lands in Blechinglie ... xiiij*s*.
The Prior of Merton, for lands there... ... ... iij*s*. iiij*d*.
The King, for lands at (left blank) ... ... xxxiiij*s*. v*d*. ob.
The Abbot of Battle, at his Manor of Brodeham ... xij*d*.
Archdeacon of Surrey for procurations and synodals of the Church of (left blank) this year, as in previous year ... ... xvij*s*. vj*d*.
In remuneration of the said Accountant Bailiff and Collector of rents of all lands and tenements, by discretion of the King's Commissioners (as last year) ... ... xl*s*.
Salary of Clerk of Auditor, for writing this account, as usually allowed to the Clerk of the Auditors of the Duchy of Lancaster ... ... ij*s*.
In remuneration of John Skynner, Seneschall of the Court there (as last year) ... ... xiij*s*. iiij*d*.
Payments allotted for the expenses of himself and other Officials of the King, as by account of particulars ... ... xx*s*.
Payments made by the Accountant to John Mores, the King's Receiver of Augmentations for the County of Surrey from outgoings of his office for the year to Michaelmas in the King's 29th year as per account signed by His Majesty's Receiver ... ... xlij*s*. vj¾*d*.

The total of all allowances and payments xl*l*. v*s*. 11¾*d*. and debit xlij*s*. xj¾*d*. paid to John Reade, to same date, by virtue and force of Letters Patent dated 2nd January following, and enrolled.
It was thus balanced.

The accounts undermentioned of the year's rent were rendered by tenants holding for unexpired terms under Leases which had been granted to them by the Prior and Convent. In each case they claim to have paid the rent for half of the year to John Reade by virtue of his Letters Patent, and the other half to the King's Receiver, whereby the account was balanced; and they respectively state that there were no arrears, as shown at the foot of the previous account.

Nicholas Carne, for rent of lands in domain ...	xxv*l*. vj*s*. viij*d*.
Thomas Bance, for rent of the Manor of Rokesnest with a house called le Tyle House held by him under Lease given under the seal of the Prior and Convent, and dated the last day of October in the 26th year of King Henry VIII (1534), to hold from Michaelmas following that date, for 21 years at a rent of	ix*l*. vj*s*. viij*d*.
George Topsell, for rent of a messuage or tenement in Tanredge, called Sowthlonds, held by him under Indenture given under Seal of the Convent and dated 16th September in the King's 15th year (1523); together with rent of 5 cows; for a term of 4 years from Michaelmas following that date, at a rent of	lxxvj*s*. viij*d*.
Alice Huntley for rent of lands called Chamberlonds Scott's Croft, Myllfelde, Harteslonde, and Downlonds, in Tanridge, held by her under Indenture given under Seal of the Convent and dated 20th March, in the King's 21st year (1529–30), for a term of 40 years	l*s*.
Richard Topsell for rent of a tenement called Botelers, in the parish of Tanridge held by him under Indenture given under seal of the Convent and dated 20th March in the King's 21st year (1529–30), to hold from Michaelmas 1531 for a term of 21 years	iiij*l*.
Henry Cowper for rent of land called Thomlyn's Lands in the parish of Oxstedd, held by him under Indenture given under seal of the Convent and dated 26th March in the King's 18th year (1527), for a term of 21 years	l*s*.
Thomas Alyn (or Aleyne) for rent of two tenements and certain lands and closes in Oxstede, held by him under Indenture given under seal of the Convent and dated 26th October in the King's 27th year (1535), for a term of 30 years ...	lxxvj*s*. viij*d*.
Robert Darby, for rent of the half part of the Rectory of Godstone, together with tithes of all corn in the parish of Wolkhamstedd, held by him under Indenture given under seal of the Convent and dated 12th August in the King's 22nd year (1530), by equal half-yearly payments at the feasts of the Nativity and of St. John Baptist ...	lxxj*s*. viij*d*.

William Barbour, for rent of the Manor of Godstone, with all lands, tenements, meadows, and pastures, in the parish of Blechinglye, held by him under

Indenture given under seal of the late Priory on 28th June in the King's 14th year (1522), for a term of 31 years	iiij*l*. vj*s*. viij*d*.
John Gaynsford, knt.,[1] and Edward Lee, clerk, for rent of the Rectory of Crowhurst, Surrey, with all its pertinents, held by him under Indenture given under Seal of the Convent on 21st September in the King's 8th year (1516), for the life of the said John Gaynsford...	liij*s*. iiij*d*.
John Haywarde, for rent of the Manor of Sentie, in the parish of Hartfelde, Sussex, held by him under Indenture given under seal of the Convent on 27th February in the King's 12th year, for a term of 61 years	iiij*l*.
William Comporte, for rent of a tenement with all lands, meadows, feedings and pastures, with all pertinents held by him under Indenture given under seal of the Convent on (date blank) for a term of 26 years, and payable by quarterly payments	iiij*l*. xiij*s*. iiij*d*.

I do not propose to trace further the history of the possessions of the Priory beyond noticing that the last remains were disposed of by authority of the Parliamentary "Commissioners for selling the Fee Farm Rents belonging to the Commonwealth of England," on the 25th March, 1651.[2] The task would, to the Writer, be simply a wearisome and distasteful one; probably wearisome also to the Reader: but if any one should wish to trace upwards their history they will no doubt find all that they want, up to the date of Manning and Bray's invaluable County History, in the carefully wrought-out studies of that work, and subsequently continued in the recent reprint and continuation of Brayley's *History of Surrey*.[3]

---

[1] Sir John Gaynesford, of Crowhurst, was Sheriff of the County in 1500 and again in 1517: he married 6 times and had 20 children, and died in 1543, and was buried at Guildford. (Paper by late G. R. French in *Surrey Archæological Collections*, III, p. 60.)

[2] Augmentation Office, Deeds of Sale of Fee-Farm Rents, K. 1, No. 13.

[3] Brayley's *History of Surrey*; reprint and continuation by Walford, published in 1882, Vols. III and IV.

Having now set forth the historical records of the Priory, it may be well to refer to the unrecorded, private life of the Canons who dwelt there.

It seems strange, at first sight, though it is a fact, that we know very little indeed of life in a mediæval monastery: but on consideration it is not strange, since the events of ordinary, daily, common-place life are just those which are the least likely to be recorded. Even as regards secular life in the middle ages, there is little known except what we can pick up casually, especially from such writers as Froissart and Monstrelet, the Chroniclers, the Homilists, and, perhaps more than all, from the Story-tellers. Amongst such of their works as have come down to us we note little bits, which at length being sorted, compared, and harmonized, give up what upon the whole is no doubt a fair general picture of the life of secular persons; especially, of course, those of the upper classes; and later on, when diaries began to be kept, the information to be extracted from them (the Diaries of Machin and Pepys, for example) is invaluable. But of the rarely eventful life of a monk, no such record has reached us, if any ever existed.

On a general view of the subject it is not therefore so strange, as at first sight might appear, that we really know very little of life in a mediæval monastery. There were certain well-known general rules of obedience, poverty, and chastity; the due performance of Divine Service at the Seven Canonical Hours; and the observance of Ecclesiastical fasts; and other duties, to which the inhabitants of all monastic establishments were bound; but the actual, definite rules were few, and their requirements differed greatly according to the particular Order to which the House belonged; beyond this it would appear that the minor rules, important as they were to those whose whole lifetime, from morning to night, and night to morning, from youth, perhaps, till old age and death, were governed by them, absolutely depended on the will of each House as from time to time enacted in Chapter; though probably, as a matter of fact, what had been originally agreed upon became fixed, and was rarely, if ever, altered.

There was, however, very great difference in the austerity or ease, and habits of the various branches of the great monastic communities. Some were distinguished by bitter severity and self-mortification; others, leading an easier life, did vast service to the Church and world by study and learning; while some devoted themselves almost exclusively to preaching, teaching, or works of charity. In the category I purposely omit the friars, through whom, mainly, discredit was brought upon monastic life in general, and to whom the scandalous stories of the early story-tellers and satirists refer; so that when the King, like Ahab, coveted the possessions of others, there was less public feeling shown in favour of monasteries than would otherwise have been manifested, even at the hazard of vengeance from his tyranny.

Leaving monastic life generally, we must limit ourselves to a short notice of the Canons Regular of the Order of St. Augustine, who were for the sake of brevity commonly called Austin Canons. Their communities may, in a few words, be described as small joint-stock companies, who, in partnership, farmed and let their land, and lived a religious, regular, quiet, bachelor life.

"Among them," said a writer in the 13th century, "one is well shod, well clothed, well fed. They go out when they like, mix with the world, and talk at table."[1] And so we find them favourably referred to by a very early author of a sober tone of mind, viz., in Piers Plowman's Crede, where, after severely censuring the Franciscans as then so widely strayed from "Fraunceses rewle," he adds:[2]—

"But Austines ordynaunce was on a good trewþe."

Of course there were Rules which formed the basis of the system under which the Austin Canons (and various other Orders of Monks) were primarily bound, and

---

[1] Satire by Guyot de Provins, quoted in Fosbrooke's *British Monachism*, p. 65.
[2] Piers Plowman's Crede, line 509 (Early English Text Society's Ed., p. 19).

which were subsequently somewhat extended. It appears to have taken centuries before the numerous communities of monks, hermits, and recluses settled down into anything like a systematic classification; but a Rule was laid down by St. Augustine of Hippo (who died A.D. 430), to which various Orders bound themselves as the basis of their organization; though even as to this the particular document in which the ordinance was comprised is a controverted point.[1] The several writers on the subject have never been able to agree about the true Rule of St. Augustine, whether it consisted in two Discourses of his, or in his 109th Epistle directed to Religious Persons. Be that as it may, all those that follow the Rule of St. Augustine, as well monks as nuns, acknowledge no other Rule but that 109th Epistle. His Rule, which was stated to be for the purposes of avoiding differences and discords, was, briefly, as follows:—

In the first place, he says, the members of the convent assembled together should dwell in the house and be of one mind, one heart, and one soul in God. None to claim anything as of his own, but all things to be in common: and to each be distributed food and clothing, not alike to all, but as the needs of each require, as we read in the Acts of the Apostles (IV, 32—35). What everyone joining the community possesses, to be thenceforward held in common; and if they possess nothing, not to be proud of their position in sharing its goods. To observe the settled hours and times of prayer, and to perform no other work in the Oratory, but that no impediment be placed in the way of any who wished to pray there at other times: Psalms and Hymns, with Prayer to God, to be there poured out with heart and voice; to sing only what is directed to be sung.

Let them mortify their flesh by fasting and abstinence as much as health will permit (with exception of the sick); and take no food except at meals. At table listen to what is customarily read, without noise or strife:

---

[1] Dugdale, *Monasticon Anglicanum;* Stevens' Supplement, II, p. 65.

and use, then, their jaws for eating only, and their ears for hearing the word of God. But the sick and infirm to be otherwise treated in respect to food and other matters.

Let them not be remarked by their habit, nor endeavour to please by their clothing, but by their behaviour. The head and hair be covered and carefully arranged.

When going out, two to walk together: on arriving at their destination there remain until their return. Conduct themselves with modesty of eyes and behaviour, for immodesty of eye tells of immodesty of heart.

The clothing of the community to be kept in one place, under the care of one or more of them, and delivered out publicly; and its washing to be done under order of the Præpositus.

Anything requisite obtained from the Cellarer, whether clothing or books, to be served out by him without grudging, but, as a rule, at fixed hours.

There be no strife, or malediction; obedience be given to the Superior; and all to live in fragrant conversation.[1]

Even in the 11th century there were Regular Canons of the Rule of St. Augustine, but it is certain that they did not begin to make solemn vows till the 12th century. Pope Innocent II, in the Lateran Council, A.D. 1139, ordained that all Regular Canons should submit to that Rule, and then they all took the name of Regular Canons of St. Augustine.

The most universal reformation which concerned all the different bodies of Regular Canons was made in 1339 by Pope Benedict XII, who, to that effect, drew up Constitutions containing 64 Articles or Paragraphs, which he directed should be universally observed.

Some pretended that these Constitutions were abrogated by Pope Clement VI, successor of Benedict; though probably not.

These Constitutions run to a very great length, but

---

[1] Migne, Patrologiæ cursus : S. Augustin ; Epistolarum, Classis III, ccxi (olim 109). Vol. II, p. 958.

their nature may be gathered from the headings to the several chapters into which they are divided, and these I must only stay to indicate still more briefly, as follows :—The making of Canons; their profession; prohibited from holding any preferment; the claustral prior; daily assembly in chapter; annually in a larger chapter, and from time to time in chapter of all the Houses in the Province; as to visitors; subventions; students in churches and monasteries; providing students and their maintenance; occupation of benefices; sick and infirm; continued observation of old customs; horses and servants not to be kept on the premises;[1] provision of benefices for those in Orders; wearing of honest habit;[2] entering or leaving the House only by permission; alienation of property forbidden; various directions as to letting and management of property; food and abstinence; dormitory without separate cells; privileges and dispensations; celebration of masses, confessions, and communion; Relics and care of ornaments; trial of certain causes prohibited; hunting forbidden;[3] against delators; precaution against collapse of churches and monasteries; Canons not to act as dealers and merchants; conspiracies in the House, and fugitives from it.[4]

The daily Chapters were an important and perhaps almost an essential element in the welfare of a House, since everything of however small importance was there discussed. In the annual Chapters matters of a wider range were discussed with other Houses of the Order; while the triennial General Chapters of the Province

---

[1] In the wealthier monasteries, at least, each of the Canons had his servant and often his horse; but, possibly, they were not kept on the premises.

[2] Extra septa ecclesiarum . . . Capas seu mantellos honestos, vel rodondellos, seu clochias talares, &c. Surplices a cubit wide, at the least, and hanging to the middle of the thigh, and having long sleeves.

[3] Possibly the rules were, in later times, more often broken in this particular than in any other : it would be easy to give references to repetitions of these injunctions, as referred to in a subsequent note.

[4] Cotton MS. *Vespasian*, D. 1, Art. 2.

were in their nature calculated to be of great value; but the impediment of journeying in those days from all parts of the kingdom to the place appointed, and the very heavy cost, and the time occupied, were so great that we need not wonder if repeated Injunctions were necessary in order to maintain the observance of the Rule which required attendance. Thus, in 1281, Archbishop Peckham, in his Constitutions of that date, refers to excuses made by many Houses, on account of their having formerly belonged to Mother Churches beyond the sea, though long since separated, or by reason of their ceremonies differing from other Houses of the same Order in the Province of Canterbury; and he directs that they be admonished by the Bishops that they duly assemble in General Chapter to treat concerning the government and reformation of the Order, and of ceremonies, and any other, if any, notable diversity in substantials of religion.[1] It may be noted that the only diversity mentioned in the gloss relates to costume. But, so far as we find, the Acts of General Chapters seem to have been chiefly directed towards keeping the numerous and scattered monasteries comprised in the body, up to the due observance of the general Rules. In this it does not appear clearly that much more was performed than by the Bishops who, as visitors, from time to time addressed Injunctions and Admonitions to the monasteries within their respective dioceses, as to themselves seemed fit.[2]

[1] Constitutions of Archbishop Peckham, 1281: Wilkins, *Concilia*, II, p. 58.

[2] For example, the Bishop of Winchester, on the 27th September, 1387, addressed Letters to the Convent of Merton (so nearly allied with Tanridge in its earlier days), exhorting them to adhere more closely than they had been doing to the original Constitutions of St. Augustine. They extend to very great length and refer to attendance at Divine Service, vain conversation, performance of omitted Masses, secular persons passing in the monastery, the care of the church and monastery doors, insufficient knowledge of some of the Canons and the Constitutions of Othobon, old clothing, absence without leave, arrangements in the dormitory, forbidding hunting, reproving non-attendance of Officers at Divine Service, reduced numbers, care of property, half-yearly accounts and repairs, forbidding grant of corrodies

It requires little knowledge of human nature to be aware that, however well organised any institution may be, and however thoughtfully ruled, things will certainly exhibit a downward tendency, and as time rolls on some kind of reformation becomes necessary in order, at least, to regain the original position. The misfortune generally is, 'that Reformers in their well-intentioned zeal frequently work serious harm, or even destruction. Amongst the Austin Canons (and, no doubt, all the Monastic Orders) in the course of time grave reforms had become needed. Thus it was that, at the General Chapter of the Order held at Leicester in 1513, there were passed certain Resolutions (as we should call them) to the effect that a thorough reformation of the whole Order both in head and members had become necessary, in order to preserve it from impending ruin. But it is difficult to see how things could have fallen into what we should consider a really serious state, since, had there been any grave or serious cause of complaint, it must have become, at all events to some extent, known publicly; such was clearly not the case, since at the same Chapter was announced the fact that the King (Henry VIII) himself and his Queen (Catherine of Arragon), the Princess, the Cardinal (Wolsey), the Queen of France (Mary, sister of King Henry VIII, relict of King Louis of France), and her husband, Charles, Duke of Suffolk, and many others, had been received as (what we should call Honorary) Brothers and Sisters of the Order.[1]

The final Code of Regula was dated 12th March, A.D. 1519-1520, and the eleventh of King Henry the Eighth,

without licence, directing chantries to be filled up; as to almsgiving, care of sick Canons, punishments by order of Chapter, pittances, sale of Woods, care of Common Seal, restraint as to shoes, eating only in refectory, chaplaincy, election of Officers, valuable furs interdicted, offices abroad forbidden without leave of parish priest, ornaments of the altar, pawning goods, study of Scripture and other works, hospitality to relatives of Canons, and directing that these Rules be enrolled and be recited twice a year. (Bodleian Library, Laud MS. 723, fol. 52.)

[1] Minutes of the General Chapter of the Order held at Leicester, 1513. Cotton MS. *Vespasian*, D. 1.

and were issued by Thomas Wolsey, by the title of St. Cecilia, Cardinal priest of the Holy Roman Church, Archbishop of York, Primate of England, and Legate of the Apostolic See: as Chancellor of the Kingdom of England and legate of the Pope, Leo X, to the most Serene and Powerful Prince and Lord, Henry, by Divine Providence King of England and France and Lord of Ireland; and made by special Commission and Indult dated at St. Peter's, Rome, and relating to all monasteries and religious houses, whether exempt, or not exempt. First it is directed that all Canons Regular (some of whom had held themselves segregate) should meet in Chapter: then follows a form of profession by the Novice who binds himself for life to follow the Rule of St. Augustine and promises obedience to the Abbot and Prior of the House and their Canonical Successors under pain of the wrath of Almighty God. The Novice to be duly instructed by the Officials; and as to obedience, and abnegation of individual property. It directs that the Canons be provided with healthful and suitable food and clothing according to the means of the House, and in other competent necessaries, from the common stock, as often as need be, by the Prepositor or other Officer appointed for the purpose; but fixing the cost at not exceeding 60s. per annum for any Canon-priest or Officer, or 30s. for a Canon not a priest, and reserving power to the Prior to make a larger allowance for any famous Doctor of Laws. No woman of whatever age, propinquity of relationship, or condition, to be permitted access to the Dormitory, Infirmary, Cloister, or Cells or Chambers of the Canons, or any other private place, but only to the place appointed for guests, or to the dwellings (*hospicia*) of prelates, or, in great monasteries, the apartments of the Prior: not forbidding them to enter the church for the purpose of devotion. Clothing to be washed by one of the Canons or some person appointed for the purpose, but no women to be admitted on that pretence. Canons, and Probationers during their year, not to go out without leave of the Prior, and then to return within a reasonable time, and only to go in company with one or two, and habited suitably. None to keep dogs or birds for hunting or sport.[1] Not to eat or drink in any neighbouring town unless on account of illness supervening, except by licence specially granted; not to go a journey other than as assigned, and then to be provided with money for the purpose from the common fund. It being fitting that all of the Rule should have a habit of one colour and form and a uniform tonsure, it was ordered all should use honest clothing according to the Benedictine statutes, of only white, brown, black, or almost black (quasi nigri) colour, and the form of clothing and shoes to be determined by the head of the House, so that all therein should be uniform: Rochets of small price, not curiously plaited, and shoes not like those of the laity: no rare or fine furs, excepting in the case of prelates such as might be suitable.[2] The tonsure to be like that of secular Clergy, but more ample.

All to sing the psalms and other things pertaining to Divine Service, not hastily or slowly, but with attention to the pointing, and distinctly, plainly, and devoutly. To observe the Canonical Hours, especially Matins and High Mass. Strictly forbidding that "pricksong"[3] be permitted to be sung in choir; and no laymen, or secular clerks, or singers, whether men or boys, be admitted into the Choir, but that at Masses of the B. Virgin and the Name of Jesus, such persons might be allowed, outside the Choir, to sing "*cum cantu fracto, seu diviso,*" and with organs; but none of the Canons, except the Celebrant, to be there. Permitting also the Canons (alone) to sing less simple melodies on Sunday and festivals at Mass and Vespers, but so that the integrity

---

[1] If space permitted, it would not be uninteresting to note how constantly both monks and secular clergy had to be admonished against hunting; a sport which, in itself, cannot be deemed more harmful than fishing, which is a recreation admitted by all to be innocent.

[2] Piers Plowman's Crede strongly, and at some length, rebukes the lavish fashions in dress and furs then used by the Franciscans; the passage is well worth referring to. (Early English Text Society's Ed., Lines 290 to 301.)

[3] Ornate Plain-song. (*Walcott.*)

of the chant and the expression of the words be not omitted. If necessary, an honest laic or secular priest, might be employed to play on the organ, but the Canons not to treat him with too much familiarity. Allowances made in respect to the performance of the offices, where the number of Canons be very small.

After Compline, all to receive Holy Water from the person appointed, and then pass to the Dormitory where silence is to be maintained, and none to leave without permission. Each to have his separate cell there, but open at the end.[1]

All to eat together in the Refectory, except Officers and Prelates, who eat at their own table or elsewhere, whether within or without the bounds of the Monastery; and a lection be heard in silence.

Abbots and Priors to be very careful that these Rules be observed. To hold a daily Chapter, at which any merited punishment be ordered, and imprisonment if necessary. To set example of attendance at Divine Service and especially at Mass, and in all things; nor be absent from the House without good cause.

Recreation to be taken with moderation and not to be allowed to interfere with other things. No players to be admitted. Recreation in sufficient numbers together, and under supervision of a grave Senior; not in villes, lanes, or taverns, but in open spaces not distant, and keeping apart from laics, whose houses should not be entered for eating, drinking, or dining. Not to remain out at night, unless with prelates at the manors.

Accounts to be prepared quarterly or half-yearly, by one of the most skilled seniors, and exhibited to the Ordinary or his Vicar General, at the Visitation; and if unsatisfactory, under pain of suspension. But monthly or weekly accounts, where usual, to be continued.

Exterior persons, with a Canon nominated by the Seneschal, may be appointed to collect rents and other claims.

---

[1] Apparently what we should call a cubicle: a part partitioned off from the general dormitory.

And, moreover, notwithstanding the Rules, the food and clothing for the mind in the form of learning is not well taught or understood; It is ordered that in the Chapter House, in the time of Chapter, the Brothers speak in Latin or French, unless any stranger be present, or on account of a great Feast day. The Convent to send one from amongst them most fit to be sent, to the University of Oxford or other suitable place, with a Student's pension, so that the man, being learned, may impart his learning: and this under a penalty of 10 marcs per annum.

Finally it is ordered that the number of Canons and Novices on the original foundation be kept up, or at least so many as the present net income of the House can maintain; and the Prelate straightway look to and see that on the death of a Canon or diminution of the number in any way, he endeavour to fill up the vacancy, under such penalty as may be assigned at the next General Chapter.

The Cardinal, then, as Legate, orders by supreme authority that these Rules be published and observed in every Monastery and House or Priory of Canons Regular of the Order, in either Province, whether exempt or not exempt, within the octave of the Feast of Corpus Christi next; but not desiring to impose them prior to the Feast of the Holy Trinity.[1]

As we have said, these Rules run to a very great length, and are here merely outlined; but they will be found to be but little more than an amplification of those by which the Order had always been bound: together they afford us the most complete account obtainable of life in a mediæval monastery.

It will be seen that the Rules were applicable to all Communities of the Order, whether large or small. At the time of the Dissolution of Monasteries, there were in England 173 Priories of Austin Canons and Priories of Augustinian Nuns, and, with the exception of the

---

[1] Cotton MS. *Vespasian*, F. IX, fol. 22: a contemporary manuscript. See also Dugdale's *Monasticon*, II, p. 564.

Houses of Benedictine Monks and Nuns which were slightly more numerous (amounting to 186), they very nearly equalled the number of all other Orders put together.¹ Some Houses were composed of 30 or 40 Canons, but many were very small, and contained but few inmates; thus at Tanridge we do not at any time find any record of more than five Canons. They were commonly called Canons, Concanons, or Confraters. The head was the Prior who was responsible for the observance of the Rules, and the good governance of the Community, and his power was considerable, but tempered by the daily meetings in the Chapter.

According to the Rule which we find in use at Hexham, no Canon could be lawfully elected to be Prior unless he was of good life and character, a priest, a person of education, of proper age, born in lawful wedlock, and a freeman : and the election must be by the voice of two-thirds of the Convent, and without contention. When the suffrages had been taken, the Canon presiding declared the result in a formal manner, and received authority to announce it to the public. All then proceeded to the High Altar, conducting thither the Prior Elect, and singing the *Te Deum* as they went. That finished, the bells rang out, and the Prior being prostrate before the Altar, the Sub-Prior offered over him a set prayer; and then the choice of the Convent was declared to the Convent at large.²

Only two Priors of the Order of Austin Canons were entitled to wear a mitre, viz., the Priors of Waltham and Cirencester:³ in a manuscript in the British Museum, dating probably between 1430 and 1450, or rather earlier, is an illumination representing a Prior habited in a black cope and white mitre, and bearing in the left hand a gilt pastoral staff, crook outwards, and a book in the right;⁴ presumably one of the Order of Austin Canons.⁵

---

[1] Fox, *English Monasteries*, Appendix No. 2.
[2] Priory of Hexham ; *Surtees Society*, Vol. I, pref. Cxxxi.
[3] Godwin, *Handbook of Archæology*.
[4] Cotton MS. *Tiberius*, III, fol. 148.
[5] So assumed in *Illuminations in British Museum*, by Birch & Jenner.

It would appear that, where the means of the House would afford it, the Canons generally had their servants and horses; of course it will be borne in mind that, considering the general nature of roads existing up to modern times, horses were essential to locomotion. At Tanridge, in 1312, when the Priory was evidently in serious financial difficulties, the Prior was directed to content himself with one only servant.[1]

The Sub-prior came next after the Prior, and acted as his lieutenant, and, as such, was commandant in his absence: in so small a House as Tanridge it seemed hardly likely there would be such an Official,[2] but in the Bishop's Visitation Articles in 1306[3] he directs them to appoint a Sub-prior; and the term also occurs in two other formal documents:[4] almost each Canon had an official title, as well as a duty. In a large House there were also the following officers. The Precentor, who had rule of the choir, archives, and library: at Tanridge he seems to have been next in authority to the Prior, and to have been the Superior of the Convent during a vacancy.[5] The Cellarer managed the domestic affairs, and frequently acted as Commissary or Proctor; this is very clearly shown by the records of Tanridge: in the Injunctions consequent on the Bishop's Visitation in 1306, he, with the Prior, was enjoined to render accounts of their respective administration to the Chapter, twice a year;[6] so he is referred to in the Visitation enquiries in 1308;[7] while in the following year he was removed from his office for neglect in this particular.[8] The Seneschal was next in importance, and sometimes held Manorial Courts; at Tanridge, it was he who kept the

---

[1] Diocesan Register, *Wodelok*, fol. 175.

[2] It would almost remind one of the Scotch lad who told his father he was always second in his class; and on further enquiry said the class consisted of "me and a lassie."

[3] Diocesan Register, *Wodelok*, fol. 148 *v.*

[4] Ibid., fols. 109 and 175.

[5] Ibid., fols. 41 *v* and 110.

[6] Ibid., fol. 149.

[7] Ibid., fol. 96 *v.*

[8] Ibid., fol. 101 *v.*

accounts of the rental.[1] The Treasurer received rents, paid expenses, and kept accounts. The Sacristan's duties were in the Church, where he slept. The Almoner's duties were chiefly such as his name implies. The Hostellar had the care of visitors. The Kitchener was responsible for the provisions, especially those for the sick, the care of whom in other respects rested with the Infirmarer. The Chamberlain's duty was the provision of clothing, bedding, and such matters. The Refectioner managed the scullery department. And finally, the Porter and his assistants, who had charge of and slept at the gate. Sometimes, also, were included the Pitanciar, the Gardener, and others. These, with deputies and assistants, formed the staff of a large House;[2] in a small one, like Tanridge, no such subdivision of duties was needed: in fact, we hear of no official other than the Prior, except that, in one instance (in 1323), the Precentor acted as head at the election of a Prior to fill a vacancy,[3] and in another the Seneschal is mentioned as having kept the Rental.[4]

Quite at the commencement of the 12th century there arose in England what might almost be called a mania for monastic establishments, and they multiplied and spread all over the country, while the nobles and the wealthy seemed almost to vie with each other in founding and endowing them; and gifts continued to be made from time to time subsequently. The natural tendency of this was that, since land was the only permanent investment, there arose a danger lest too large a part of the land should become vested in them—for by their rules they were stringently forbidden to alienate property, and therefore all accretions were permanent. To guard against the risk of mischief, both social and political, which in course of time must necessarily have resulted, there were passed divers Statutes of Mortmain, which rendered void the absolute grant for charitable purposes of

---

[1] Ministers' Accounts, 28 Henry VIII, No. 108. (*Appendix*, XLI.)
[2] Mackenzie Walcott, *Church and Conventual Arrangement*.
[3] Fox, *English Mon.*, p. 139; Winchester Reg., *Stratford*, fol. 3.
[4] Ministers' Accounts, 28 Henry VIII, No. 108.

any Real Estate, without the King's licence—a provision in force at the present day. Such licences however, made by Letters Patent, were very frequently granted, and probably in many cases for the sake of a valuable consideration to the King, or his officers. One would suppose that under such circumstances, with property increasing from time to time and never diminishing, all monasteries must infallibly become constantly more and more wealthy, but such was by no means the case. Probably we may account for it partly by their great charities, and partly, perhaps, because they were (as Corporations generally are) more liberal than private owners are to their tenants. The poor, the sick, and aged, had in those days nothing to look to for shelter, or preservation from starving, except the Religious Houses, and casual relief from the rich, who, it must be borne in mind, were proportionately far less numerous than now; when the monasteries were dissolved, workhouses and public relief for the poor and necessitous had to be provided at the cost of the nation. Partly, no doubt, from the heavy imposts laid upon them by Kings and Popes; sometimes from the granting of improvident Corrodies;[1] and no doubt in other cases from want of judicious management of the property, which was more especially likely to happen in the case of the smaller Priories—at Tanridge, for example, out of the five Canons, which seems to have been their highest

[1] A Corrody was, as already mentioned, somewhat in the nature of a life annuity—a provision of food, lodging, and raiment for a valuable consideration. One would assume that ultimately the House would derive benefit from the land, which generally formed the consideration, but such does not appear to have been generally the case; on the contrary, they so frequently did themselves such serious harm by improvident grants of the kind that the authorities interfered to forbid it: thus Archbishop Langton, in his Constitutions dated in 1222, orders that no Corrodies should be given or sold, or stipends for life or for a given time be granted, unless for urgent necessity, and with the Bishop's consent (Wilkins, *Concilia*, I, p. 591): and Archbishop Kempe, in his Constitutions issued for the Province of York in 1444, makes a similar provision, directing that such grants be only made after a diligent and mature consultation of two days, at least, in Chapter, and then upon licence from the Diocesan. (Wilkins' *Concilia*, III, p. 671.)

number, it was probable (and records indicate the fact) that from time to time none of them would be possessed of the requisite business capacity and education needful for a due administration of their estate consisting of land and tenements and manors, of varying and complicated tenure, and requiring very good system and book-keeping. Temporary needs would naturally lead to mortgage or other alienation of property, although at that period interest ranged high, and a recovery would be difficult. The pecuniary difficulties of the Convent were evidently great in 1309 and 1312, in which latter year the Bishop intervened and appointed a Supervisor of their temporalities;[1] and again in 1330, when he appointed a coadjutor and interdicted the Prior himself from interference in the administration of the goods of the House:[2] and in 1461 the Common-Law Court, evidently interfering on behalf of a creditor, issued a Sequestration of their property.[3] From one cause or other it happened that many monasteries, including some of the most flourishing, were at times in great need, and when the period of their dissolution arrived it was found that very few possessed any large, and none an extravagant, amount of property. Taking Tanridge as a fair average example, the entire value of the estates given to the House, and accumulated during a period of much more than three centuries, produced a net income of only £78 : 16s. 10¾d.; which, even after making full allowance for the difference between the value of money towards the middle of the 16th century and at the present time, is no great amount.

The dress of the Canons differed not a little in different Houses of the Order: in this and divers other things there was no rigid rule of conformity, but within somewhat wide limits they managed their own affairs. The best evidence we could desire is provided by the famous Canonist Lyndwode, in his gloss upon a constitution of Archbishop Peckham (dated 1281), in which he mentions among ceremonies (or usages) of which even the

[1] Diocesan Register, *Wodelok*, fol. 96 v. (*Appendix*, XII.)
[2] Diocesan Register, *Stratford*, fol. 51. (*Appendix*, XXVI.)
[3] Diocesan Register, *Waynflete*, I, fol. 68*. (*Appendix*, XXXIX.)

General Chapter could not deprive them : such as that some of the Order wore a linen rochet and above it a black, open, cope; others entirely white linen, or wool; others a black cope fastened with a cross upon the breast; and others white raiment with a cross set upon it. And so with food. Some eat flesh, some none; some fasted at stated times, others not; some wore untanned leather shoes[1] (ocreis) like monks, while others wear boots (sotulares) like secular clergy.[2] And, as we have seen, the Canons were not even limited to the black and white, but simply to a sober hue. By the Canons made under Archbishop Hubert Walter in the year 1200, it was ordered that no Black Monks, or Canons, or Nuns, use coloured copes (or cloaks) but black only; nor any facings but black or white made of the skins of lambs, cats, or foxes.[3] And further, in 1220, it was ordered that neither Monks nor Canons Regular should wear girdles of silk, or garnished with gold, or silver, nor use burnet, or any irregular cloth.[4] The Constitutions of Pope Clement V merely inhibit inordinate or finely adorned clothing, and excess in eating and drinking.[5] The Canons of Pope Benedict XII relating to dress are limited to strictly inhibiting any Canon wearing, when beyond the bounds, any clothes over their habits, except "capas, seu mantellos honestos, vel rodondellos seu clochias talares."[6]

---

[1] This I take to be the meaning, but do not find the word *Ochrea* in Ducange, or minor glossaries. *Sotulares*, subtalares, calcei, nostris *souliers*; used mediævally to mean half-boots.

[2] Lyndwode's *Provinciale* ; Oxford Edition, 1679, p. 213. Lyndwode was the Official of the Prerogative Court of Canterbury, afterwards Keeper of the Privy Seal, and finally Bishop of St. David's; he died in 1446.

[3] Canons, A.D. 1200; Wilkins' *Concilia*, I, p. 508. As regards such furs, they had previously been forbidden to abbesses and nuns by the Canons made under Archbishop Peter Corboyle in 1127. (Wilkins, I, p. 411.)

[4] Canons, A.D. 1220; Wilkins, I, p. 574.

[5] Constitutions of Pope Clement V: Sec. De statu monachorum; Basle Ed., 1476. The section was addressed to the School of Bologna.

[6] Cotton MS. *Vespasian*, D. 1, Art. 2. *Rodondella;* vestis species, v. cloca. *Clochia;* vestis species, quæ equitantum, et peregre euntium propria est. (Ducange.)

At Tanridge we find that the Bishop's Injunction, issued in 1308, consequent on his Visitation, merely prohibits clothing different from and unfit for their Order, and directs that they should only wear such as the Rules, and propriety of Religion, required, and with the provision (showing that there was no rigidly fixed and definite dress) that they should all wear a uniform habit.[1]

The Austin Canons were in the habit of wearing beards, and covering their heads with a four-sided cap, instead of the cowl or hood of an ordinary monk.[2] Their tonsure was like that of a secular priest, and hair cut short at half the depth of the ear.[3]

Certain Monastic Orders had a special predilection for a particular type of site for the foundation of their establishments,[4] but it can scarcely be so said of the Austin Canons, though they appear to have preferred the suburbs of towns, and then to have selected a fertile plain watered by a clear, flowing stream, in default of which fishponds were essential. At Tanridge, a clear spring, issuing from the hill-side, flows into a basin forming a pond below, and thence through a succession of ponds some acres in extent.

The general plan of their type of church, and of the grouping of the conventual buildings around it, is given by Rev. Mackenzie Walcott, but it scarcely seems to me sufficiently definite to be laid down as a general type. In the case of Tanridge, there are no records discoverable containing, or from which we can deduce, any idea of the arrangement, and, perhaps with one exception, there is not one stone standing on another above ground; possibly some day, archæological zeal, or some more utilitarian cause, may lead to excavations showing us the foundations of the buildings. The exception referred to is about a dozen feet

---

[1] Diocesan Register, *Wodelok*, fol. 149.   [2] Wolsey's Ordinances.

[3] Walcott, *Conventual Arrangement*, p. 40.

[4] "Bernardus valles, Colles Benedictus amabat; Oppida Franciscus, magnas Ignatius urbes." (Quoted in Jameson's *Legends of the Monastic Orders*, Introd., p. xxxix.)

SECTION.

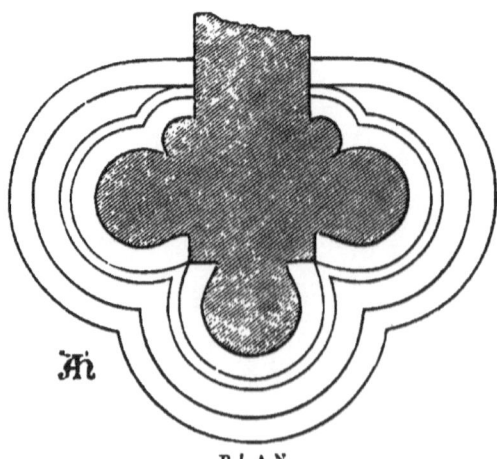

PLAN.

To face page 77.

frontage under the bushes, between the more modern house called "the Priory" and the second pond, within which are remains of a flooring of strong lime and sand; but this may date subsequently to the destruction of the Priory.[1] The cause of the entire and almost instantaneous destruction of monastic churches and buildings by those who had purchased them from the Crown was, no doubt, partly in order quickly to realize the profits on the transaction, but probably still more from the fear that the tide might turn again and that some equally arbitrary enactment might rob them of their share of the spoil.

All that we know concerning the buildings which formed the Priory of Tanridge is, that, subsidiary to the Church which we may with great reason assume to have been dedicated in honour of St. James, there was a Chapel with its altar dedicated to the Blessed Virgin.[2] At the time of the Dissolution there was a church, and a belfry tower, and a cemetery, which was probably the garth in the midst of the cloisters.[3]

One small fragment is all that is known to exist: a little capital from which, probably, sprang the inner arch of a window: wreathed around its bell is graceful foliage of oak leaves, with acorns, just sufficiently conventionalized for true art, and wrought with admirable skill: its date is about the middle of the 14th century. The illustration at the commencement of the present monograph is of full size: the elevation and plan are given on the opposite page.[4] Some ornamental paving tiles

---

[1] On the brow of the hill beyond the ponds, are some ponderous detached masses of unwrought stone, and there is there one small piece of carved work, evidently part of a cornice of revived classic date.

[2] Mentioned in Pedes finium, 47 Henry III, Case 2, No. 177. It is of course possible that when the Institution was changed from a Hospital to a Priory, or when a Chapel was rebuilt, there might have been an altered dedication; but we may assume that in such case, the altar mentioned would have been referred to as the high altar, had it been so: and, in fact, in 1461, we find the House spoken of as the Priory of St. James.

[3] These were amongst the property sold by the King to John Rede on 2nd January, 1538. (Harl. MS. 4786.)

[4] I am indebted to Mr. Percy Wigram, whose family formerly resided on the spot, for the loan of the elegantly carved capital from which these illustrations were made.

found on the site were, within memory, preserved in a frame at the house built on the premises, but have disappeared; a few other fragments both of glazed paving tiles and others, devoid of ornament, were turned up a few days since.

Still, one may hazard the conjecture that the cloister was situated immediately below the bushes just mentioned, since, upon some excavation being commenced there, many human bones were found, and in consequence work was discontinued and the excavation filled in again.[1]

The broken remains of two gravestones or coffin-lids are still there. The pieces composing the most perfect of these, when put together, present a quadrilateral form sloping from head to foot and want but one piece more to complete; the length is 6 ft., and the width at the head 2 ft. 6 in., diminishing to 1 ft. $3\frac{1}{2}$ in. at the foot. Unhappily, it is of Petworth or Sussex marble, and the action of the weather upon it, during three centuries and a-half, has so completely disintegrated the surface, that there is no appearance of any inscription, but there is visible the lower part of an incised cross, consisting of two steps and a plain narrow stem. It is clearly impossible to specify the date with any approach to certainty, but it may probably be placed quite early in the 14th century. A former occupant of the Priory House had a penchant for antiquities, and no doubt he had the pieces put together and the vacancies filled in with Roman cement, fragments of which remain, though the pieces of stone have been again separated and until now thrown aside and half buried: it is, however, Mr. Borradaile's intention to have them reset and preserved.

The other gravestone was of the same form, but only two fragments remain and they bear neither ornament nor inscription.

---

[1] This information was given by the Rev. R. H. Borradaile, M.A., F.S.A., a member of this Society, who is now the occupant of the house called the Priory.

Among the various errors regarding the middle ages into which we inconsiderately fall, there is, perhaps, scarcely one which is more deeply seated, or more widely spread, than the commonly entertained view of monastic life.

So strong is the prejudice on this subject, that few persons can be persuaded to look upon an ancient monk as anything better than a personification of all that is sensual in our corrupt nature, and in whom self-indulgence was the great business of his life, aggravated by concealment beneath the uninviting cloak of an austere discipline. Let us see what was the case.

First; as to the observance of the Canonical Hours which were spent in devotion; this rule, alone, contradicts the charge of self-indulgence, for no one who cared for ease and comfort would select daybreak and midnight at all seasons of the year for attendance in chapel. The Canonical Hours were daybreak, or 6 o'clock in the morning, 9, 12, 3, 6, 9, and midnight.

The diet of the monks was another austerity, which in these days would not be submitted to, even by the most indigent. Fasting, even on one day in the week, would be regarded as a great hardship (or self-restraint), if imposed on those who are well fed and fare sumptuously. It can then be scarcely denied that it must have been a severe trial and self-mortification, to men who fared scantily at all times, and rarely enjoyed a good, substantial meal, to endure the rigid and frequent fasts which the monastic discipline of many of the Orders prescribed. The common opinion that the monkish dietary was the reverse of this is groundless, and may be classed among our vulgar errors. The truth is, that the daily diet of the monastery was remarkably frugal, and usually consisted of herbs, eggs, fish, bread, cheese, butter, and ale or beer.

Punishment usually consisted in a diminution of their rations of food, or a diet of bread and water, and imprisonment; and not infrequently by removal temporarily or permanently to some House of the Order: thus, at Tanridge in 1309, the Cellarer was, by order of the Bishop as Visitor, deprived of his office and transferred to Newark Priory, where he suffered imprisonment and was fed on bread and water:[1] and there are references to like punishment in the House itself, by order of the Prior and Chapter.

The dress which the inmates of the monastery wore had as little in it to excite pride as their general mode of living had to foster gluttony.[2] It was wisely made distinctive, while, as we have seen, it was limited in pattern and restrained to white, black, grey, or brown colour.

As regards the value of the monks to the outside world (for I must not here trespass upon the religious side of the question as affecting themselves personally), it may be put briefly, that they set the example of skilful cultivation even of the waste lands of the country; they were beneficent lords to their tenants and servants; protectors of the liberties of the people in the midst of the tyrannies of the feudal ages; the great cultivators of learning and the arts; the great educators of the people; the centres of religious zeal;[3] they were the chief almoners of the nation, and types of hospitality.

It is no exaggeration to say that solely to the monasteries are we indebted for the preservation of the Books of the Holy Bible, the writings of the Early Christians, and even all classic learning and literature: this fact alone shows the affection with which the Scriptures and other learning were regarded—an affection that could not have arisen or been maintained without a full knowledge of their value.[4] But for those amongst their communities who possessed a moderate amount of learning, and some skill and feeling for art, ample work was provided in the Scriptorium in copying books (often borrowed on the security of a heavy bond for their due return) and illuminating them with a patient industry,

---

[1] Diocesan Register, *Wodelok*, fol. 103 v. (*Appendix*, XIV.)
[2] Fox, *Monks and Monasteries*, p. 118.
[3] Cutts, *Turning Points in English History*, p. 139.
[4] I must content myself with a general reference to Berington's *Literary History of the Middle Ages* and Maitland's *Dark Ages*.

an ability, fidelity, and artistic taste which gives them in no few instances, even in the present utilitarian age, a very large and increasing money value. These, of course, were simply the work of the scribe and artist; but it is clear that this laborious work would never have been performed except for the value felt of a work copied, or as an indication of the honour in which were held the Bible and books used in Divine Service.

Isaac Taylor (who, as a Nonconformist, will not be accused of any special predilection for monastic institutions) remarks, that monastic institutions seemed as if framed for the special purpose of transmitting the remains of ancient literature, sacred and profane, through a period in which, except for so extraordinary a provision, they must inevitably have perished.[1] When learning declined among the people, the Religious Houses became the chief receptacles of books; for in almost every such establishment there were individuals who still cultivated literature and the sciences with ardour: every convent and monastery had its library, its librarian, and other officers employed in the conservation of the books.[2] And so, in the words of an eminent modern writer, Dr. Cutts:—" In the earlier centuries of the mediæval period, the monastic system was, in God's hands, the most powerful agency for preaching the Gospel and establishing the Church of Christ among the barbarous nations of Europe; and in the later centuries the monasteries were the centres of civilisation, learning, and art, as well as of religion."[3]

In illustration of the importance attached to learning by the Austin Canons, we may note that the famous Walter de Merton took his name from the Austin Priory of Merton, in this county, for, although it does not appear whether he was one of the Canons, yet he was intimately connected with the House, and his first scholastic endeavours were established by means of a grant made to

---

[1] Isaac Taylor, *History of Transmission of Ancient Books*, p. 8¼.
[2] Isaac Taylor, p. 16.
[3] Cutts, *Turning Points of English Church History*, p. 190.

him for the purpose by the Priory of their Manor of Maldon, together with the advowson of the Church there;[1] and which foundation, a few years later, he developed into Merton College, Oxford, in 1274, one of the earliest, and probably at that time the most completely organised college at either of the Universities.

And renewed attention was called by Wolsey's Injunctions to the Rules and Constitutions as to reading of Latin (and French, he adds); and he directed that (under penalty of a fine) where the income of the House would permit, they should select and send a student to the University, who being thus adorned with learning might communicate it to the others.[2]

By most of the religious corporations throughout the country, schools were maintained, in which, while the children of the rich might find a ready and accessible training, the instruction of the poor was not forgotten. Instruction was given gratuitously in these seminaries in singing, reading, and writing, and perhaps in some of the more advanced arts of the age; and the generosity with which they were conducted seems to have warranted the name by which they were generally known —the name of Free Schools. When the monasteries were falling, many petitions are said to have been received, that the Free Schools might stand. The loss fell most heavily on the poor.[3] The credit, therefore, due to King Edward VI and Queen Elizabeth, for the foundation and endowment of Public Schools, from Christ's Hospital to local Grammar Schools, is limited to the return by them, for educational purposes, of a portion of that which the Crown had despoiled education as an incident to monastic work.

We must bear in mind also that the larger monasteries were the recorders or chroniclers of the events of the period, and, from the fact of their being corporations,

---

[1] Merton Cartulary; Cotton MS. *Cleopatra*, C. ix, fol. Cxlij, v.
[2] Wolsey's Ordinances, 1519: Cotton MS. *Vespasian*, F. ix.
[3] Rev. Richard W. Dixon, *History of the Church of England from the Abolition of the Roman Jurisdiction*, Vol. II, p. 226.

were enabled to continue their work from year to year through many centuries, and it is to them almost exclusively that we are indebted for any consecutive narrative of public or important events of history: not a few of such chronicles have come down to us, such as the Chronicles of Matthew of Westminster, Roger of Wendover, Florence of Worcester, and Matthew Paris: and there can be no doubt that the histories collected in many familiar printed folios, such as those of Fabyan, Grafton, Holinshed, Baker, and Stow, were compiled solely from monastic chronicles.

A Martyrology kept at Tanridge is casually mentioned in 1308: the Bishop directed his Statutes to be enrolled there so as to be permanently placed on record.[1]

Then, much legal work was needed in the management of the affairs of the House. In those days investments were not made with "the beautiful simplicity of the three per cents;" land, houses, and stock were the only form of permanent property, and the singularly complicated nature of the tenures, and the difficulties arising from the frequently disturbed state of the country occasioned innumerable misunderstandings, doubts, and disputes; beside which, the properties and the Livings permitted to be appropriated to a House were often situated far away, necessitating the appointment and occasional supervision of a proctor or agent, or else the negotiation and grant of a lease, and then a receiver of rents. Nor must we forget that, on the occasion of the decease or resignation or removal of the Head of the Monastery, there were long and careful formalities to be performed, and their enrolment made in the Bishop's Court, and various sanctions obtained, before he could be replaced by a permanent successor. The form of Corredy granted by this Priory, about the year 1500, was that selected by some lawyer as a precedent.[2] The

---

[1] The Martyrology was the volume in which, very usually, the Obituary and Regula were entered with other things desired to be kept upon record. (Vide Ducange's *Glossary*.)
[2] Harleian MS. 4785.

amount of legal business involved in the affairs of the House was therefore very considerable.[1]

Then as to the management of the property much labour was involved. The greater part was let at small rentals, and necessarily required a survey from time to time to see that the houses or cottages were properly kept in repair, and that the land was fairly treated. Various farms, which remained in the hands of the House to be cultivated by a bailiff or steward, needed still closer supervision; while the larger Houses had outlying properties in which were established little branches or cells inhabited by two or three of their number, who undertook the cultivation or management, and had from time to time to be relieved from their isolated position by other members of the House.

The building and repairs of their churches and conventual buildings must have involved a constant attention and labour, even if no one of the House acted as architect, though that was certainly the case in many instances of church building, and no doubt was usual in minor matters. Building was a much more arduous undertaking in early days when there were no great contractors ready to tender for works of any cost up to hundreds of thousands of pounds; but the greater part of the materials and arrangements had to be prepared on the spot.

Besides their noble alms-deeds to the poor, the sick, and the aged, monasteries, especially the larger and more wealthy among them, were frequently called upon to furnish hospitality to the King or members of the Royal family or other travellers of less degree: in the absence of inns capable of more than extremely rough and limited accommodation, it was customary for travellers of rank to rest at a monastery, and perhaps for some time together; and the visitors on departing might, or

---

[1] If we take the large Priory of Merton as an illustration, it will be seen that the work must necessarily have been very great: they had properties or rents or appropriations in 15 counties, viz.: Surrey, Kent, Essex, Hertford, Huntingdon, Bedford, Buckingham, Lincoln, Sussex, Hampshire, Wiltshire, Dorset, Devon, Somerset, and Cornwall.

might not, make any reasonable remuneration for the cost of their entertainment: a few days' visit from a King or Cardinal with a hundred retainers would put the House to no trifling cost, nor was it likely to be adequately reimbursed. The Archbishop of Canterbury was stopping at Tanridge on 14th March, 1296–7.

Nor did monasteries escape being heavily taxed towards the expenses of the King and State; when Parliament called on the laity to contribute a tenth or fifteenth of their income or goods to the necessities of the Kingdom, Convocation was summoned to meet and make a similar assessment upon ecclesiastical income or property, and also to collect it. Beside which, there came demands from the Pope for contributions for his needs, and various other objects; while, perhaps, their most valuable preferments were unjustly grasped by him and given to his favourites or dependants, who frequently did nothing but receive the income without ever visiting the locality or kingdom. No wonder, then, that monasteries, large or small, were often in a state of poverty.

No unimportant part of the benefit which the public derived from monastic institutions, was, that a portion, and generally by far the largest portion, of each of their churches was free to the whole world, who were thus enabled to participate freely and constantly in the Divine Service. Most of our cathedrals were built and maintained by monasteries, and worship conducted by them without the cost of a penny to anyone but the limited number of monks or canons comprised in the establishment. Thus, in cities, thousands were benefited, and in the country, perhaps, the advantage was still greater; as in localities such as Tanridge, where the churches and services were often scanty, and the incumbent not rarely non-resident. No doubt many of the donors of endowments to monasteries were more influenced by this fact than by the preservation and dissemination of learning, for which many wealthy men cared little, though perhaps it may be found, as social life in the middle ages becomes more fully and accurately known, that the upper class were by no means an illiterate, ignorant class, as supposed by popular prejudice. A careful, painstaking, and learned description of life in the middle ages, prepared from a study of the stores of information now open to the student, would be, indeed, a heavy undertaking, but one remaining to be undertaken, for we have as yet nothing but most meagre and unworthy, if not prejudiced, sketches of the subject.

I must not dwell more on this side of the topic before us, nor pause to advert to the many minor matters in which the monastic institutions wrought vast good to the nation; but will turn to the other side of the question, and consider, very briefly, how far the idea, which floats vaguely in the public mind, adverse to monasteries, is justified or otherwise. And, first, a wide distinction must be drawn between monks and friars which in the public mind are synonymous; the former possessed property, but it was held by the community absolutely in common: the latter professed to have, and in fact for some time after their institution, had no property, and subsisted upon casual alms. A very little consideration will show that when the members of the Mendicant Orders became numerous, their thousands roaming all over the country subsisting on chance charity, and practically without personal supervision, could not fail to lead to gross abuses; and perhaps it may fairly be said that the friars, by rapacity and greed, by fraud and frequent immorality, and still more by the prejudices which they more or less intentionally raised against the monks (for whom they entertained a feeling of bitter rivalry), and by the hostility which their conduct created amongst the parochial clergy and their supporters, had weakened the people's affection and esteem for the other Orders and had prepared the way for the total destruction of monasteries, by thus destroying the feelings of wide-spread reverence and esteem which the latter had so well merited, and which otherwise might have rendered their destruction dangerous or impracticable. It may be noticed that in the collections of jests and humorous tales which have come down to us from the middle ages, in which ribaldry and scandalous ecclesiastical stories form no inconsiderable part, it is constantly the friars who figure as chief characters. The popular belief unfortunately tars all with the same brush: monks and friars of all Orders, and even the parochial or secular clergy were often alike condemned for sloth, sensuality, ignorance, and irreligion. It has been already shown that the life of a monk was the most unlikely to attract men even ordinarily affected towards those characteristics.

Let us first see what evidence has been found in proof of such charges as those adverted to. Among the vast number of monks scattered broadcast over the length and breadth of the country, often in small communities and in outlying cells of some of the larger communities, perhaps but two or three together, with little more than a nominal supervision practicable, one might not unfairly anticipate that under circumstances so favourable to laxity, frequent scandals would result, especially as a revulsion from the more or less rigid discipline to which they were bound when at home. On the arrival of the time when, through the King's power, Parliament passed Acts for the Dissolution of Monasteries,[1] the commonest show of decency required some pretence for what otherwise must appear to the world in the light of highway-robbery. It was therefore, clearly, on the King's behalf, and on the part of the wealthy and powerful who benefited by obtaining grants of monastic property at small, and sometimes little more than nominal prices, the duty of the Commissioners appointed for carrying out the work, to note and report every iniquity that reached their ears respecting the Houses they visited, and whether confirmed by evidence or not; and, considering who many

[1] First, for the suppression of the small monasteries possessing property producing a revenue less than £200 per annum; like robbing the little boys too small to protect themselves: and two years later—when the proceeds of this vast sacrilege had been squandered, and more money was needed to supply the wants of the profligate monarch, the moral support of all the smaller houses and that of their patrons being gone—the larger houses thus left standing alone were too weak to ward off their own ruin.

of the Commissioners were, one might anticipate that in default of genuine charges they would not hesitate to invent some. Let us note what happened.

It was evident from the first, as we now see it, that it appeared clearly to the monasteries that their doom was sealed, and there remained no hope of earthly intervention to preserve from spoliation the property which their House had in the course of centuries received from the pious for the purposes of religion, or to save themselves, after solemnly devoting their life to the duties of the cloister, from being turned adrift, and mostly penniless, on the wide world. A few of the larger Houses, indeed, more sanguine, bolder, or more desperate, joined themselves to risings of the populace against the despotism by which they were ground down—such as "The Pilgrimage of Grace"—and their Abbots or Priors paid for it by forfeiture of their heads upon the block. Others firmly, but temperately, refused to surrender what (even if there had been no deeper motive of duty involved) was not theirs to surrender; since the property was the property of a corporation, and they personally had, at the utmost, but a life interest in it: and for such their refusal they were arrested and executed; among these martyrs were the Abbots of the famous Monasteries of Reading, Glastonbury, and Colchester,[1] who were perhaps selected on account of their eminence, *pour encourager les autres*. But very generally, the monasteries altogether gave way, and affixed their hands and the Conventual Seal to the surrender of their Houses, lands, and property to the Crown; in return for which, if the surrender were pleasantly done, the head and perhaps one or two others received some small pension for life, or until they obtained from some other source a stipend of equal amount. There were formerly high-minded banditti in Italy, who, after despoiling travellers who made no defence, and ransacking their baggage, made them a present of a scudo or two to carry them on their road. If the monastery could not be frightened or

---

[1] Fox, *Monks and Monasteries*, p. 403.

cajoled into a surrender, the result was the same, except that they got no pensions and were kicked out of their Houses, and perhaps personally ill-treated.

Hopeless, reckless men, under these circumstances, were not unlikely in some cases to be induced by an unscrupulous Commissioner to endeavour to curry favour by confessing to all sorts of enormities. An example of this kind happened at the Cluniac Priory of St. Andrew, Northampton, where the monks duly executed a confession " as bloated, fulsome, and rotund as " an Act of Parliament, volleying forth endless convolu- " tions of phraseology; it seemed to consist of nothing " but words. Never was penitence so well ordered."[1] This is the solitary example of such a confession, and even here the form is vague, and may mean nothing more than a worldliness and neglect of their duties. Curiously enough, the same Commissioner had visited the House previously, and had then noted no evils but debt and involvement.

At Bittlesden, a Cistercian Priory in Buckinghamshire, there was executed a formulated confession (whether supplied to them or invented by their own ingenuity), but it contained nothing that can be construed into an admission of moral depravity: and the same form of words was used in other cases, making six Houses in all.[2]

These are the only known instances.

Proof, therefore, of those charges against monasteries in general which rankle in the public mind, is altogether wanting, while the almost entire absence of them, in spite of every incentive to the production or invention of scandalous tales, furnishes the strongest possible evidence in their favour. And finally, we may note the fact that the last Abbots or Priors of dissolved monasteries, in many cases became the first Deans in new

---

[1] Dixon, *History of the Church of England*, II, p. 19. He adds that Weaver (*Funeral Monuments*, pp. 106—110) appears to have believed, without seeing, that there were many other confessions like it. The important part of the confession is reprinted by Dixon in a foot-note to p. 20.

[2] Dixon, *History of the Church of England*, II, p. 36.

Corporations, *e.g.*, Durham, Winchester, Worcester, Rochester, Carlisle, and Ely; and so in the new chapters of Chester, Peterborough, and Westminster. Many new Canonries and Prebends were filled by the appointment of former monks. The Bishops of most of the new Sees, such as Oxford, Peterborough, Gloucester, and Bristol, had previously been Abbots, Priors, or Provincials. At Canterbury, although the head of the House was deprived, no less than twenty-nine of the Convent were appointed to offices under the new foundation, and all the rest received pensions or promotions.[1]

And finally, we may again refer to the fact that, at the General Chapter of Austin Canons, held at Leicester in 1513, King Henry VIII himself, and his Queen Catherine, the Princess, the Cardinal Wolsey, the ex-Queen of France, and her husband the Duke of Suffolk, and many others, were enrolled as associates of the Order;[2] affording the strongest proof they could very well have given of the high esteem in which they held the Austin Canons.

THE PRIORS OF TANRIDGE.

THOMAS. The earliest Prior[3] of whom we find mention was named Thomas, who held that office on the octave of the Purification (9th February), 1225-6, when a Concord was entered into in a Law Suit.[4]

ADAM. Prior Thomas was, presumably, succeeded by Adam, who, in the autumn of 1235, entered into a Concord in a Law Suit.[5]

HUMPHREY. Humphrey apparently was the successor of Adam; we find him mentioned as Prior in a pro-

---

[1] Dixon, II, p. 225.
[2] Cotton MS. *Vespasian*, D. 1.
[3] These three earliest Priors have not hitherto been recorded. The list and particulars given by Manning and Bray are very good and full, but now considerably supplemented in the present monograph. A few of the dates differ slightly from those given by Dugdale.
[4] Pedes finium, 10 Henry III; Surrey, No. 74. (*Appendix*, V.)
[5] Pedes finium, 19 Henry III; Surrey, No. 181. (*Appendix*, VI.)

ceeding before the Justices Itinerant ended in January, 1262-3.[1]

WALTER.- Walter de Pedeleshurst was appointed 4th June, 1306, by the Bishop, on lapse, having first vacated his election for want of due form.[2] On the 12th March, 1309, the resignation of Prior Walter was admitted by the Bishop:[3] in the proceedings on the appointment of his successor, on 17th June following,[4] he is spoken of as Walter de Hetfeld. It seems improbable that this was another Walter.

THOMAS. Thomas de St. Alban, a Canon of Newark, from which Priory he was transferred by the Bishop in May or June, was appointed 4th June, 1309, by the Bishop, on lapse, the House not having elected according to the Bishop's mandate dated 15th March, 1309. There was a mandate to induct him 17th June. On 22nd November, 1312, Charles (de Seggeford), Rector of Colesdon, was made his coadjutor, the Priory having been much wasted by his simplicity or negligence.[5] He resigned in 1322.[6]

HENRY. Henry de Pecham appears to have been possessed of abilities which raised him to a position which his merits do not seem to have justified. Up to the 4th February, 1309, he was Cellarer and Supervisor of extrinsic affairs, as assistant to William de Shyre, who had been specially placed in the House to manage its business:[7] but on that day the Bishop removed him from his office, and on 10th March transferred him to Newark Priory, and on the 13th March gave directions as to his custody in solitary confinement and on short allowance.[8] Two months later the imprisonment was remitted, on

---

[1] Pedes finium, 49 Henry III; Surrey, Case 2, No. 177. (*Appendix*, VII.)
[2] Diocesan Register, *Wodelok*, 40 *v* to 41 *v*.
[3] Ibid., fol. 104.
[4] Ibid., fol. 110.
[5] The various documents in reference to this transaction are entered in the Diocesan Register, *Wodelok*, fols. 108 *v*, 109 *v*, and 110.
[6] Diocesan Register, *Asser*, 22 *v*.
[7] Diocesan Register, *Wodelok*, fol. 101 *v*.
[8] Ibid., fols. 103 *v*. and 105 *v*.

account of the patience and humility with which he had borne his punishment;[1] and at another interval of two months he was permitted to return to Tanridge, but still with certain legal disabilities.[2] Apparently, he continued in the House from this time without any further complaint and acquired the respect of his Brethren, for we find that on the 10th February, 1323, they elected him as Prior, and though the election was declared void for irregularity, the Bishop on the 31st March following appointed him to the Office;[3] but too late, for he died soon afterwards, and on the 17th March, 1324, a Citation issued for the election of a new Prior to fill the office vacant by his decease.[4]

JOHN. John Hansard, a Canon, was elected, but the election was judicially declared by the Bishop to be invalid, and the appointment thereupon devolving upon him, he appointed the said John Hansard to the Office: the proceedings lasted from the 17th March to 2nd April, 1324.[5] Whether from age or lack of ability, he became incapable of managing the affairs of the House, the Bishop about the end of May, 1330, interdicted him from doing so, and appointed one Laurence de Rustyngton.[6] Becoming worse, he on 4th September, 1335, resigned his Office to the Bishop, who was making a visitation of the House.[7]

PHILIP. On 4th September, 1335, when Hansard resigned, the Canons placed the appointment in the Bishop's hands, and he appointed Philip de Wokyngham as his successor. He was previously a Canon of the same Order at Newerk, in Priest's Orders, and described as a prudent and discreet man, and very circumspect in temporal and spiritual matters.[7] To him the Bishop, on the 17th December, 1338, granted Letters of Adminis-

---

[1] Diocesan Register, *Wodelok*, fol. 108.
[2] Ibid., fol. 112.
[3] Diocesan Register, *Asser*, fol. 22 v.
[4] Diocesan Register, *Stratford*, fol. 3.
[5] Ibid. (*Appendix*, XI.)
[6] Diocesan Register, *Stratford*, fol. 51. (*Appendix*, XXVI.)
[7] Diocesan Register, *Orleton*, I, fol. 26 v. (*Appendix*, XXVIII.)

tration to the Goods of John de Walden, in accordance with the wish expressed by the deceased in his last illness.[1] But he neglected his duties to the House, and a Citation was on 17th January, 1341, issued against him on complaint of non-residence, but he could not be found, and the Citation was otherwise served; and in the end, on 24th September, 1341, the Bishop decreed his deprivation.[2]

JOHN. John de Merstham, a Canon, was elected on 12th November, 1341, and the judicial proceedings took place before the Bishop's Commissioners, in Farnham Church, and his election was confirmed on the following day.[3] He resigned in 1380.[4]

RICHARD. Richard French was elected, and a Commission to enquire into the regularity of the election was issued 8th May, 1380.[4] He died 9th December, 1403.[5]

WILLIAM. William Sonderesh was elected 14th March, 1404; but, on presenting himself to the Bishop to be confirmed, the Bishop declared his election void, and collated him on his own authority the same day.[5]

(The Bishop's Registers, 1415-1446, are lost.)

JOHN. John Fremyngham was Prior in 1441.[6]

JOHN. John Hamond resigned about 1458.[7]

JOHN. John Graunesden, Canon of the Priory or Conventual Church of the Holy Trinity in London, was elected; and on 15th May, 1458, was confirmed by the Bishop.[7] He resigned 1463.[8]

JOHN. John Odierne (perhaps from Odiham, Hants),

---

[1] Diocesan Register, *Wykeham*, II, fol. 69.

[2] Diocesan Register, *Orleton*, I, fol. 108. (*Appendix*, XXIX, XXX, XXXI, XXXII.)

[3] Ibid., fols. 109 and 109 *v*. (*Appendix*, XXXIV, XXXV, XXXVI.)

[4] Diocesan Register, *Wykeham*, II, pt. 3, 186 *v*.

[5] Ibid., I, 344 *v*.

[6] This appears by a casual mention in Letters Testimonial, Diocesan Register, *Wayneflete*, I, fol. 15* *v*.

[7] Diocesan Register, *Wayneflete*, I, fol. 90 *v*.

[8] Ibid., 108 *v*.

the fourth successive Prior of the name of John, had previously been the Sub-prior; he was appointed by the Bishop, to whom the Convent had given up their right of election.[1] He was nominated on 14th July, and the election was confirmed on 16th July, 1463.[2] He died 1464.[3]

WILLIAM. William West, a monk of the House, was appointed by the Bishop, by a like devolution of the power, 22nd December, 1464.[3] He resigned 1467.[4]

JOHN. John Kyrton, Canon of Sandelford Priory, Berkshire, was elected by the Convent 16th April, 1467, and confirmed by the Bishop at Southwark, on the 5th June;[4] resigned 1469; and on 19th April in that year a sequestration was granted to Hugh Heghstall or Hextall, Rector of Blechingly.[5]

ROBERT. Robert was cited to attend in Convocation in 1470, 1472, and 1474.[6]

WILLIAM. William was cited to attend in Convocation in 1478.[7]

ROBERT. Robert was cited to attend in Convocation in 1495:[8] and Sir Robert Mitchell was cited to Convocation in 1499. He resigned this Priory upon his appointment by the Bishop on the 13th July of that year, to be Prior of Reigate; and on 19th November following was elected Prior of St. Mary Overie. (But see *post*.)

ROBERT. Sir Robert Wodd, or Wode, was nominated by the Bishop, at the request of the Chapter, on 9th July, 1499.[9] He was cited to attend in Convocation in 1500; and on 18th July, 1500, the Bishop nominated him to be Prior of St. Denys near Southampton, in which

---

[1] Diocesan Register, *Wayneflete*, I, fol. 108 *v*.
[2] Ibid., fols. 126 *v*. to 127 *v*.
[3] Ibid., 135 *v*.
[4] Ibid., 154.
[5] Diocesan Register, *Waynflete*, Vol. I, pt. 2, fol. 96.
[6] Ibid., fols. 142 and 156 *v*.
[7] Diocesan Register, *Langton*, fol. 15 *v*, at foot.
[8] Ibid., fol. 56 *v*.
[9] Diocesan Register, *Langton*, fol. 51, et seq.

office he was confirmed on 3rd August following, and took the Canonical Oath of obedience to the Bishop on the 15th of the same month.[1]

JOHN. The Convent empowered the Bishop to fill the vacancy, and he accordingly on 11th August, 1500, appointed Sir John Forster, a Canon of the Order.[2] He was cited to attend in Convocation in 1510, 1512, and 1523,[3] and is mentioned in the Court Rolls of Bersted and Tanridge Manors from Michaelmas 1502 to 1513.[4]

ROBERT. Robert Mitchell appears to have again become Prior of the House. He is mentioned in the Court Rolls of Bersted from 28th February, 1521, to 19th May, 1524.[5] He resigned on 24th February, 1525.[6]

JOHN. On the resignation of Robert Mitchell, the House commissioned John Farent, LL.D., John Lacy, Prior of Merton, and John Lyngfeld, a Canon of St. Mary Overie, to appoint to the vacancy; and they appointed the said John Lyngfeld on the 21st February, 1524-5.[6] He is named on the Bersted Court Rolls from June, 1525, to 11th October, 1529:[7] in the latter year he was summoned to attend Convocation.[8] Upon the Dissolution of the House the King, on 2nd July, 1536, granted him a pension of £14 per annum.[9]

I am indebted to Mr. Baigent for searches in the Diocesan Registers at Winchester, and copies of the important documents there, which are printed in the Appendix; my own time not permitting me to undertake this part of the work: in order to insure accuracy, these and the other documents printed in the Appendix have, since setting up in type, been collated with the originals.

---

[1] Diocesan Register, *Langton*, fol. 54.
[2] Ibid., fol. 55.
[3] Diocesan Register, *Fox*, II, fol. 144; III, fol. 20 *v*; V, fol. 16 *v*.
[4] Court Rolls of Bersted, Harl. MS. 4785, fols. 3—8.
[5] Harl. MS. 4785.
[6] Diocesan Register, *Fox*, V, fol. 95.
[7] Harl. MS. 4785, fols. 13—16.
[8] Letters and Papers, Hen. VIII: Record Office Publ., IV, p. 2651.
[9] Augmentation Office, Miscellaneous Books, 244, No. 127. (*Appendix*, XXXVII.)

APPENDIX.

LIST OF DOCUMENTS.

I. Deed of Gift by Odo, son of William de Dammartin, to the Hospital of St. James in the Ville of Tanregge. (Dugdale's *Monasticon*, VI, p. 604.)

II. Further Gift by same to same. (Dugdale's *Monasticon*, VI, p. 604.)

III. Charter by Walter, Prior of Merton, in favour of Benefactors to the Hospital of St. James of Tenrigge. (Cotton MS. *Cleopatra*, C. vii, fol. 86.)

IV. Gift by Odo, son of Odo de Danmertin, to the Hospital of St. James of Tunregge. (Harleian MS. 2044 [Randall Holmes' Collections], fol. 114.)

V. Concord in the *Curia Regis*, between John and Alicia de Wauton and the Prior of Tenrugge. (Pedes finium, (10) Henry III, Surrey, No. 74.)

VI. Concord in the *Curia Regis*, between Gillebert and Richalda Oisel and the Prior and Church of Tenrigge. (Pedes finium, (19) Henry III, Surrey, No. 181.)

VII. Concord in the *Curia Regis*, between the Prior of Tanrigge and Thomas de Warblington. (Pedes finium, (47) Henry III, Surrey, Case 2, No. 177.)

VIII. Permission by Roland de Oksted for Grant by William de Oksted to the Priory. (Inquisition *post mortem*, 12 Edward I, Surrey, No. 49.)

IX. Licence in Mortmain for Henry de Guldeford to grant to Prior and Convent of Tanrigge the Advowson of Crawehurst Church. (Patent Roll, 30 Edward I, m. 3.)

X. Injunctions, 20th December, 1308, consequent on Visitation. (Winchester Diocesan Register, *Wodelok*, fols. 148 *v* to 149 *v*.)

XI. Commission of Enquiry as to conformity with Injunctions: 25th November, 1308. (Winchester Diocesan Register, *Wodelok*, fol. 97 v.)

XII. Report of Commission: 5th December, 1308. (Winchester Diocesan Register, *Wodelok*, fol. 96 v.)

XIII. Ordinance to avoid Strife: 30th November, 1308. (Winchester Diocesan Register, *Wodelok*, fol. 96 v.)

XIV. Further Commission for Visitation (1308). (Winchester Diocesan Register, *Wodelok*, fol. 103 v.)

XV. Deprivation of Henry de Pecham of Office of Cellarer, and appointment of another in his place: 4th February, 1309. (Winchester Diocesan Register, *Wodelok*, fol. 101 v.)

XVI. Order for Banishment and Imprisonment of Henry de Pecham, late Cellarer: 12th March, 1309. (Winchester Diocesan Register, *Wodelok*, fol. 103 v.)

XVII. Orders to Priory of Newark as to Treatment of Prisoner: 23rd March, 1309. (Winchester Diocesan Register, *Wodelok*, fol. 105 v.)

XVIII. Order for Amelioration of Punishment: 27th May, 1309. (Winchester Diocesan Register, *Wodelok*, fol. 108.)

XIX. Permission for Him to return to Tanridge: 16th July, 1309. (Winchester Diocesan Register, *Wodelok*, fol. 112.)

XX. Order for Payment for Expenses of Prisoner: 16th July, 1309. (Winchester Diocesan Register, *Wodelok*, fol. 112.)

XXI. Letters of Request to the Prior of Newark to permit Thomas de St. Alban, one of his Canons, to leave the Priory, in order to become Prior of Tanrugge. (Winchester Diocesan Register, *Wodelok*, fol. 108 v.)

XXII. Licence for the Transfer, &c. (Winchester Diocesan Register, *Wodelok*, fol. 109 v.)

XXIII. Appointment of Coadjutor for Temporal Affairs: 22nd November, 1312. (Winchester Diocesan Register, *Wodelok*, fol. 175.)

XXIV. Proclamation of Election of John Hansard to be Prior: 17th March, 1324. (Winchester Diocesan Register, *Stratford*, fol. 3.)

XXV. Process of the Election; Mandate for Induction; and Monition of Obedience: 31st March, 1324. (Winchester Diocesan Register, *Stratford*, fol. 3.)

XXVI. Commission of Coadjutor to Prior: 31st May, 1330. (Winchester Diocesan Register, *Stratford*, fol. 51.)

XXVII. Inquisition *ad quod damnum*, for gift by Henry att Donne to the Priory of 5 acres at Okstede. (British Museum, Add. MS. 6167 [Symm's Collections], p. 415.)

XXVIII. Episcopal Visitation of the Priory when John Hansard resigned and Philip de Wokyngham was appointed Prior: 4th September, 1335. (Winchester Diocesan Register, *Orleton*, I, fol. 26 *v.*)

XXIX. Commission to cite Prior Philip for Non-Residence: 17th January, 1341. (Winchester Diocesan Register, *Orleton*, I, fol. 108.)

XXX. Citation of same "by ways and means:" 28th July, 1341. (Winchester Diocesan Register, *Orleton*, I, fol. 108.)

XXXI. Commission for Deprivation for Non-Residence: 22nd September, 1341. (Winchester Diocesan Register, *Orleton*, I, fol. 108 *v.*)

XXXII. Sentence of Deprivation: 26th September, 1341. (Winchester Diocesan Register, *Orleton*, I, fol. 108 *v.*)

XXXIII. Inquisition *post mortem*, of John de Warblyngton, who died on 13th February, 1351. (Inquis. P. M., 25 Edw. III, 1st Nos., No. 54. [Add. MS. 6167, fol. 416.])

XXXIV. Process of Election of John de Merstham to be Prior, the morrow of St. Martin, 1341. (Winchester Diocesan Register, *Orleton*, I, fol. 109.)

XXXV. Confirmation of the Election: 13th November, 1341. (Winchester Diocesan Register, *Orleton*, I, fol. 109 *v.*)

XXXVI. Mandate for Installation: 13th November, 1341. (Winchester Diocesan Register, *Orleton*, I, fol. 109 *v.*)

XXXVII. Letters Testimonial to William Wiltshire: 4th July, 1452. (Winchester Diocesan Register, *Wayneflete*, I, fol. 15* *v.*)

XXXVIII. Sequestration of Income of the Priory : 14th October, 1461. (Winchester Diocesan Register, *Wayneflete*, I, fol. 68*.)

XXXIX. Episcopal Sequestration on Vacancy : 10th April, 1469. (Winchester Diocesan Register, *Wayneflete*, I, fol. 96*.)

XL. Grant of Pension to Prior on Dissolution of the Priory : 2nd July, 1536. (Augmentation Office, Miscel. Books, Vol. 244, No. 127.)

XLI. Ministers' Accounts : year ending Michaelmas, 29th Henry VIII (1537). (Ministers' Accounts, 28-29 Henry VIII, No. 108.)

I.

DEED OF GIFT BY ODO, SON OF WILLIAM DE DAMMARTIN, TO THE HOSPITAL OF ST. JAMES IN THE VILLE OF TANREGGE.

(Dugdale's *Monasticon*, VI, p. 604.)

Universis sanctæ matris ecclesiæ filiis ad quos præsens scriptum pervenerit, Odo de Dammartin, filius Willielmi de Dammartin, salutem. Noverit universitas vestra me dedisse et concessisse et hac præsenti carta mea confirmasse, pro salute animæ meæ et uxoris meæ, et puerorum meorum; et pro animabus patris et matris meæ; et antecessorum et successorum meorum, Deo et Hospitali S. Jacobi in villa de Tanregge, et tribus presbyteris in perpetuum ibidem Deo servientibus, et confratribus ejusdem Hospitalis, totam terram meam de Warlinggeham, ad suscipiendum et sustentandum infirmos, et pauperes, et peregrinos, hospitio indigentes in liberam et puram elemosinam; cum molendino ad ventum, et cum omnibus pertinentiis suis, sine aliquo retinemento, in croftis, in pictlakes, in bosco, in gravis, in plano, in pratis, in pascuis, in semitis, in viis, in aquis, in maris, in sepibus, in clausturis, in communibus pasturis, et in omnibus libertatibus; habendam et tenendam libere et quiete, finaliter, ab omni servitio et exactione seculari quod debeo hæredibus Willielmi de Hammes; scilicet xx^s sterlingorum et due calcaria deaurata de pretii sex denariorum, vel sex denarios annuatim ad duos terminos; scilicet ad Pascha decem solidos et calcaria; et ad festum S. Michaelis decem solidos, sine calumpnia; et salvo servitio quantum pertinet ad quartam partem feodi unius militis pro omnibus servitiis et demandis. Et ego et heredes mei debemus defendere et warantizare præfatam terram et donationem atque confirmationem contra omnes homines et omnes fœminas. His testibus, Radulfo capellano de Rigata, Henrico capellano, Hamone de Turbeville, Radulfo Pimpe, Luca de Laundecote, Petro de Perefricht, Willielmo de Danmartin, Gralando et Baldrico fratribus, Petro de Thaleuurthe, Radulfo de Turneham, Radulfo parcario, Johanne Bolle, Nicolao de la Dene, et pluribus aliis.

II.

FURTHER GIFT BY SAME TO SAME.

(Dugdale's *Monasticon*, VI, p. 604.)

Sciant presentes et futuri, quod ego Odo de Dammartin, filius Willielmi de Dammartin, dedi pro salute animæ meæ, Deo et Hospitali

S. Jacobi de Tanregge, omnes reliquias meas, et duos cifos argenteos ad calicem faciendam, et vestimenta, et omnes libros, cæteraque omnia capellæ meæ. Insuper, dedi præfato Hospitali ix boves, et unum taurum, et suem cum porcellis, quæ sunt ad Suevic' in computatione xii boum; quos divisi eidem hospitali, habendos de melioribus bovibus terræ meæ. Et ut hæc donatio mea rata sit et stabilis, eam præsenti cartû meâ atque sigillo confirmavi. Hiis testibus, Rob. capellano, Will. capellano, Thoma de Wllst priore de Meretuna, Radulfo decano, et pluribus aliis.

III.

CHARTER BY WALTER, PRIOR OF MERTON, IN FAVOUR OF BENE-FACTORS TO THE HOSPITAL OF ST. JAMES OF TENRIGGE.

(Cotton MS. *Cleopatra*, C. vii, fol. 86.)

W[alterus], Prior Meritoñ τ ejusdē loci c'vēt', univ̄sis Xp̄i fidelibus p̄sntes lifas inspᶜtʳis, sīt in d̄no. Noṽit univ̄sitas v̄ra, nos divine pietatis intuitu, Dn̄m Odonē de Dammartī fūdatorē τ ōes fres τ sorores τ ōes Benefactores Hospitalis sc̄i Jacobi de tenrig̃ in fr̄nitatē dom' n̄re de M?etoñ, sp̄atr suscepisse τ cōcessisse in ip̄i ptē τ cōmūionē nob̄cum h̄ant ī ōib3 or̄onib3 Elemosinis, Jejuniis, Vigiliis, Disciplinis, in Missar3 celebrat̄onib3, in Religionis τ Ordinis observat̄onib3, τ ī ōib3 Aliis Bonis τ Beneficiis que ī domo n̄ra τ in Omnibus Domibus Religiosis fuerī τ in ppetuū fient. In huj' fr̄nitatis testimoniū sigillū n̄rm p̄senti scripto duximus apponendū. Valt. Dat̄ anno d̄ni M.CC.xvij°, xv kt Julii.

IV.

GIFT BY ODO, SON OF ODO DE DANMERTIN, TO THE HOSPITAL OF ST. JAMES OF TUNREGGE.

(Harleian MS. 2044 [Randall Holmes' Collections], fol. 114.)

Sc. τc. Ego Odo de Danmᵃtī fīt Odonis de Danmertin dedi τ p Salute aīa mee et p aīab3 p̄ris et m̄ris mee et ancesŝ et successorȩ meorȩ Deo et hospitali Sc̄i Jacob̄ de Tūregge et fr̄ib3 ibidē deo τc̄. dimidiā acr̄ t̃re v̄. le Brome in villa de Chepsted, q̃m Alfriȩ Soxere tenuit de me cū domib3 q̃m hᵗ cum ip̄a t̃ra : ħend et tenendā τc : et ego warantī3. τc : tesf̄ Wilt de Dam̄ertin, Rob̄t Burnard, Radulf de Pi'pʳ, Rob̄t fil Pagani, Wilt de Sc̄o Joħe, Petᵒ Talewrth, Ada de Talewrth, Eustachio de Wlkest, Wilt de Novat̄ra, et plurib3 aliis.

V.

Concord in the Curia Regis, between John and Alicia de Wauton and the Prior of Tenrugge.

(Pedes finium, (10) Henry III, Surrey, No. 74.)

Hec est finalis concordia fĉa in Cuṝ Dñi Regis apud Westm̃ in Octaḃ Purificaĉõis Beate Marie anno Regni Regis Henṝ fił Regis Joħis, decimo; coram Martino de Paℓhiłł, Thoṁ de Muleton̄, Thoṁ de Heiden̄, Roḃ de Lexinton̄, Warino fił Johelis, Justiĉ, ⁊ aliis Dñi Regis fidelibʒ tūc ibi ꝑsentibʒ; Inℓ Joħm de Wauton̄ ⁊ Aliciā uxorē ejus petñtes p Thomā de Grava positū loco iꝑius Joħis ad lucᵃn̄ vł pđū ⁊ p Wiłłm de Kingestun̄ positū loco iꝑius Aliĉ ad lucᵃn̄ vł pđū. Et Thomā Priorē de Tenruggᷓ tenentē, de qᵃℓ viginti acris bosci cū ptin̄ in Tenrugge. Unde placitū fuit inℓ eos in eađ cuṝ, scił qđ ꝑdĉi Joħs ⁊ Aliĉ remiserūt ⁊ quietū clamaⱴūt de se ⁊ heredibʒ iꝑius Aliĉ, iꝑi Priori ⁊ successoribʒ suis ⁊ eccłie de Tenrugge totū jus ⁊ clamiū quod habueṝt in ꝑdĉis quater viginti acris bosci cū ptin̄ imppetuū. Et pro hᵃc remissõe quieta clamancia fine ⁊ concordia ꝑdĉus Prior remisit de se ⁊ successoribʒ suis eisđ Joħi ⁊ Aliĉ ⁊ heredibʒ iꝑius Aliĉ pessonā ad triginta porcos qᵃm hūit in bosco eorundē Joħis ⁊ Aliĉ ex dono Odonis Danmartin senioris. Et chaciam cū tresdeci canibʒ ⁊ sex leporariis, quam hūit ex dono Odonis Danmartī Junioris, in warenna eorundū Joħis ⁊ Aliĉ ⁊ hr̃đū iꝑius Aliĉ imppetuū.

VI.

Concord in the Curia Regis, between Gillebert and Richalda Oisel and the Prior and Church of Tenrigge.

(Pedes finium, (19) Henry III, Surrey, No. 181.)

Hec est finał concordia fĉa in Cuṝ dñi Reḡ apđ Bermundeꝫ a die Sĉi Miĉħ in tres septim̃, anno Regni Reḡ Henṝ fił Reḡ Joħ decimo nono; corā Wiłło de Eboṝ, Wiłło de Insula, Rađo de Norwiĉ, ⁊ Huḡ de Playʒ, justiĉ itiñantibʒ, ⁊ aliis dñi Reḡ fidelibʒ tūc ibi ꝑsentibʒ. Inℓ Gilleḃ Oisel ⁊ Richalđ uẋ ejus petentes, ⁊ Adam Priorē de Tenriḡ tenentē, de sexdeci acr̄ ℓre cū ptin̄ in Tenriḡ. Unde assisa mortis antecessī sum̄onita fuit inℓ eos in eadem cuṝ, scił q̄d ꝑdĉi Gilleḃs ⁊ Richalda recognoⱴūt totam ꝑdĉam ℓrā cum ptin̄ esse jus iꝑius Prioris ⁊ Eccłie sue de Tenriḡ. Et p hac recogniĉõne, fine ⁊ concordia, idem Prior cõcessit ꝑdĉis Gilleḃ ⁊ Richalde novē acr̄ ℓre cū ptin̄ de eađ ℓra, scił illas novē acr̄ ℓre quas Roḃs de Shortehał quondā tenuit. Habenđ ⁊ tenenđ iꝑis Gilleḃ ⁊

Richalde ꝛ hedibȝ iꝑius Richalde de βdco Priore ꝛ succ̃ suis ꝛ eccłia
βdc̃a inppetuū. Reddendo inde annuati duodeci deñ ad festū Sc̃i Mich̃ ꝑ
om̃i ſvic̃o ꝛ exaccõne. Et ꝑᵗea idem Prior dedit βdc̃is Gilleb ot Richalde
dimid́ marc̃ argēti.

VII.

Concord in the Curia Regis, between the Prior of Tanrigge and Thomas de Warblington.

(Pedes finium, (47) Henry III, Surrey, Case 2, No. 177.)

Hec est final concord́ fc̃a in cuꝛ̃ dñi Reg̃ apud Geldeford́ a die Sc̃i
Hillaꝛ̃ in quindecim dies, anno regni Reg̃ Henꝛ̃ fił Reg̃ Joh̃is qᵃᵈᵃgesio
septio; coram Mᵃrtino de Littilbyꝛ̃, Walᵗo de Bersted, Galfrido de
Leukenoꝛ̃, Ric̃o de Hemington, Justic̃ Itiꞅłant, ꝛ aliis dñi Reg̃ fidelibȝ
tūc ibi βsentibȝ. Inꝉ Humfrid́ Priorē de Tanrigge queꝛ̃, ꝛ Thomam de
Warblington̄ inpedientē, de uno mesuag̃, qᵃtuordeci acꝛ̃ ᵗre ꝛ duodeci acꝛ̃
pastʳᵉ cū ꝑtinenc̃ in Tannerigge. Unde placitū warant carte sum̃ fuit
inꝉ eos in eadem cuꝛ̃, sc̃t q̃d βdc̃us Thom̃ recogñ βdc̃a tenem̃ta cū
ptinenc̃ esse jus iꝑius Prioris ꝛ eccłie sue de Tannerigge ut illa que idem
Prior ꝛ eccłia sua βdc̃a h̃nt de dono iꝑius Thom̃. Hñd́ ꝛ tenend́ eidē
Priori successoꝛ̃ suis ꝛ eccłie sue βdc̃e de βdc̃o Thom̃ ꝛ hedibȝ suis in
libꞅam puram ꝛ ꝑpetuam elemoſ inppetuum. Et βdc̃us Thom̃ ꝛ heredes
sui warant acquiet ꝛ defendent βdc̃o Priori successoꝛ̃ suis ꝛ eccłie sue
βdc̃e, βdc̃a tenem̃ta cū ptiñ ut puram ꝛ perpetuam elemoſ suam, libam ꝛ
quietā ab omni seculari ſvic̃o ꝛ exaccõe, contᵃ om̃es hom̃es inppetuū.
Et ꝑᵗea idē Thom̃ concessit ꝑ se ꝛ hedibȝ suis q̃d iꝑi deceᵗo reddent
singuł annis βdc̃o Priori succ̃ suis ꝛ eccłie sue βdc̃e, viginti solidos ad
duos ᵗminos, sc̃t medietatē ad festū Nativit̃ Sc̃i Joh̃is Bapt̃, ꝛ alᵗam
medietatē ad Natale Dñi. Et si ita contingat q̃d́ βdc̃us Thom̃ vł hedes
sui in solucõe βdcoꝝ denaꝛ̃ ad aliq̃d ᵗminū defec̃t, bene licebit eidem
Priori succ̃ suis ꝛ eccłie sue βdc̃e, distⁱngꞅe βdc̃m Thom̃ ꝛ hed suos ꝑ
omnia catalla sua in omnibȝ ᵗris ꝛ tenem̃tis suis in maꞅio de Tenrigg̃
inventa, usqȝ ad plenam solucõnem denaꝛ̃ qui a retro fuꞅint. Et βdc̃us
Prior concessit ꝑ se succ̃ suis ꝛ eccłia sua βdc̃a, q̃d iꝑi deceᵗo invenient
quendam canonicum suū capełłm qui in eccłia sua βdc̃a ad altare Bē
Marie, ꝑ aꞅabȝ iꝑius Thom̃ antecessoꝝ ꝛ hed suoꝝ, quolibet die divina
celebrabit.

VIII.

Permission by Roland de Oksted for Grant by William de Oksted to the Priory.

(Inquisition *post mortem*, 12 Edward I, Surrey, No. 49.)

Pateat uniṽsis hoc sc¹ptū visuŕ vł auditur̄ q̃d ego Rolandus de Oksted, concessi ⁊ p me ⁊ ħredibus meiꝫ cōfirmavi . . P¹ori de Tenregg ⁊ eiusdm loci conventui, ingressū in ƚris et tenemt̄ cū ptiñ q°s petūt de gr̄a d̄ni Regꝫ recipe de dono Wiłłi de Oksted de feodo meo. In villa de Oksted. Hn̄d ⁊ tend̄ de me ⁊ ħredibus meis vł meis assigªtis faciendo inde m̊ ⁊ ħredibus meis om̄ia ẛvicia inde de jure debita ⁊ cōsueta, put in sc¹ptis inƚ nos ad mod cirogªpħ c'fectis plenius c'tinetʳ. In cui' rei testimōū ꝑsenti sc¹pto sigillum meum apposui. Daɫ die Jovis pxı̄a ante festum Sc̄i Edmūdi C'fessoŕ, Anno r' Regꝫ Edward ƚcio deciō.

IX.

Licence in Mortmain for Henry de Guldeford to grant to Prior and Convent of Tanrigge the Advowson of Crawehurst Church.

(Patent Roll, 30 Edward I, m. 3.)

Pro Priore ⎱ ꝶ om̄ibꝫ ad quos ⁊c, salt̄m. Licet de com̄uni consilio
de Tanrigge. ⎰ regni nr̄i statůimus q̃d nō liceat viris religiosis seu aliis ingredi feodū alicujus ita q̃d ad manum mortuam deveniat sine licencia nr̄a ⁊ capitalis d̄ni de quo res illa immediate tenetʳ; p finem, tamen quem dilc̄us nobis in Xp̄o Prior de Tanrigge fecit nobiscum coram veñabili pr̄e Walƚo Coventr̄ ⁊ Lych̄ Ep̄o, Theẛ nr̄o, concessimus et licenciam dedimus, quantum in nobis est, Henr̄ de Guldeford q̃d ip̄e advocacõem ecctie de Crawehurst dare possit ⁊ assignare ꝑfatis Priori ⁊ Conventui ejusdem loci, tenendam ⁊ ħendam sibi ⁊ successoribus suis imppetuū. Et eisd Priori et Conventui q̃d ip̄i advocacõem illam ꝑdc̄õ Henrico recipere possint tenendam ⁊ ħendam sibi ⁊ successoribus suis ꝑdc̄is, sicut ꝑdc̄m est tenore ꝑsenciū, similitʳ licenciam dedimus spaɫem. Nolentes q̃d idem Henricus vel heredes sui aut ꝑdc̄i Prior ⁊ Conventus seu successores sui, rōne Statuti ꝑdc̄i p nos vel heredes nr̄os inde occōnentʳ in aliquo, vel gªventʳ. Salviẛ tamen capitalibus d̄ñis feodi illius ẛviciis inde debitis et consuetis. In cujus ⁊c. T. ꝶ. apud Westm̄ xiiij die Novembr̄.

X.

INJUNCTIONS, 20TH DECEMBER, 1308, CONSEQUENT ON VISITATION.
(Winchester Diocesan Register, *Wodelok*, fols. 148 *v* to 149 *v*.)

Tanrugge. Fr̃ H[enricus, pmissione divina Wintoñ ep̄us,] dilc̄is filiis .. P̶ori de Tanrugg' n̄re dioc̄, v̄l ejus vices gerenti:⸲ ꝉ ejusd̃ loci Conventui, salt͞m, gr̃am ꝉ bn̄. Nup nos die Jovis px post f͞m Sc̄i Edwardi Regę ꝉ Confessore, anno Dn̄i MᵒCCCᵐᵒ octavo, vos et moñ v̄rm put n̄ro pastorali incumbit officio visitantes:⸲ qued̄a inł vos correc̄õe digna repim⁹, que sub forᵃ que subsequitʳ, decrevim⁹ corrigenda. In p̶mis, ordinamus, statuim⁹ ꝉ ꝑcipimus, q̃d divinū officiū, tam de die qᵃ de nocte, cū õi sollempnitate, qua convenit, de cełᵒ celebretʳ, saltim q singlis diebʒ, cum missis ad quas p scriptū, v̄l p juramentū tenemini, p bn̄factoribʒ celebrentʳ, videt́ missa una de Sc̄a Maria cū nota, ꝉ alt́a cum nota, que dicitʳ missa major ad quā tenei̇ ex observancia regulari, ꝉ quicuq ad dc̄as missas celebrandas p bn̄fc̄toribʒ sive alias cū nota f͞uint intitulati, nisi p se, seu suppõitas personas iṗas celebraṽintː⸲ volumus eodem die in pane et aqᵃ jejunant ꝉ nichõ⁹ per alios misse celebrētʳ antedc̄e, ne ppł eoʒ maliciam, divinū officiū subtᵃhatʳ, ꝉ nullus ab officio divino, absq cã r̃onabili ꝉ legı̄a se absentet, ꝉ tunc de sui p̶oris licencia sp̄ali. Item, vestigiis bone memorie d̃ni Ottoboni dudum Apᶜᵉ Sedis legati in Angł inherentes:⸲ statuendo ut supᵃ ꝑcipimus, q canõici inł vos ꝑfessi ꝉ in sa͞ddocio constituti frequenł confiteantʳ suo priori, v̄l alteri ejusd̃ ordinis de ip̄ius licencia, ꝉ divina celebrent in locis ad hoc deputatis ꝉ hacten⁹ cõsuetis. Item, ꝑcipim⁹ q suppᶦor sc̄d̄m anteqᵃ consuetudinē, inł vos usitatam in v̄ro collegio de v̄ro consensu unanimi ꝑficiatʳ. Pꝛcipim⁹ eciā q silenciū inł vos locis ꝉ temporibʒ sc̄d̄m regulā v̄ram de cełᵒ artius observetʳ, ꝉ q hostia 'claustri, horis debitis, claudantʳ ꝉ clausa eisdem tempibʒ custodiantʳ. Item, ꝑcipim⁹, q nullus absq licencia sui p̶oris claustrum v̄l moñ exire quoquo modo ꝑsumat, nec supior ille ita de facili ut consuetū est fr̃em aliquē licenciet ad exeund absq c̃a justa ꝉ r̃onabili, ꝉ tunc sic exiens, honestum comitem p p̶orem sᶦ adjunctū h̃eat, ꝉ limitato sibi tempe redeat sine mora. Item, ꝑcipim⁹ ut sᵃ, q nūs fr̃um put cõvenit augeatʳ qᵃcici⁹ ad id facultas se optulerit, ꝉ ydonei valeant repiri. Inhibem⁹ eciā ne quis v̄rm decełᵒ utatʳ veste aliqᵃ ordini suo dissimłi ꝉ indecenti, sʒ tali quā regt́a v̄ra ꝉ religionis honestas exigit ꝉ requirit, ꝑviso q õmi sit h̃itus uniformis. Inhibem⁹ ꝉ ne qui v̄rm cortinas h̃eant in domitorio circa lectos, sʒ ita jaceant singłi ut videri valeant a quolibet transeunte. Item, ordinam⁹ ꝉ statuend́ ꝑcipimus, q infirmi confr̃es v̄ri sc̄d̄m eoʒ indigenc̄iā ꝉ v̄ram regulam visitentʳ, ꝉ sc̄d̄m fᵃterne humanitatis debitū decełᵒ ꝑcurentʳ, ac elemosina debita ꝛ consueta, plus solito flat in fut̃ʳm. Item, inhibem⁹ ne deceł̃o, fr̃ib3 existentib3 in mēsa inhoneste psone seculares refectoriū ingᵉdiantʳ, ꝛ comedant, sive sint domestici, sive exᵃnci s3 exspᵉtent usq̃ post refecõm fratrum, v̄l loc⁹ ali⁹ ꝑ eoɀ refeccõe eis deceł̃o deputetʳ. Item, inhibem⁹, ne com̃essacõos ꝛ potacõos post cubitū fr̃um, quisqᵃ v̄rm teneat in refectoris, vel alibi, nᶜ de cōsuetudie, absq̃ rōnabili cā reficiatʳ, nˡ horis debitis et cōsuetis. Item, statuendo ꝑcipim⁹, q̃ null⁹ fr̃um cū muliere suspᶜta, v̄l de qᵃ possit ħeri suspicio, sive seculari, sive religiosa, locis ꝛ tempib3 suspᶜtis colloqⁱū ħeat, nᶜ ad domū iꝑius, quoquo mᵒ accedat, ne ex hoc scandalū in pp̄lo oriatʳ. Item, statuim⁹ ordinam⁹ ꝛ ꝑcipim⁹ q̃d quolibet anno semel admin⁹ statū moñ v̄ri in capitł̃o puᶜᵉ coŕ fr̃ib3, ꝓut statuta scõɀ patrū exigūt, prior ꝛ celarius, qui ꝑ tempe fũint ostendant, ꝛ de administᵃcõc sua reddant plenaŕ rõem, ꝛ circa exoñacõm eris alieni, in quo moñ obligatʳ, in qᵃntū est possibile laborent, ꝛ com̃odū moñ v̄ri pcurent deceł̃o ꝓut possunt. Item, statuimus ordinam⁹ ꝛ ꝑcipim⁹, q̃ scd̄m antiqᵃ consuetudinem hacten⁹ inł̃ vos usitatā, ꝛ v̄ri ordinis regulam in esculentis ꝛ poculentis, vestib3 ꝛ aliis nᵉcciis, juxᵃ facultates eccie v̄ro voɓ provideatʳ, ꝛ si que illicite alienata fũint, ꝑ virib3 revocentʳ, ꝛ majora negocia monasteŕ v̄ri, ac sigillū v̄rm cõe de voluntate ꝛ assensu majoris ꝛ sanioris ptis conventus, tractentʳ, exceāntʳ, fiāt ꝛ deceł̃o pcurentʳ, ꝛ q̃ nemora v̄ra ñllaten⁹ ꝑsternantʳ, nᶜ arbores in eisdem dentur nisi de c'sensu unanimi, ꝛ ex cā ŕonabili vobis pⁱmit⁹ exꝑssa, ꝛ ꝑ majorem ptē v̄ri collegii approbata. Pꝛmissa õia ꝛ sinḡla voɓ mittim⁹ sub sigillo ñro patent̃ signata, ꝑ vos ꝛ quēlibet v̄rm qᵃten⁹ vos cōjunctim, ꝛ divisim tangūt, seu tanḡc poł̃unt in fut̃ʳm, in virtute scē obedīe dilige̅nł̃ ꝛ fidelił̃ observanda ꝛ quolibet anno qᵃter, videł̃t, qᵒlibet qᵃterio anni semel coram voɓ in pleno capitł̃o v̄ro, scilicet, in pⁱma Dñica Adventus Dñi, ꝛ in Dñica medie Qᵃdragesime, ꝛ in ƒo Ascencõis Dñice, ac ccīa infra octaɓ Nativĩ Bē Marie virḡ plene, disticte ꝛ apte, publice recitanda, ne quis v̄rm sup ꝑmissis v̄l eoɀ aliquib3 seu aliquo, ignorancīa ꝑtendere. Valeat quoquomodo. Datt apud Essher', xiij k̃ɫ Decembŕ, anno Dñi sᵃdc̃o. Consñre, qᵃrto.

XI.

COMMISSION OF ENQUIRY AS TO CONFORMITY WITH INJUNCTIONS: 25TH NOVEMBER, 1308.

(Winchester Diocesan Register, *Wodelok*, fol. 97 *v.*)

Commissio de Tanrugge. Fŕ H[enricus] ꞇc̄, diłcis fił, pⁱori de Tanrugg' ñre dioc̃, v̄l ejus vices gerenti, ꝛ ejusđ loci coñ. Salm̃, grãm t bn̄. Ad t'minand̄ felicr, ac modestiori quo pot'im', p honore religionis, ea que in v̄ro mon̄, nup in n̄rᵃ visitac̄oe invenim' corrigenda, religiosis viris, Fr̄ Laur̄ de Glouc̄, sacre theologie p̄fessori, t frī Ad Saȝ monacho Sc̄i Swithi Wint, comittimus vices n̄ras, cū coh̄c̄ois canōice p̄tate. eosd̄ ad vos p̄senciatr dirigendo, vob̄q̄ ōibȝ & sing̃lis in virtute sc̄e obeđie p̄cipim' t mandam', qᵃtin' eis sing̃lis que emendac̄ōm status domus v̄re contig̃̃e pot'unt ac in ōibȝ, que ex pte n̄ra vob̄ injungent quo ad tempalia t sp̄ualia, plenius peatis t humilit' intendatis. Vat̄t. Daī ap̄d Farnhᵃm, vij kt̄ Decembr̄, anno t̄c̄ [MᵒCCCᵐᵒ octavo].

XII.

Report of Commission: 5th December, 1308.

(Winchester Diocesan Register, *Wodelok*, fol. 96 *v.*)

Acta ejusdem. Md̄ q frēs L[aurencius] t Ad[am] feria quinta p̄x ante fm̄ Sc̄i Andr̄, anno Dn̄i MᵒCCCᵐᵒ Octavo, mane in capitulo de 'Tarugg' corā pᶦore, celerar̄ et toto cōventu p̄misso v̄bo Dei, pᶦmo.∕ exhibũũt decᵉtum d̄ni H[enrici] Dei grᵃ Wint ep̄i, t ilt̄d in sing̃lis suis artic̄lis diligenci' exposũũt. Sc̄do.∕ q̄sier̄t ab eis certificator̄ mandatᵉ dc̄i patᶦs sup c'poto redd̄ citᵃ certū diē. Et quia nō certificarũt penā tante inobediē debitā d̄ni Wint ep̄i arbitᶦo, reservar̄t. Tertio.∕ inq̄ᶦsier̄t an celerariᶦ comp̄ reddiderit et inveñunt q a tempe fundac̄ois domᶦ nᶜ tēpe celer̄ nūc existentᵉ nᶜ alt'ius unqᵃ comp̄ reddebatʳ. Ita q nesciebat valorē domᶦ, s̄mᵃ reddit' anni nec exitū cujᶦcunq̄ gᵃngie, nᶜ sum̄a seminis sem̄ per annū in quocunq̄ geñe gᵃni, nec exitū cujᶦcūq̄ tass̄ bladi, nᶜ s̄mᵃ blad̄ ad furniend̄ p annū, nec ad brac̄, nec libac̄oes famulo₃, nec aliud sciebant prior, celerarius v̄l alii q̄d ad statum ptinere debuit. Quarto.∕ fec̄unt celerariū redd̄?e comptū coram priore t conventu t incipientes a pᶦmo anno sue administᵃc̄ois, tot invener̄t negligencias t falsitates, q̄d vix infra spaciū multoȝ dieȝ illū compotū t'minassent, iō seq̄nti die incepunt ab ultimo anno sue administᵃc̄ois, t inventis falsitatibȝ detestabilibȝ fecerũt p manus Simonis de Schirford ordinem compoti unius anni pro exemplo reddendi comp̄ p futᵘo. Quinto.∕ dc̄s fr̄ A[dam] cum W[illelmo] de Schire, canonico t eorum ballīo per ordinac̄oem dc̄i L[aurencii] viderūt ptem nemoȝ t invenerūt q̄d possunt vend̄?e in loco quē viderunt de vet'ibȝ quercubȝ ad valorem viginti marcaȝ p empc̄oe bladi t debitis acquitand̄ t hoc absq̄ dampnū domᶦ. Sexto.∕ quia ministri eoȝ sectares numq̄ᵃ p talt v̄l juramentū fũrũt oñati, eos oñarūt p utᵐq̄ t sup hoc et aliis ordinac̄oem fec̄unt in forᵃ que sequitʳ in sedula huic adjuncta. Septimo ordinarūt dñm Henr' tauq^a supvisorē rex ext^{i}nsecax, et dñm Willm de Schire receptorem oīm spectanciū [infra] prioratum ᴛ hoc sub for^a in q^{a}dam sedula contenta ᴛ status autē dom' ᴛ ordinacōem comp̄ apparent in q^{a}dam cedula laℓali. Octavo ipis existentib3 in dissencōe, dc̄s L[aurencius] om̄es reduxit ad concordiā.

Nono injunxit eis q̄ poħent in martilog̃ statuta d́ni Wintoñ ᴛ ordinacōes ipox, ᴛ p̄misso v̄bo Dei dimisit eos in pace, ac sc^{i}psit d́no Roƀo de Stang^{a}ve, militi, q̄ pmitℓet dñm W[illelmum] de Schyr' stare domi.

XIII.

Ordinance to avoid Strife: 30th November, 1308.

(Winchester Diocesan Register, *Wodelok*, fol. 96 v.)

Ordinacio facta apud Tanrugge. Fr̄ Laurencius de Glouc' ᴛ Ad́ Sax monach' Wint, com̄issar' veñ p̄ris d́ni H[enrici] Dei gr̃a Wintoñ ep̄i, dilectc̣ in Xp̃o .. p^{i}ori de Tanrugg' v̄l ejus vices gerenti, ᴛ ejusd́ loci convētui, salt in eo quē pepit uℓus v^{r}ginaℓ. Volentes inℓ vos caritatē, que finis religionis ēē dinoscit^r cōfov̄e, lites ᴛ dissensiones cōpesc̄e, quib3 plexq̄ unitas ᴛ concordia dissolvūt^r, statuim^9 ᴛ ordinam^9 ut nħs v̄rum cū alio litiget, aut cōtendat, seu alℓi confr̄um contumeliā inferat q^{o}q^{o}modo q̄ si q^{i}s v̄rum iu ƥmissis deliquerit, p p^{i}orem, vℓ alterum ƥsidentē capiℓlo corā ōib3 corripiat^r. Et si ter sup hoc reƥhcn^9 se nō emendav̄it, p subt^{a}ccōm sui ferculi puniat^r, ita q̄ crescente culpa crescat et pena, quousq̃ in hoc füit emendat^9. Per ƥmissa autē nō intendim^9 inhibere q^{i}n frem delinq̄ntem p^{i}or v̄l alℓ corripiat modestia semp in omnibus observata. Iℓ, statuim^9, q̄ fr̄ cui cura expensax coq̄ne v̄re com̄ittit^r, in fine cujusl3 septīmane de administr^{a}cōe sua, p^{i}ori suo reddat plenar̄ rōm. Iℓ, ordinam^9 q̄ minist^i v̄ri seculares, ᴛ in officiis constituti, videℓ, in g^{a}ngiis, ᴛ g^{a}narℓio, ac eciā ad custodiā aīaliū v̄rox deputati, sint p talliam oñati, ᴛ se faciant p talliā exoñare de receptis, ƥstentq̃ sac^{a}mentū corporali q̄ fideliℓ admīst^{a}būt, recipiendo, recepta custodiendo, ᴛ ead́ aliis libr̄ando, n^{c}non de exitib3 aīaliū fideliℓ respondendo, ᴛ dc̄i minist^i secular' sing̃li ad hoc q^{a}ten^9 eos cōtingūt p p^{i}orē v̄l frem cui tempaliū cura com̄ittit^r, cōpellant^r. Premissa oīa et sing̃la vobis injungim^9 firmiℓ observanda, ᴛ cū decreto veñabit p̄ris ƥdc̄i d́ni Wint ep̄i corā voƀ ōi q^{a}rter' anni in v̄ro capiℓlo pu$^c^e$ recitanda Daℓ ap̄d Tanrugg' die Sc̄i Andr̄ ap̄li, anno Dñi M^{o}CCC^{mo} octavo.

XIV.

Further Commission for Visitation (1308).

(Winchester Diocesan Register, *Wodelok*, fol. 103 v.)

Commissio de Tanrugge. Fr̃ H[enricus] ɫc̃, dilcis filiis . . priori et convent̃ de Tanrugg', n̄re dioc̃, salɫm ɫc̃. Prop⌢ quedā visitac̃ŏm n̄ram apud vos nup f̄cam contingencia, dilc̃os nob̃ in Xp̃o, Mag̃ros Pħm de Barton̄, arcħm nr̄m Surr̄, ꞇ Laur̄ de Glouc̃, monachū Sc̃i Pet¹ ej⁹dē (*sic*) sacre theologie p̄fessorē, vob̃ destinam⁹ canoĩce ſ̃minanda, q¹bȝ in hᵃc pte vices n̄rᵃs comitt̃, cū conc̃õis canoĩce p̃tate. Vob̃ injungentes, qᵃtiñ eisd̃ in hiis ꞇ aliis, que penes vos invener̃int corrĩgẽda, peatis sicut nob̃. Scientes q censuras quas tulerit in rebelles, faciem⁹ auctore Dño inviolabilif observari. Daɫ ɫc̃. [MᵒCCCᵒ Octavo.]¹

XV.

Deprivation of Henry de Pecham of Office of Cellarer, and Appointment of Another in his Place: 4th February, 1309.

(Winchester Diocesan Register, *Wodelok*, fol. 101 v.)

. . *Priori et conventui de Tanrugge.* Salɫm, grām ꞇ bñ. Cum nos visitacõis n̄re officiū, inſ vos jur' diocẽs nup exc̃entes, frem H[enricum] tūc celerariū v̄rm, multis rõibȝ id poscentibȝ ab officio suo β̃dc̃o amoṽim⁹ ꞇ eundem supvisorē rex ext'nsecax, in subsidiū frĩs Will̃i de Shire quẽ p utilitate mon̄ v̄ri, v̄rm ordinavim⁹ receptorē deputaṽim⁹, quousq aᵈ in hac pte duxim⁹ statuend. Volẽtes, quod sᶜ p nos gestū ꞇ semiplene, plenariū sorciatʳ effc̃m, vob̃ mandam⁹ in virtute sc̃e obediẽ firmif injungentes, qᵃt⁹ β̃dc̃m frem Henr̄, quẽ tenore β̃senciū ab ōi admīst̃ᵃc̃ōe tempaliū certis ex cāis absolvim⁹, a β̃dc̃a cur̄ celerar̄ amoventes, ip̃m de tempali admīnistᵃc̃ōe intᵒomitɫe n̄llaten⁹ pmittatis, nᶜ cepta v̄ri pⁱorat⁹ exire, quousq aliud a nobis ħueritis in mandatis. Dc̃m vero frem W[illelmum] de Shyre in officio celerar̄ loco suo substituatis. Frem Joħm de Gothᵃm, vel aliū v̄ri collegii ad hoc ydoneū p gerenda cura rex infᵃ limites pⁱoratus existenciū β̃fato Will̃o adjũgentes, ut vices gerat receptoris, et de consilio ejusđ frĩs W[illelmi] ad utilitatē v̄re eccĩe admīstret. Sic' vos ħntes in β̃missſ ut m̃ito de negligencia redargui minime valeatis. Daɫ apđ M˜ewell, ij non̄ Febr̄, anno Domini mil̃lo CCCᵐᵒ Octavo. Cons̄ n̄re, qᵃrto.

---

¹ The succeeding entry in the Register is dated 1st March, 1308-9, and is written with the same ink.

XVI.

ORDER FOR BANISHMENT AND IMPRISONMENT OF HENRY DE PECHAM, LATE CELLARER: 12TH MARCH, 1309.

(Winchester Diocesan Register, *Wodelok*, fol. 103 *v*.)

Littera pro fratre H. de Pecham, canonico de Tanrugge. Frater H[enricus] ℞c, dilĉis fit . . Priori ⁊ convent' de Novo loco, saltm, ℞c. Quia frem H[enricum] de Pech^am, canōicum de Tanrugg' certis, ⁊ legittimis ex caīs, honorē religiōis, ⁊ sue aīe salutē contingentibʒ a domo sua p̄dc̄a, duxim⁹ emittend vob firmit injungendo mādam⁹, qᵃtin⁹ visis p̄sentibʒ, ip̄m ad temp⁹, apud vos, sumptibʒ pⁱorat⁹ de Tanrugg' p̄dc̄i moraturū, benigni⁹ admittatis, ita, q̄ in certa camā cū nᵃcciis vite tm̄ moram tᵃhat nᵉ sⁱ certum locum exire liceat aut cū secularibʒ here tᵃctatū, nisi de pⁱoris aut suppⁱoris licencia sp̄ali, ⁊ p visum duoʒ confrum vroʒ etatis mature ⁊ cōp̄sacōis honeste, quos auctoritate n̄ra ip̄i⁹ custodie continue deputetis. P?missa vice n̄ra, effc̄ualiter exequētes, quousq̄ aᵈ a nob s̄r hiis hūitis in mand̄. Daī ap̄d Essher, iiij Iđ Mᵃrcii, anno Dn̄i miltio CCCᵐᵒ Octavo.

XVII.

ORDERS TO PRIORY OF NEWARK AS TO TREATMENT OF PRISONER: 23RD MARCH, 1309.

(Winchester Diocesan Register, *Wodelok*, fol. 105 *v*.)

Pecham. Frater Henricus ℞c, dilĉis . . Priori et conventui de Novo loco, saltm, gr̄am et bn̄. Cum nos nup visitacōis n̄re officiū jure dioces in pⁱoratu de Tanrugge n̄re dioc̄ exĉentes, Fratⁱ Henrico de Pech^am ejusdem pⁱorat⁹ canōico, suis demītis id poscentibus p aīe ip̄ius salute, penitenciam injuximꝰ infrascp̄tam, usq̄ ad n̄re volūtatis bn̄placitū apud vos pagendam⸝ vidʒ q̄ in secreta, ⁊ separata camā, solus absq̄ socio sub custodia duoʒ cōcanoicoʒ vroʒ, bone opinionis et etatis mature ip̄m frem Henr̄ vicissim custodiencium, et claves ip̄ius camē deferencium, comōretʳ, ⁊ q̄ idem in qualibet sexta feria, sinḡlis ebdomadabus, in pane cervisia ⁊ potagio tm̄, jejunet; aliis vero diebus dū apud vos remanserit, pane, cervisia, et potagio cū uno ferculo tm̄mᵒ sit contentus, nᵉ cepta camē p̄dc̄e exeat quoquo modo, nisi cā inevitabilis ⁊ r̄onabit, hoc exposcat, nᵉ eciā divina infra dc̄m tempus celebrare quovis modo p̄sumat, seu cū aliqua p̄sona seculari seorsum, sive religiosa, nisi in p̄sencia custodū ip̄ius, seu alterius eoʒd̄, p vos ut p̄mittiʳ deputādoʒ, colloquiū h̄eat quoquo modo, p cujus nc̄ciis, s̄b forᵃ qᵃ p̄mittiᵗʳ, eiđ p vos ministᵃndis, sinḡlis ebdomadabus, qᵃ diu inl̄ vos

I

morā tᵃxerit, duodecim denar̃ a . . Priore t̃ capit̃lo de Tanrugg' βdc̃is,' voḃ solvend̃, duxim⁹ statüend̃. Vobis mandamus in virtute sc̃e obedĩe t̃ sub peᵃ districc̃ois canoīce, firmiꝑ injũgendo, qᵃtin⁹ dc̃m fr̃em Henr̃ devote admittentes, eidē cam̃am, t̃ custodiã, ac ceꝑa, nᵃccia, juxta formā supius exp̃ssam exhibere, n̄llaten⁹ omittatis. Taliꝑ in βmissis vos h̃ntes, ne sup inobediencia, fraude, seu negligencia, vos redargũe, quoq° modo nos contingat in futᵘm. Val̃t. Dat̃ apud Novū locum, ix kt̃ April̃, anno Dn̄i milt̃o CCC^{mo} octavo. Cons̃ n̄re, quarto.

XVIII.

Order for Amelioration of Punishment: 27th May, 1309.

(Winchester Diocesan Register, *Wodelok*, fol. 108.)

Littera priori de Novo loco pro fratre Henrico de Pecham directa.
Sal̃m, gr̃am t̃ bn̄. Quia intellexim⁹ q̃ fr̃ H[enricus] de Pekhᵃm, apud vos de mandato n̄ro moram tᵃhens, p̃niam s̃ⁱ imp̃oitā, cū humilitate sustinuit paciens̃ꝑ, ita q̃ in eo, certa sue emendac̃ois indicia jā appent, voḃ manda[m]⁹ qᵃt⁹ ip̃m, liḃantes a cam̃a in qᵃ detinet̃ʳ, pmittatis eundē seq̃ⁱ Convent̃ in choro, dormitorio, refectorio, ceꝑisq̃ locis infᵃ clausū, sub certo custode p vos sue custodie deputando, sic q̃ claustr̃ᵐ nō exeat, quousq̃ t̃c̃. Val̃t. Dat̃ apud Al̃t Cler̃, vj kt̃ Junii, anno Dn̄i milt̃io CCC^{mo} nono.

XIX.

Permission for Him to Return to Tanridge: 16th July, 1309.

(Winchester Diocesan Register, *Wodelok*, fol. 112.)

Pecham. Fraꝑ H[enricus] t̃c̃, dilc̃is filiis . . Priori t̃ Conventui de Novo loco n̄re dioc̃, sal̃m, gr̃am t̃ bn̄. Cum p̃nia, nedū, sc̃d̃m qᵃntitatē excessus, s3 eciā sc̃d̃m penitentis contric̃om, juxᵃ βsidentis arbit̃ⁱum, pvide sit moderand̃, t̃ si necesse fũit penitus relaxand̃, ac nos p t̃ras v̄ras intelleximus, quod Frater Henr̃ de Pechᵃm, canoīcus de Tanrugge, quē vobis alias tᵃnsmisimus, p̃niam s̃ⁱ certis decãis, p nos imp̃oitam, sub certa forᵃ inꝑ vos pacturus, paciens̃ꝑ, t̃ cū ōi humilitate et contric̃oe magna, in eadem pagenda, se gessit, ita q̃ certū sue emendac̃ois indicium penes vos om̃s appet manifeste. Nos igit̃ʳ devoc̃oe βfati fr̃is Henrici, sic ut βmittit̃ʳ penitentis, t̃ laudabile testimonio, quod de ipsius vita phibetis, consideratis,' volentes p̃niam per nos eidē imp̃oitam, ex cãis βmissis relaxare,' voḃ mandam⁹ qᵃtinus, ip̃m cū suo pⁱore, ad moñ de Tanrugg' t̃ locū ppⁱū redire liḃe pmittatis. Cui ad dc̃m moñ redeund̃ liḃam in

Dño tenore p̄sencꝰ concedim’ facultatē. Scientes insup q̄ ūre occurrit bñ memorie, qᵃliſ p suis necessariis, qᵃmdiu inſ vos morā fecit, voɓ sing̃lis ebdomadabʒ, duodeci deñ a suo pⁱore de Tanrugg’ solvend̃, duxim’ ordinare, sup cujꝰ pecūie solucōe, voɓ celeriſ faciend̃ .. Priori suo memorato, lr̃as ūras monatorias, destinavim’. Dat̃ apud Essher’, xvij kt̃ Augusti, anno Dñi MᵒCCCᵐᵒ nono.

XX.

ORDER FOR PAYMENT FOR EXPENSES OF PRISONER: 16TH JULY, 1309.

(Winchester Diocesan Register, *Wodelok*, fol. 112.)

Littera .. Priori et conventui Novi loci pro fratre Henrico de Pechᵃm directa. Fr̃ H[enricus] t̃c, dilc̃is filiis .. Priori ⁊ conventui de Tanrugg’, salt̃m, gr̃am [⁊ bñ]. Cū nos alias fr̃em H[enricum] de Pechᵃm, cōcanouicū vr̃m, cui suis demitis id poscentibʒ in ultr̃a visitacōe ūra, quā nup inſ vos excuim’, p̃niam injūxim’ salutarē, .. Priori ⁊ conventui de Novo loco ūre dioc̃, p hiꝰ p̄nia sub certa forā inſ eos pagenda, duxim’ destinare, p suis necessariis ministᵃndis cid̃, sing̃lis ebdomadabʒ a voɓ duodeci denar̄ solvend̃ qᵃmdiu inſ eosd̃ morā fecit, eisdem statuentes. Et nos ad instanciā .. prioris ⁊ conventus Novi loci de ip̃ius cōtricōe ⁊ devocōe animi, in eadem penitentia pagenda, laudibile testimoniū phibenciū, penitenciā eid̃ impōitam, jā duxim’ relaxare; vobis mandā’ ⁊ districte monem’ in Dño, qᵃtꝰ dc̃m fr̃em Henr̃, inſ vos benigne admittentes, habita computacōe solerti sup ip̃ius mora inſ canōicos monasterii Novi loci, juxta p̄tactam taxacōm ūram celeriſ p ip̃ius fr̃is H[enrici] nᵃcciis satisfaciatis eisd̃, ita q p̄textu hiꝰ ip̃os de voɓ impostez noɓ conquer’ non coutingat, ⁊ ip̃m sicut fr̃em claustᵃlem, tractetis, ita q̃d de ūris intⁱnsecis v̄l extⁱnsecis negociis ut ballȋs v̄l obedienciarius ñllaten’ se intᵒmittat, quousq̃ de ip̃ius gestu laudabili inſ vos in monast̃io v̄ro recepim’ fidem pleniorē. Dat̃ ap̃d Essher’, xvij kt̃ Augusti, anno Dñi milt̃io CCCᵐᵒ nono.

XXI.

LETTERS OF REQUEST TO THE PRIOR OF NEWARK TO PERMIT THOMAS DE ST. ALBAN, ONE OF HIS CANONS, TO LEAVE THE PRIORY, IN ORDER TO BECOME PRIOR OF TANRUGGE.

(Winchester Diocesan Register, *Wodelok*, fol. 108 v.)

Littera priori de Novo loco pro fratre Thoma de Sancto Albano directa. Fr̃ H[enricus] t̃c, dilc̄o fit̃ .. Priori de Novo loco ūre dioc̃, salm̄, gr̃am ꞇ bn̄. Quia fr̃em Thomā de Sc̄o Albano cōcanōicū vr̃m in pⁱorē monasterii de Tanrugg' n̄re dioc̄, put nob̄ incūbit ista vice, licet invitū ꞵficere intendim⁹, quod absq̧ licencia ṽra sp̄ali fac̄e volūtatis n̄re non existit, cū nᶜ ip̄e absq̧ vob̄ in hoc licite valeat cōsentir', vos attente requirim⁹ ꞇ rogam⁹, qᵃtⁱ dc̄m Thomā, ab obedīa ꞇ subjecc̄oe, qua, domui ṽre est astrictus absolventes, eid̄ hiⁱ ꞵfixioni n̄re consenciendi, ꞇ ad dc̄m Moñ de Tanrugg' tᵃnseundi, licenciā p ṽrᵃs patentes ƚras concedere velitis sp̄alem. Vaƚt. Daƚ ꞇc̄.

XXII.

LICENCE FOR THE TRANSFER, &c.

(Winchester Diocesan Register, *Wodelok*, fol. 109 v.)

Littera directa fratri Thome de Sancto Albano. Fraƚ H[enricus] ꞇc̄, dilc̄o filio fr̃i The de Sc̄o Albano, salm̄, gr̃am ꞇ bn̄. Cum constet nob̄ pⁱorē tuū Moñ de Novo loco, de consensu conventus ejusdem, ab ōi subjecc̄oe et obediencia quibus moñ ꞵdc̄o astrictus extiƚas, in forᵃ juris te absolvisse, ꞇ ad Moñ de Tanrugge n̄re dioc̄ tᵃnseundi, licenciam p suas ƚras patentes concessisse sp̄alem, ac nos te in pⁱorem Moñ de Tanrugg' ꞵdc̄i put nob̄ ista vice incūbit ꞵfic̄e decrev̄imⁱ, dño cōcedente.꞉ Tibi mandamus, qᵃtinⁱ hac instanti die Mᵃrtis mane ap̄d Essher' ad nos dirigas gr̄ssus tuos, factur' et receptᵉ in ꞵmissis, quod ordo posƚlat r̄ois. Vaƚ. Dat ꞇc̄.¹

XXIII.

APPOINTMENT OF COADJUTOR FOR TEMPORAL AFFAIRS:
22ND NOVEMBER, 1312.

(Winchester Diocesan Register, *Wodelok*, fol. 175.)

Tanrugge. Frater H[enricus] ꞇc̄, dilc̄is filiis . . Prior ꞇ conventui de Tanruggh', n̄re dioc̄, saluƚe ꞇc̄. Cum nup p discretos viros Magr̃m Laurenciū de Gloucesƚ, monachū, sacre pagine pfessorem, ꞇ . . Offic̄ n̄rm, pⁱoratū ṽrum tam in capite qᵃm in membr̃, mandav̄imus visitari: Iidemq̧ visitac̄ois officiū, debite exc̄entes, invenissent pⁱoratū ꞵdc̄m, p simplicitaƚe ꞇ negligenciam Prioris qui de dilapidac̄oe ex c̄tis cāis suspectus hēbātur in tantū collapsum q̄d vix adic̄e poƚit ut resurgat dñm Carolū, Rectorē ecc̄lie de Colesdoñ, virū utiq̧ p̧vidū ꞇ discretū, eidem . . Priori coadjutorē, vob̄ ꞵsentibus, ꞇ hoc instanƚ postulantibꜝ

---

¹ Placed between entries of 14th and 15th June, 1308.

deputarunt, sine cujus consilio ꝛ assensu nich eoꝝ faɛet que ad administraꝯoem ptinent temporalē ordinantes q̃d idem . . Prior in refectorio cum fratᶦbus cotidie comedat ꝛ in dormitorio de nocte jaceat ꝛ in sp̃ualibus dūtaxat eisdem diligenꝉ intendat q̃d q̨ fraꝉ Joħes de Pende cōcanōicᵍ vester vices gerat celerarii oĩa agens de consilio et assensu dñi Caroli supᵃdc̃i: Proviso q̃d sigillũ vr̃m cōe s̃b tᶦbus clavibus custodiretʳ fideℏ, quaꝝ una penes pᶦorem alꝑa penes rectorem, ꝑcia penes suppᶦorem inꝉim remañet. Nos igitur q̃d in hac pte a ꝑfatis comissar̃ ñris pvide fc̃m est ratũ ꝛ gᵃtum ħntes. Voƀ in vᶦtute obediencie firmiꝉ injūgendo mandamᵍ, qᵃtinᵍ ea que p ipᵒs ibiđ ordinata sũt inviolabiliꝉ observantes, om̃ia que ꝑfatus dñs Carolus, in hiis que ad ministraꝯoem respiciũt temporalē p v̄ra utilitate rite duꝗit, ordinanđ, studeatis efficaciꝉ adimplere quoadusq̨ duꝗimᵍ aliꝉ providenđ: nolumᵍ tamen q̃d ipe v̄l vos, sine ñro bñptito ꝛ assensu ad aliquas alienacōes faciendas inꝉrim pcedatis. Volumᵍ ꝛ ꝛ mandamᵍ q̃d dc̃us Prior cui usum cujᵍcumq̨ sigilli ad mutuũ contᵃhendũ inꝉdicimᵍ, uno solo s̃viente sit contentus. Presentes autē lr̃as penes dc̃m dñm Carolũ volumᵍ remañe. Daī apud Suthwerk', x kℏn Decembr̃, anno Dñi miltimo CCCᵐᵒ duodecimo. · Consr̃ ñre, octavo.

XXIV.

PROCLAMATION OF ELECTION OF JOHN HANSARD TO BE PRIOR: 17TH MARCH, 1324.

(Winchester Diocesan Register, *Stratford*, fol. 3.)

Joħes ꝛc̃, dilc̃o filio .. offic̃ archĩ Surr̃, salℏm grām ꝛ bñ. Vacante nup pᶦoratu de Tanrigg' nr̃e dioc̃ p mortē Henr̃ de Pechᵃm ultimi prioris ejusdem... Suppᶦor ꝛ ejusdem loci cōcanonici, Fr̃em Joħm Hansard dc̃e domᵍ concanōcᵘ in pᶦorem dc̃e ecc̃lie de Tanrigg'; licencia eligendi a dc̃i pᶦoratus patrono, petita pᶦmitᵍ ꝛ optenta, concordiꝉ ꝛ canōᶜᵉ, ut asℏitʳ, eleg?unt. Cum gⁱ ad exaīacōnem negocii eꝉccõis memorate qⁱnto die juridico post instans fm Annũc'ƀte Mᵉ in ecc̃lia convēℏi de Suthewerk nr̃e dioc̃, favente Dño, pcedꝑe intendamᵍ ꝛ ulꝉius quod nr̃o incumbit offic̃o pagꝑe in hac pte: Vobis firmiꝉ injūgendo mandamᵍ qᵃtī citetꝑ seu citar' fac' pemptorꝗ oppōitorem v̄l oppōitores si qui sint noīatⁱ in spe, ac & om̃is alios in geñe, in ecc̃lia dc̃i pᶦoratᵍ qui se voluerint oppoñe contᵃ dc̃i electi psonā seu eꝉccōis formā ꝑdc̃e, ipam eꝉccōm palam ꝛ puᶜᵉ denūciando, q̃d cōpeant cor̃ noƀ v̄l .. comissar̃ nostr̃ die ꝛ loco ꝑdc̃is, ꝑcise ꝛ pemptor', ꝑpōitur' ꝛ ostensur', quicqⁱd ꝑpoñe v̄l obiɛe voluĩnt contᵃ electi psonam ut ꝑdicitʳ v̄l eꝉccōis formā, si sibi viderint expedire factur'q̨ ulſius in dĉo neḡo cum c'tinuaĉone et progaĉone dieʒ ſbsequenciū, quod canoce dictaverint sancŧones. De die recepṫ ṫĉ. Dat' apd Sutherwerkᵱ, xvjᵐᵒ kln April, anno Dñi MᵒCCCᵐᵒxxiiijᵗᵒ. (*sic* pro xxiijᵒ.)

XXV.

PROCESS OF THE ELECTION; MANDATE FOR INDUCTION; AND MONITION OF OBEDIENCE: 31st MARCH, 1324.

(Winchester Diocesan Register, *Stratford*, fol. 3.)

Process of the Election.

Acta corͬ noḃ Joħne, pmissione dīa Wyntoñ eр̄s, in eccłia conˡⁱ de Suthewerkᵱ nr̄e dioĉ, die Veñis pẋ pͥ fm Anñc ɓe Mᵉ anno Dñi Miłłio CCCᵐᵒxxiiijᵗᵒ in neḡo eŧcĉois de fr̄e Joħne Hansard cōcanocᵒ pˡoraꝉ de Tanrigg' nr̄e dioĉ, p ꞵcentorē ᷓ cōcanoᶜᵒˢ ejusdem domͥ in pˡorem dĉe domͥ nūc vacantᵱ, nup celebrate, electo. Lecta lra ſtificat' offiĉ d́ni archi Surr̄ p quam constabat oppoitores quoscūqͺ qⁱ cᷓᵃ dĉm eŧcm seu eŧcĉois formā de eo fĉam se oppoñe aut diĉe volῦint, ad dĉos diem ᷓ locū coram noḃ v̄l comiss' nostr̄ pemptorͬ fuisse vocatᵱ, ꞵcise ᷓ pēto⁰ quicqⁱd diĉe, ꝓpoñe aut obiĉe voluerint contᵃ dĉm eŧcm seu eŧcĉois formā cum effectu ꝓpoitur' ᷓ ostensur', ulſiͥ q͂ factur' ᷓ receptur' cū c'tinuaĉōc ᷓ progaĉone dieʒ sequenciū quod canoce dictav̄int sanctōnes. Precetorq͂ ᷓ cōcanonici de Tanrigg' ꞵdĉi, p fr̄em Joħm de Pende dĉe domͥ cōcanoᶜᵘ, ad- psequend dĉe eŧcĉois neḡm per eosd pcur̄ łie c'stitutū 'ac dĉo eŧco psoᵗͥ compenᵇʒ, ac exhibitis p eundē pcur̄ pcuratorio suo, decreto eŧcĉois p eos celebrate ᷓ pitate quadā cōpmissar̄ facta de eligendo eis pˡorem dĉe domͥ, nᵒnon quadā lra a patᵒno dĉe domͥ de licencia eligendi ab eo petita ᷓ optēta ; factaqͺ puᶜᵃ pclamaĉōe ad hostiū ecclie conˡᵐ ꞵdĉe q͂d siqⁱ essent q͂ contᵃ dĉm eŧcm seu eŧcĉois formā de eodem Joħne fĉam quicqᵃ diĉe aut ꝓpoñe voluerint, q͂d corͬ noḃ tunc cōperent ꝓpoitur' qⁱᶜqⁱd ꝓpoñe volῦint in hac pte ipisqͺ sepiͥ ꞵconizatis ᷓ diuciͥ exspᶜtatis, ñlloqͺ cōpente nec aliqⁱd cᷓᵃ dĉos eŧcm ᷓ eŧcĉois formā dicente v̄l ꝓpoᵗᵉ, ñllis eciam instructoribus in hac pte pductis, nec aliqᵒs pduĉe volentᵱ se nichil in dĉo neḡo diĉe v̄l ꝓpoñe qᵒvismᵒ, factaqͺ publicaⁿᵉ decreti ᷓ exhibitoʒ ꞵdĉoʒ de c'sensu eŧci ᷓ pcur̄ ꞵfaṫ,' ꞵfigimͥ dĉis pcur̄ ᷓ eŧco diem Sabɓti pẋ tunc seqñ loco qᵒ pˡus ad faciᵈ ulſius in dĉo eŧcĉois neḡo corͬ noḃ, quod justicia suadebit. Quibʒ die ᷓ loco, dĉis pcur̄ ᷓ eŧco ut pˡus compenᵘᵇʒ, ꞵconizatis eciā oppoitoribʒ ħiͥ q͂d ꝓpoñent cᷓᵃ dĉos eŧcm ᷓ eŧcĉois formā quicqⁱd diĉe aut ꝓpoñe voluerint, ñlloqͺ licet łie ꞵconizato ᷓ diuciͥ expᶜtato quovismᵒ cōpente, ꞵclusaqͺ via dĉis oppoitoribʒ ᷓ omibʒ aliis viam quicqᵃ ulſiͥ in hac pᵗᵉ pponēdi p decretū, dĉoqͺ decreto eŧcĉois, ꝓpṫ iꝓius ineptitudinē ᷓ ñllitatem in eodem contentᵱ, m̄ltipliciꝉ ipugnato, tand̄ iidem et̄cus ꝉ p̄cur̄ cor̄ nob in judic̄o, pso͞tꝰ constituti, dc̄e et̄cc̄oi de ip̄o et̄co fte ꝉ oī. juri r̄one ejusdem ip̄i et̄co cōpetenti v̄l cōpetituro, ac p̄cessui corā nob h̄ito, pure simp͞r ꝉ absolute resignarūt ordinac̄oi ꝉ gr̄e nr̄e in hac pte totalit̄ submittētes. Et quia nob constat dc̄am elc̄om ꝉ et̄cc̄ois formā m̄ltip͠r fuisse ꝉ esse n̄llam ꝉ oīo invalidam꞉ p̄t̄atem eidem ecc͠ie de p͡iore p̄videndi nob rite ꝉ ͠lic fuisse et esse hac vice pleno jure devolutā꞉ p̄nūciam⁹ in hiis sc͡iptis p̄testantes exp̄sse eid̄ ecc͠ie de p͡iore p̄vid?e, put ad nos ptinet hac vice pleno jure, p̄figim⁹ꝙ dc̄o et̄co ꝉ p̄cur̄ diē Lune p͞x tunc seq̄n̄ loco quo p͡ius ad facid͠ ꝉ recipid͠ in eodē neḡo quod justicia suadebit. Postmod̄ vero die Lune adveᵗᵉ loco quo p͡ius p̄t͡ibunali sedentes, dc̄m fr̄em Joh̄m Hansard in p͡iore dc̄e ecc͠ie p̄fecim⁹ s̄b hac forᵃ. In Dei noīe, Amen. Nos Johannes, p̄missione dīa Wyntoñ ep̄us, cum ad nos p̄videndi p͡ioratui de Tanrigg' nr̄e Wyntoñ dioc̄ de p͡iore sit canoᶜᵉ hac vice devoluta p̄tīas, Nos volentes quatē⁹ cum Deo possum⁹ p̄vid?e ip̄i p͡ioratui de te fr̄e Joh̄ne Hansard, ip̄ius ecc͠ie concanoᶜᵒ, in obs̄vancia regulari exp̄sse p̄fesso ꝉ in sac̄doc̄o c'stituto, p̄videm⁹ ꝉ te in p͡iorem ecc͠ie de Tanrigg' memorate, admīst̄ᵃtōm tā in sp̄ualib3 qᵃm in ͠ipraᵇ3 t͡i coh̄͠ttētes.

Mandate of Induction.

Joh̄nes p̄missione dīa Wyntoñ Ep̄s, dil̄co filio .. Offic̄ arch̄i Surr̄, sal̄tm grām ꝉ bn̄. Quia nos frem Joh̄em Hansard ecc͠ie de Tanrigg' nr̄e dioc̄ cōcanoᶜᵘ, in obs̄vancia regulari exp̄sse p̄fessum ꝉ in ordine sac̄docii constitutū, ip̄i ecc͠ie p̄videndi p͡ioratui c̄tis de causis ꝉ leḡis ad nos hac vice p̄t̄iate ͠lie devoluta p̄fecim⁹ in p͡iorem꞉ vob comittimus ꝉ mandam⁹ qᵃtin⁹ eund̄ fr̄em Joh̄em Hansard in corp̄alem poss'onē dc̄i p͡iorat⁹, juriū ꝉ ptinenciaȝ suaȝ, inducatis ꝉ defendatis inductū. Contᵃdc̄ores vero ꝉ rebelles, si qui fū̄int, in hac pte p censurā ecc͠iasticā compescendo. Dat̄ ap̄d Suthewerk̄e, iiijᵗᵒ non̄ April, anno Dn̄i MᵒCCCᵐᵒxxiiijᵗᵒ.

Monition of Obedience.

Joh̄nes, p̄missione dīa Wyntoñ ep̄us, dil̄cis filiis .. Precentori ꝉ cōcanoᶜⁱˢ de Tanrigg' nr̄e dioc̄, sal̄tm grām ꝉ bn̄. Quia nos fr̄em Joh̄em Hansard, ecc͠ie vr̄e de Tanrigg' p̄dc̄e, in obs̄vancia regulari exp̄sse p̄fessum ꝉ in ordine sac̄docii constitutū, ip̄ius ecc͠ie jure nob p̄videndi de p͡iore dc̄i loci hac vice p̄t̄iate ͠lie devoluta, canoᶜᵉ p̄fecim⁹ in p͡iorem꞉ vob injūgim⁹ ꝉ mandam⁹ qᵃtin⁹ eidem fr̄i Joh̄i tanqᵃm p͡iori vr̄o sitis in om̄ib3 intendentes parit̄ ꝉ obedientes, put ord̄is vr̄i regula docet, exigit ac requirit꞉ Scientes q̄d sn̄ias quas rite tulerit in rebelles, ratas h̄ebim⁹ ꝉ faciem⁹ auctore Dn̄o inviolabilit̄ obs̄vari. Dat̄ ap̄d Suthewerk̄e, iiijᵗᵒ Non̄ April, anno Dn̄i mil̄timo CCCᵐᵒxxiiijᵗᵒ. Et cōn̄s̄ nr̄e, p͡imo.

XXVI.

Commission of Coadjutor to Prior: 31st May, 1380.

(Winchester Diocesan Register, *Stratford*, fol. 51.)

Johs ϯc, dilco filio dño Lauȓ de Rustyngtoñ, saltm, grām ϯ ƀn. Priore ϯ friƀʒ domus de Tanrigg' nr̃o dioc̃ p nos nup, modo debito visitatis, ℥tis ϯ legĩs de cāis admĩstrac̃õm bonoʒ dc̃e dom⁹ pᶦori inᵖdixim⁹ memorato, donᶜ aliud de statu suo duxĩm⁹ ordinanđ. Te igitr de cuj⁹ fidelitate ϯ industria fiduciam reportam⁹, coadjutorem dc̃o pᶦori inᵖim deputam⁹. Nolentes qd sine consilio ϯ assensu tuo, pᶦor seu qᶦvis alius de bonis dc̃e dom⁹ aliquatr intᵒmittat, custodiamq̨ ϯ admĩtrac̃õm bonoʒ dc̃o dom⁹ tibi tanqᵃm coadjutori legĩo, donec aliud ordinaѷim⁹, cõmittim⁹ p ƥsentes. In cujus ϯc. Dat̃ apud Esshᵉe, ijᵒ ktn [Junii], anno Dñi mitto, CCCᵐᵒ tᶦcesimo. Et cons̃ nr̃e, vijᵒ.

Eisdem die, loco ϯ anno sc̃ᶦpt̃ fuit pᶦori ƥdc̃o q̨d intendȝet eidem Lauȓ tanqᵃm coadjutori suo legĩo ĩ hac pte.

XXVII.

Inquisition *ad quod damnum*, for Gift by Henry att Donne to the Priory of 5 Acres at Okstede.

(British Museum, Add. MS. 6167 [Symm's Collections], p. 415.)

Juratores dicunt q̨d licet Escaetor đni Regis in Comitatu Surȓȝ p quandam Inquisicõcm coram ipso ex officio suo captam invenerit q̨d Prior de Tanrugge appropriavit sibi ϯ domui sue quinq̨ acras terre cum ptiñ in Okstede ex donacõue ϯ concessione Henȓ att Donne de Warlyngham fc̃is domui ƥdc̃e tempore dñi Regis p̃ris đni Regis nunc, post publicacõem Statuti de terris ϯ teñtis ad manū mortuam non ponenđ editi, licencia ip̃ius đni Regis sup hoc non obtenta. Dicunt tamen q̨d idem Prior de ƥdc̃is quinq̨ acris terre, tanquam de·pcella dc̃e carucate a tempore donationis ϯ assignacõis earundem seiś̃tus fuit quousq̨ ƥdc̃us Escaetor ƥdcas quinq̨ acras terre p virtutem Inquisicõnis ƥdc̃e cepit in manū đni Regis. In cujus rei testimoñ ϯc.

XXVIII.

Episcopal Visitation of the Priory when John Hansard resigned and Philip de Wokyngham was appointed Prior: 4th September, 1385.

(Winchester Diocesan Register, *Orleton*, I, fol. 26 v.)

Mᵈ. q̨d iiijᵗᵃ die mensis Septēbȓ, anno Dñi, mitto, CCCᵐᵒxxxvᵗᵒ.

Veñ p̄r dn̄s A[dam] Dī grā Wyntoñ ēpus in domo cap̄lari Priorat' de
Tanrugge, ord̃is Sc̃i Augusti, sue dioc̄, psonaliꝑ constitut', ip̄m prioratū
in capite ⁊ in mēbr̃ ex sui officii debito canoᶜᵉ visitavᵗ, ⁊ s̄bsequenꝑ
ibid̄e de exꝑssa c'ssu frĩs Johĩs Hansard, tūc ej'd̄e pⁱoratᵒ prioris, qui p̄p̄
sui corpis debilitatē ⁊ sue insufficiēciā psone, coram eodem p̄re ejusd̄e
pⁱoratᵒ regimini pure ⁊ sponte cessit: ceꝓꝛq̃ oñm ⁊ singloꝛ canōicoꝛ
dc̃i pⁱorat' juxᵃ effc̃m cessionis hi' p ip̄m p̄rem admisse ⁊ canonice
acceptate: de frē Pho de Wokyngh᎑m in monasⱱio de Novo [Loco]
eoꝛd̄e ordinis et dioc̄ canōico exꝑsse ꝑfesso ⁊ in ordine sac̄dotali c'stituto,
viro utiq̃ ꝑvido ⁊ discreto, ⁊ in sp̄ualibꝫ ⁊ tepalibꝫ p̄limū cⁱcūspecto, de
c'ssu ⁊ licencia pⁱoris sui de Novo Loco tūc ibid̄e p̄sentĩ: dc̄o prioratui
de Tanrugge ⁊ fribꝫ inibi Deo ꝫvientibꝫ, ꝑvidit, ⁊ ip̄m ejusd̄e pⁱoratᵒ ⁊
frm̃ ꝑdcoꝛ in pⁱorē ꝑfecit ⁊ pastorē sub hac forma. IN DEI NOMIE, AMĒ.
Nos Adā pmissione divina Wyntoñ Ēpus, admissa cessione religiosi
viri frĩs Johĩs Hansard nup.. pⁱoris de Tanrugge ord̃is Sc̃i Augusti ñro
dioc̄ in manibꝫ ñris sponte fc̃a, ⁊ potestate ad ꝑvidend̃ eidem domui de
psona ydonea in pⁱorē ⁊ pastorē ejusd̄e ab eod̄e Johc̃ ⁊ oĩnibꝫ aliis ⁊
singlĩs fribꝫ ejusd̄e pⁱoratᵒ noꝯ exꝑsse concessa: Xp̄i nōīe invocato
religᵗ virū frēm Phm̃ de Wokynghᵃm in moᵃsⱱio de Newerkᵖ dc̃i ord̃is
exꝑsse ꝑfessum ⁊ in ordīe sac̄dotali c'stiᵗᵘ virū ꝑvidū ⁊ discretū, ac in
sp̄ualibꝫ ⁊ tempalibꝫ cⁱcumspectū, dc̃e domui de Tanrugge ⁊ canoᶜⁱˢ inibi
Deo ꝫvientibꝫ in pⁱorē ꝑficimus ⁊ pastorē. Acᵗ sunt h̃, anno, die ⁊ loco
ꝑdc̃is. Pʒsentibꝫ Maḡris J[ohanne] Lowe, juris civilᵗ ꝑfessor' ⁊ Henr̃
de Lond̃ rᵒ eccᵉ de Withihame, Cic̃ dioc̄; ac Wilⱱo de Alresford' ⁊
J[ohanno] de Beautre, apⱱica aucᵃⱱe noᵃriis publicis testĩ, ⁊c̃.

XXIX.
COMMISSION TO CITE PRIOR PHILIP FOR NON-RESIDENCE: 17TH JANUARY, 1341.
(Winchester Diocesan Register, *Orleton*, I, fol. 108.)

Adā, ⁊c̃. Maḡro A[de] de Wambergh'.. offic̃ nr̃i comissar̃
geñali, salⱱm, gᵃ ⁊ bñ. Licet ꝑlati ad regend̃ eccᵃˢ dī poscit gregē
dñicū pascᵉ ⁊ a lupi rapacis invasionibꝫ ꝑtegᵉ, juraq̃ ⁊ facultates
ecctie illesa ꝫvare, cū omī vigilantia teneatʳ. Fr̃ tn̄ Phs pⁱor eccᵉ
convenⁱʳ de Tanrugge' nr̃e dioc̄ put ex dilc̄oꝛ fil canoᶜᵒꝛ ejusd̄e eccᵉ
gᵃvi q̃rela recipimᵒ, ministⱱiū sⁱ in cad̄e creditū pinpendēs, eccliam et
gregē sibi comiss' curaq̃ ⁊ regimē utⁱusq̃ p̄pⁱa temⁱⱱᵉ p nōmodica
tēpa desᵘuit ⁊ absq̃ licencia debita, seu cā rōnabli vel honesta, ab
ecctia ꝑdc̃a se fraudulenꝑ absentaviꝑ ⁊ in locis incognitis demoratʳ
hucusq̃. Ne igitʳ discipline ⁊ recti regim̃is gub̃nac̃o in dc̃a eccᵃ

derelicto, naufragetᵣ, q̃d absit, ibidem religio, ipaq̃ ecc̃lia pacintᵣ aliquā in suis facultatibʒ lesionē, h̃iʸ pic̃tis remediis oportunis qᵃntū cū dō possumʸ duximʸ occᵣrend̃. Qᵃobrē vobis in vⁱtute obedie fᶦmiľ injūgēdo mādamʸ qᵃᵗ frēm Pħm pⁱorē p̃dc̃m in locis ubi ṽisimilius creditᵣ inveniri diligenľ, querētes, ip̃m si psonaliľ invenire poľitis in pp̃ⁱa psona, alioquin in ecc̃ᵃ p̃dc̃a corā p̃cuřē suo si quē dimiserit, ac notis familiaribʒ ꝭ amicis suis, tⁱne citac̃onis ac monicõis edc̃o pubᶜᵉ p̃põito citetę̃ eūdē, ac & moneteę̃ ꝭ efficaciľ inducatis eundē q̃d, s̃b peᵃ juris ad eccē ꝭ curā suā p̃dic̃t, infᵃ tempʸ a canōibʒ limitatū, redeat, ac & cⁱca easdē regend̃ diligenľ intendat. De die vᵒ recepⁿⁱˢ p̃s'ᵐ, citac̃onū ac monicōnum vřaʒ, modo ꝭ forma eaʒ ꝭ an dc̃us h̃iʸ monic̃oi pere neglex̃it, nos post lapsum dc̃i tēpis c̃tif p lřas v̄ras patent̃ haʒ šē continētes. Dat̃ apd̃ Essh̃ʔe, xvij die mens̃ Januař, anno Dūi MᵒCCCᵐᵒxl, ꝭ tᵃns̃onis nře, octavo.

XXX.

CITATION OF SAME "BY WAYS AND MEANS:" 28TH JULY, 1341.
(Winchester Diocesan Register, *Orleton*, I, fol. 108.)

Adam, ꝯc̃. Mag̃ro Ade ꝯc̃. ut s̃ᵃ salm̃, gřam ꝭ bñ. Cū nup audita q̃rela gᵃvi relig̃ viroʒ ac dilc̃ōʒ filioʒ canoᶜᵒʒ eccē convenľᵣ de Tanrugge ñre dioc̃, q̃d fř Pħs dc̃e ecc̃lie pⁱor minisťiū sⁱ in eadē creditū pinpendēs, ecc̃liam ꝭ gregē sⁱ com̃iss̃ curāq̃, ꝭ regim̃e utⁱusq̃ pp̃ⁱa temʔⁱᵗᵉ desŭit, ꝭ absq̃ licencia debita seu cā rõnabli v̄l honesta ab ecc̃lia p̃dc̃a se fraudulenľ absentavᵗ ꝭ in locis incognitis p tempᵃ nōmodica morabatᵣ, ꝭ ne discipline ꝭ recti regim̃is gub̃ʔnac̃o in dc̃a ecc̃lia derelicto naufragetᵣ, quod absit, ibidē religio ipaq̃ ecc̃ᵃ paľetᵣ aliquā in suis faculta᷍bʒ lesionē, voħ aľ dederimʸ in mandatis qᵃtę̃ frēm Pħm pⁱorē p̃dc̃m in locis ubi ṽisimiliʸ cred̃ʔetur inveniri diligenľ q̃reretis, ꝭ ip̃m, si personaliľ invenire potuissetis, in pp̃ⁱa psona, alioqⁱn in ecc̃ᵃ p̃dc̃a, corā p̃cuřē suo, si quē dimiẞit, ac notis familiaribʒ ꝭ amicis suis, tⁱne citac̃onis ac monicõis edc̃o pubᶜᵉ p̃põito, citaretis eundē ac & moneretis ꝭ efficaciľ inducĕtis, q̃d s̃b pena juris, ad ecc̃liam ꝭ curā suā predic̃t infᵃ tempʸ a canōibʒ limitatū rediret, ac & cⁱca easdem regend̃ diligenľ ut tenetur; et vos dc̃m Pħm pⁱorē aucᵃte mandati nři p̃dc̃i, diligenľ q̃sitū ꝭ psonaliľ non invētū, in eccē p̃dc̃a nullo p̃cuře ip̃ius invēto, corā notis familiaribʒ ꝭ amicis suis, trino citaⁿⁱˢ ac monicõis edc̃o pubᶜᵉ p̃põito, citastis monuisteʒ ꝭ efficaciľ induxistis quod s̃b peᵃ juris ad ecc̃am ꝭ curā p̃dictę̃ infᵃ tempus a canonibʒ limitatū rediret ꝭ cⁱca easdem regend̃ intenderet diligenľ, quibus quidem monic̃onibʒ, idē Pħs oĩo pere neglex̃it, put p ťras v̄ras ctificatoŕ sup hoc noƀ directas liq̃t evideñt, volentes igitr dc̄e ecc̄e indēpniti pspiĉe, ꝯ juris ordinē qui in hac pte requiritr obsɼvare. Voƀ fimiℓ injūgendo mādamᵍ, qati dc̄m Pħm diligeñt q̄rentes, ipm si psonaliℓ invēire potitp in ppia psona alioquin ipius pcurem si quē dimisit, necnō ipm Pħm in eccª ꝑdc̄a corā notis familiariƀꝫ ꝯ amicis suis pubᶜᵉ citacōnis edc̄o ppōito, citetis seu citori faciatp pemptoŕ q̃d c'peat coŕ noƀ v̄l nr̄o comīssaŕ in eccª nr̄a Catħ Wynt̄. vij die juridico post fm̄ exaltaⁿⁱˢ Sc̄e Crucis, cām si quam ħeat dc̄us Pħs rōnabilē, qªre ad ejus pivacōem ꝯ amocōem ab ecctia ꝑdc̄a minime pcedi debeat ppōitur', ultius qꝫ fc̄ur' ꝯ receptur' juxta canoᶜᶜᵒˢ sanccōes, quod natra ꝯ qªlitas hiᵍ negocii exigit ꝯ requirit, ꝯ eciā s̄niam diffinitīam pivacōis ꝯ amocōis sue ab ecctia si nlˉ canōicū qᵒd obstare potit auditurᵍ. Et de die recepⁿⁱˢ ꝑsentium ac citaⁿⁱˢ vr̄e modo q̧ ꝯ forª ejusdē, nos v̄l dc̄m nr̄m comīssaŕ dc̄is die ꝯ loco ctif' p l. vr̄as paƫ haꝫ s̆iem continētes. Daƫ apd Farnhªm, xxviij die mensp Julij, anno Dn̄i Miℓℓo CCCᵐᵒxl pimo, ꝯ tªtonis nr̄e, viijᵒ.

XXXI.
COMMISSION FOR DEPRIVATION FOR NON-RESIDENCE:
22ND SEPTEMBER, 1341.

(Winchester Diocesan Register, *Orleton*, I, fol. 108 *v.*)

Adam, ꝯc, discreto viro . . offic̄ nr̄o, saltm, gr̄am ꝯ bn̄. Cum nup fr̃ Pħs pior ecctie convenlˉ de Tanrugg' nr̄e dioc̄, ministɼiū sibi in eadē creditū pinpendēs, ecctiam ꝯ grege sibi comīss curā ꝯ regimē utiusq̧ ppia temtitate p nōmodica tēpa notorie des̆uisset, ꝯ absq̧ licencia debita seu cā rōnabli v̄l honesta, ab ecctia ꝑdc̄a se fraudulenƫ absentasset ꝯ in locis incognitis moratᵍ fuisset, nos indēpniti dc̄e ecctie pspiĉe ac hiᵍ pictis obviare cupiētes, ipm fr̄em Pħm aucªte diligeñt ubi ɼisimiliℓ credebatr invēire q̄situ ꝯ nō invētū in eccª ꝑdc̄a, xxj die mens̄ Januarii, ꝯ s̄bsequeƫ, viij die mens̄ Mªrcii, ꝯ postea penultīo die mens̄ Junii px ꝑteritp nullo pcure ipius invento corā notis familiariƀꝫ ꝯ amicis suis tine citacōnis ac monicōnis edc̄o pubᶜᵉ ppōito fecissemᵍ citari motti ꝯ efficaciℓ induci, q̃d s̄b pena juris ad ecctiam ꝯ curā suā ꝑdictp infª tempus a canonibus limitatū rediissꝫ, ꝯ cica easdē regend diligeƫ intendisset, ꝯ ꝑfatis Pħs pior hiᵍ monicōi pere neglexisset hucusq̧, ad cognoscend ꝯ pcedˉ in neḡo ꝑdc̄o juxª ejus qªlitatē ꝯ natram, ꝯ ipm Philippū a dc̄is pioratu ꝯ eccª privand ꝯ amovend ꝯ ultius faciend in toto neḡo antedc̄o, quod jurp ftit ꝯ rōnis, voƀ comittimᵍ, vices nr̄as, cū cohcōnis canōice potestate. Daƫ apud Walthªm, xxij die mens̄ Sept, anno Dn̄i miℓℓo CCCᵐᵒxlj, ꝯ ℓnst nr̄e, viij.

XXXII.

Sentence of Deprivation: 26th September, 1341.

(Winchester Diocesan Register, *Orleton*, I, fol. 108 v.)

In Dei noīe, Amen. Cum fr̃ Pħus pᵒʳ eccᵉ convenˡʳ de Tanrugge Wynt̃ diōc, minisf̃iū sibi in eadē creditū p̃inpendēs, eccl̃iam ꝛ gregē sibi cōm̃ⁱss̃, curāq̃ ꝛ regimē utⁱusq̃ p̃pⁱa temĩᵗᵉ p nōmodica tēpa deserens, ꝛ absq̃ licencia debita, ab eadē se fraudulenᵗ absentās nec valēs p̃sonalit̃ invēiri nulloq̃ p̃cūre p eum dimisso, fuisset auctᵃte veñabit̃ p̃ris d̃ni Ade, Dei gr̃a Wynt̃ c̃p̃i, loci diocesani, in eccᵃ βdc̃a, ac cor̃a notis familiaribȝ ꝛ amicis suis tⁱne citac̃õis ac monic̃õis edc̃o pubᶜᵉ p̃põito, q̃d s̃b pena juris ad eccᵃᵐ ꝛ cur̃a suā predic̃t infᵃ tempᵍ a canonibȝ limitatū rediret, ꝛ cⁱca easdem regend̃ diligent̃ intenderet, legĩe citatᵍ monitᵍ ꝛ efficacit̃ inductus. Et q̃r hiᵍ monic̃õi infᵃ semestr' tempus p̃ere neglexit, adhuc postea non valēs p̃sonalit̃ invēiri, nᵒ aliqᵒ p̃cūre p eum dimisso, citac̃õis edc̃o cor̃a notis familiaribȝ ꝛ amicis suis ac & in eccᵃ βdc̃a puᶜᵉ p̃põito, cãm rõnabilē si quã ħeret qᵃre ad ejus pⁱvac̃õem ꝛ amoc̃õem ab eccᵃ βdc̃a minime p̃cedi deberet, p̃põitur' factur' ꝛ receptur', quod natᵘa ꝛ qualitas hiᵍ negocii exiğet ꝛ requireret, ꝛ & s̃niam diffinitivā amoc̃õis ꝛ pⁱvationis ab eadem eccᵃ si qⁱd canonicū nō obviaret auditur'; aucᵗe dc̃i p̃ris, ad ctas diē ꝛ locū c'petētes, pemptoř ꝛ p̃ termino pemptoř cor̃a ip̃o v̄l suo cōmissař leĩe citatᵍ, quibȝ die ꝛ loco, videt̄, vij die juridico post fm̃ Exaltac̃onis Sc̃e Crucis in eccᵃ Cath̃ Wynt̃, dc̃o Pħo cor̃ nob̃ .. offic̃ ꝛ cōmissario dc̃i p̃ris in dc̃o negō sp̃alit̃ deputato p tⁱbunali sedētibȝ līe βconiȝato, sȝ nullo modo cōpente, ip̃m usq̃ in px̃m diē jurid̃ extūc px̃ sequētē in eodē loco duxim̄ expᵒtand̃, quibȝ die ꝛ loco ip̃m Pħm ut pⁱus cor̃a nobis p tⁱbunali sedētibȝ legĩe βconiȝatū ꝛ nō compentē, it̃ū usq̃ in px̃m diē juridicū extūc px̃ sequuturū in loco βdc̃õ, ad idē quod pⁱdē faciend̃ duxim̄ expᵒtand̃. Quibȝ die ꝛ loco, videt̄, vj kln Octobř, anno D̃ñi MᵒCCCᵒxljᵒ. Nos offic̃ ꝛ cōmissař antedc̃us dc̃m Pħm adhuc sepius ꝛ l̃co βconiȝatū ˙diuciᵍ expectatum coram nobis compere nō curātē, p̃nūciamus contumatē, ꝛ in penā ħiᵍ contumacie, ponderatis βmissis, ip̃m Pħm ab eadem eccᵃ amovemᵍ, destituimᵍ ꝛ privamus, amotū destitutū ꝛ privatū esse, s̃ñialit̃ ꝛ diffinitĩe p̃nūciamᵍ ꝛ ab eadē fore, ꝛ movend̃, ꝛ spoliand̃, ꝛ ad elecc̃õem futʳˡ pⁱoris in eadē, p eos ad quos hiᵍ electio, ptiñe dinoscitʳ p̃cedend̃ dec̃vimus in hiis sⁱcptis. Lat̃ p d̃ñm offic̃ Wyntoñ in loco cōsistoř Wyntoñ, vj kln Octobř, anno D̃ñi MᵒCCC.xlj. Indicc̃õe xᵃ, poni d̃ni B̃ñdc̃i pᵃpe xij, anno vij. P̃ȝentibȝ discr̃ viris, mağris Tħa de Enhᵃᵐ ꝛ Joħe de Ware dc̃i c'sistoř advocatis; Mağris Roğo Bryan ꝛ Roğo Scolys aucᵃte apᶜᵃ noᵉriis pubᶜⁱˢ ꝛc. testibȝ, ꝛc̃.

XXXIII.

INQUISITION *post mortem*, OF JOHN DE WARBLYNGTON, WHO DIED ON 13TH FEBRUARY, 1351.

(Inquis. P. M., 25 Edw. III, 1st Nos., No. 54. [Add. MS. 6167, fol. 416.])

Jurator. * * * dicunt q̃d ꝑdc̃um manerium de Tanrugge oneratur ab antiquo Priori de Tanrugg in xxˢ viijᵈ annui reddiť, solveñd ad Festa Pasche ⁊ Sc̃i Mich̃is p equales porcõnes, ut patet p fiñem in Curia Dñi Regis inde levatū ⁊ ostensum. Et dicunt q̃d pquisiť Curie iɓm valent per annū xijᵈ. Et dicunt q̃d ꝑdc̃us Joh̃es de Warblyngton, obiit xiij° die Februarii, ⁊c̃. Et dicunt q̃d Joh̃es de Warblyngton, filius ꝑdc̃ Joh̃is defuncti, est heres ejusdem proquinquior ⁊ etatis sex annorū,⁊c̃. In cujᵉ rei testimoñ, ⁊c̃.

XXXIV.

PROCESS OF ELECTION OF JOHN DE MERSTHAM TO BE PRIOR, THE MORROW OF ST. MARTIN, 1341.

(Winchester Diocesan Register, *Orleton*, I, fol. 109.)

Act̃ coram noɓ Joh̃e de Wolveleye, veñabiƚ p̃ris dñi Ade, Dei gr̃a Wyntoñ Ep̃i, in nego̅ elecc̃onis de fr̃e Joh̃e de Mersthᵃm canoᶜᵒ ecclie convenˡʳ de Tanrugg' Wyntoñ dioc̃ in pⁱorẽ ejᵉdc̃ ecclie jam vacantis (ut dicitʳ) celebrate comissaŕ sp̃aliť deputato in eccᵃ proch̃ de Farnhᵃm die Lune in crastino Sc̃i Mᵃrtini, anno Dñi miƚƚo, CCCᵐᵒxlj°, videƚt cū constaret noɓ p litťas c̃tificatoŕ mag̃ri Ade de Wamberg̃h, offic̃ Wyntoñ, comissaŕ g̃ñaƚ omnes ⁊ singlos si qui fuĩnt qui dc̃e eleccõi seu electo se oppoñe voluĩnt ad dc̃os die ⁊ locū fuisse citatos quicq'd obice voluĩnt in dc̃e eleccõnis formā v̄l elc̃i psonā oppositur' fc̃ur' ⁊ receptur' quod juris fuĩt et rõnis, fc̃aq̨ pubᶜᵃ pclamc̃õe si qui se c'ᵃ dc̃e eleccõnis formā v̄l elc̃i psonā ꝑpoñe seu c'ᵃ dicere voluĩnt in foribȝ ipius ecclie de Farnhᵃm, ⁊ ipis sepius ꝑconizatis ⁊ diuciᵉ expectatꝑ, nulloq̨ oppositore seu c'ᵃdc̃ore c'pente, omnibus ⁊ singlis in g̃ñe quicqᵃm in hac pte ꝑpoᵈⁱ v̄l c'ᵃdicendi viā ꝑcludim' p decretū. Exhibitꝑ q̨ decreto dc̃e eleccⁱonis ⁊ quinq̨ aliis ƚris sɓ sigiƚƚ convẽt', p fr̃em Roɓtum Scotenye ipius eccᵉ c'venˡʳ canoᶜᵘ convent̃ᵉ ejusdẽ pcurẽm ƚratorie constitutū, ac pductis p eundẽ duobȝ instructoribȝ p informac̃õe pleniori eleccõnis pdc̃e, videƚt fr̃e Joh̃e de Sontynge ejusdẽ eccᵉ canoᶜᵒ,⁊ dño Wiƚƚo capeƚƚo eccᵉ proˡʳ de Tanrugge':⁄ quibȝ admissis juratis ⁊ exaⁱatꝑ ꝑfigimꝑ elc̃o ⁊ pcuri ꝑdc̃is sc̃dm die juridicū post festū Sc̃i Mᵃrtini ꝑdc̃m ad c'pend coŕ dc̃o pre in capella castˡ sui de Farnhᵃm, ad facidʳ ꝫ recipidʳ sup p̄missis quod juris fũit ꝫ rōnis. Quib3 die ꝫ loco, electo ꝫ p̄cure p̄dc̄is cor̄ nob̄ Ada, miŝac̄oe divina Wynt̄ ep̄o, p tˡbunali sedentib3 pᵘliṽ c'penᵇ3 dc̄isq̈ ꝫ depositōib3 dc̄o᷈ instructo᷈ ad ip̄ius petic̄oem p̄curis publicatis, h̃itis & discussionib3 sup exhibitis ꝫ p̄ductis tociᵘˢ elecⁿⁱˢ negocii sᵃ scˡpti, s̄bsequenṽ c'cluso in codē tandē ad finalē pnuciac̄oem dc̄i negocii p̄cessimus in hunc modū.

In Dei nom̄ie, Amen. Nos Adam, miŝac̄oe divina Wyntoñ Ep̄us, auditis ꝫ intellc̄is ñlitis cause ꝫ negocii elecc̄onis de religioso viro fr̃e Joñe de Mersthᵃm, canoᶜᵒ eccᵉ convenˡʳ de Tanrugge ordinis Sc̄i Aug̃tini nr̃e dioc̄ in pᶦorē ejusdē ecct̃ie jam vacantis elc̄o nup fc̄e ꝫ corā nob̄ sufficienṽ examinate ꝫ discusse, q̈3 invenimus dc̄am elecc̄oem de psona ydonea concᵘrentib3 omuib3 que de jure requiruntʳ in hac pte rite ꝫ canonice celebratā, ip̄am elecc̄oem, invocata Sp̄us Sc̄i gr̃a, c'fˡmamᵘˢ, eidē olecto curam ꝫ administᵃc̄oem dc̄o ecct̃ie plenarie coīmittendo, q᷈ quidē p̃nunciac̄oe p Mag̃rm Joñem de Wolveleye de mandato dc̄i p̃ris ĩca, canticoq̈, Te Dm̃ laudamᵘˢ solēpniṽ decantato, aliis q̈3 pactis p cundē p̃rem in talib3 c'suetis, dc̄us fr̃ Joñes, electᵘˢ obediam dc̄o p̃ri p̄stitit consuetam.

XXXV.

Confirmation of the Election: 13th November, 1341.

(Winchester Diocesan Register, *Orleton*, I, fol. 109 *v*.)

Adam, ꝫc̃. Religioso viro filio in Xp̄o dilc̄o fr̃i Joñi de M?sthᵃm, canonico pˡoratᵘˢ sive eccᵉ conventuaˡ de Tanrugg', ordinis Sc̄i Augus̃ti nr̃e dioc̄, salm̃, gr̃am ꝫ bñ. Vacanto nup dc̄o pˡoratu sive eccᵃ p pˡvac̄oem ꝫ amoc̄oem fr̃is Pñi de Wokynghᵃm, nup pˡoris ejusdē, elecc̄oem de [te] in pˡorem ejusdē ecct̃ie sive pˡoratᵘˢ elc̄o concordiṽ celebratā, pontificali aucᵘte confˡmamᵘˢ legittīe p̄cedentes, ꝫ te in priorē ejusdē pˡoratᵘ sive ecct̃ie p̄ficimᵘˢ ꝫ pastorē curā ꝫ administᵃc̄oem ejusdē tibi plenarie coīmittēdo, firma concepta fiducia q̈d gr̃a divina tˡ assistente p̄picia dc̄a ecct̃ia sive pˡoratᵘˢ p tuū minisṽium fructuosū salutᵉ p̄spitatᵉ votiva suscipiet incrementa. In cujᵘˢ ꝫc̃. Datᵘ apud Farnhᵃm, xiij die mensᵉ Novēbr̃, anno Dñi MᵒCCCᵐᵒxlj, ꝫ tr̃nsĩonis nr̃e, viijᵒ.

XXXVI.

Mandate for Installation: 13th November, 1341.

(Winchester Diocesan Register, *Orleton*, I, fol. 109 *v*.)

Adam, ꝫc̃, dilc̄is filiis . . pˡori de Reygate ꝫ ppetuo vicario eccᵉ proˡʳ de Walkenestede nr̃e dioc̄, salm̃, gr̃am ꝫ bñ. Cū mag̃r Wiłłs Inge, ar¹dīatum Surr ñre dioc ꝑdc̄e de fc̄o ꞇ non de jure occupās et eidē de fc̄o incumbens sit ꞇ a diu est fuit majorum excōiⁿᵘ s̄niis ꝑ suis notoriis excessibȝ ꞇ deḽtis et criminibus rite ꞇ legīo ꝑ nos innodatus, ꞇ ꝑ sic excōiᵗᵒ puᶜᵉ in dioc̄ nr̄a ꞇ aliis diocesibȝ cōvicinis nūciat⁹, ad installand̄ put moris est in p¹oratu sive eccᵃ convenⁿ de Tanrugg' dc̄e dioc̄ fr̄em Joh̄em de Merstʰᵃm in p¹orem ejusdē eccl̄ie sive p¹orat⁹ ꝑ p¹vacōem ꞇ amocōem fr̄is Phi de Wokynghᵃm nup p¹oris ipīus vacantis, electū ꞇ ꝑ nos canonice c'f¹matū, ac ad assignand̄ eidē stallū in choro ꞇ locū in caꝑlo hactenus p¹oribȝ qui ꝑ tempe fuerunt assignatę, nᶜnon ad faciend̄ ꞇ exc̄end̄ que in ꝑmissis ꞇ circa ea nc̄cia fūint sive optuna ꞇ ad c'pescend̄, c'ᵃdc̄ores ꞇ rebelles si qui fūint in hac parte, vob̄ ꞇ cuilibȝ vr̄m insolidū com̄ittim⁹ vices nr̄as cū cohc̄onis canonice potᵉ. Dat̄ apud Farnhᵃm, xiij die mens̄ Novembr̄, anno Dn̄i sᵃdc̄o.

XXXVII.

LETTERS TESTIMONIAL TO WILLIAM WILTSHIRE: 4TH JULY, 1452.

(Winchester Diocesan Register, *Wayneflete*, I, fol. 15* v.)

Littera testimonialis quod quidam frater Willelmus Wiltshire fuit ordinem Sancti Augustini canonice professus. Universis Xp̄i fidelibȝ ꝑsentes lr̄as inspecturę v̄l auditurę, Wiltus miseratione dīa Wyntoñ Epūs, salt̄m et fidem indubiam ꝑsentibȝ adhib¹?e. Novit unv̄sitas v̄ra q̄d fr̄ Wiltus Wiltshire, canōicus regularis p¹orat⁹ de Tanrigg' in com̄ Surr̄, ñre dioc̄, c'tra quem fr̄em Wiltum, quidam Walꝑum Lathum queralā in qᵃdam curia ut dr̄ affirmavit, fuit anno Dn̄i Mᵒ CCCᵐᵒ xlj°, anno r̄. r̄. Henr̄ Sexti post conquestū, XIX° in ordinē Sc̄i Augustini in dc̄o p¹oratu rite et exꝑsse ꝑfess⁹ ac sub obedīa fr̄is Joh̄is Fremyngham ejusd̄ loci p¹oris a tūc usq̄ ad temp⁹ date ꝑsentiū cōtinue regulariꝛ ꞇ laudabilꝛ convsat⁹ ac ꝑ tali tent⁹ ꞇ habit⁹ ac notorie reputat⁹. In quoȝ oīm ꞇ singtm fidem ꞇ testm sigillū ñrm ꝑsentibȝ duxim⁹ apponend̄. Dat̄ in mañio ūro de Essher' qʳᵗo die mensę Jut, año Dn̄i Mitto CCCCᵐᵒ quiqᵃgesimo sc̄do. Et ñre cons̄, año quinto.

XXXVIII.

SEQUESTRATION OF INCOME OF THE PRIORY: 14TH OCTOBER, 1461.

(Winchester Diocesan Register, *Waynflete*, I, fol. 68*.)

Sequestracio fructuum Prioratus de Tanrigge. Wiltus ꞇc̄, diḽcto nob̄ in Xp̄o, Nich̄o Assheton̄ justic̄ de cōi banco dn̄i ñri regis, dño

Johi Hamond canōico regīi pⁱorat⁹ Sc̄i Jacobi de Tanrigge, ord̄ Sc̄i Augī, n̄re dioc̄, Witto Gaynsford ꝗ Johi Elynbrigge fratis, saltm̄ ꞇc̄. Cum nos ex officio n̄ro legīe p̄cedentes, oēs et sin͠glos fruct⁹, reddit⁹ ꞇ p̄vent⁹, ad prioratū p̄dc̄m pertiñ sive spectantes, p̄p̄ᵖ dilapidac͞oem bonoꝝ ejusd̄ priorat⁹ cor̄ dilc̄o not̄ in Xp̄o Mag͠ro Wittmo Darsset, legū doctore cancellario n̄ro in quadam inquisic͞oe p eund̄ Mag͠rm Wittum inibi auc͞ᵃte n̄ra nup faci notorie comptam, ac justas ꞇ legīas causas nos in hac pte movētes sequestᵃvim⁹, justicia id poscente. Vot̄ c'jūtim ꞇ divīs com̄ittim⁹ ꞇ mandam⁹ firmiᵖ injūgētes qᵃtin⁹ sequestrū n̄rm h̄j⁹ oïbus et sin͠glis quoꝝ inᵗest in hac pte publicantes, dicī fruct⁹, reddit⁹ ꞇ p̄vent⁹ sub arto ꞇ tulo custodiạtis seu custodiri faciatis sequesto sicuti de eisd̄ not̄ volŭitꝫ respond⁷ꝫe. Dat in palacio n̄ro de Wolveseye sub n̄ro sigillo, xiiijᵒ die Octobr̄, aᵒ Dn̄i MᵒCCCCᵒlxjᵒ, ꞇ n̄re cons̄, aᵒ quinto decimo.

XXXIX.

EPISCOPAL SEQUESTRATION ON VACANCY : 10TH APRIL, 1469.

(Winchester Diocesan Register, *Wayneflete*, I, fol. 96*.)

Sequestracio fructus Prioratus de Tanrigge vacantis. Decimo die mensꝫ Aprilꝫ aᵒ Dn̄i MᵒCCCC. lxixᵒ, directa fuit sequestᵃcio bonoꝝ ꞇ fructuū pⁱorat⁹ de Tanrigge p resignac͞oem fr̄is Johis Kyrton, ultⁱ pⁱorꝫ it̄m vacantꝫ Mag͠ro Hugoni Heghstale rectori eccl̄ie de Blechyngle ac fr̄i Robto Haysant canōico ord̄ Sc̄i Augustini ad recipiend̄ ꞇ salvo custodiend̄ fruct⁹ ꞇ reddit⁹ ejusd̄ priorat⁹, dc̄a vacac͞oe durante cū clausulꝫ nᵃciis ut in forma.

XL.

GRANT OF PENSION TO PRIOR ON DISSOLUTION OF THE PRIORY :
2ND JULY, 1536.

(Augmentation Office, Miscel. Books, Vol. 244, No. 127.)

Rex Omit̄ꝫ ad quos ꞇc̄, salutem ; cum nup prioratus de Tanrege in Com̄ n̄ro Surr̄ auctoritate pliamenti iam supp̄ssus ꞇ dissolutus existit, unde quidam Johes Lyngfeld tempore dissoluc͞ois illius ꞇ diu antea prior inde fuit ; Nos volentes r̄onabilem annualem penc͞oem sive p̄moc͞oem condignam eidem Johi ad victum ꞇ exhibic͞oem suam melius sustinend̄ provideri ; Sciatis igitʳ qd nos in considerac͞oe p̄missoꝝ de g̃ra n̄ra sp̃iali ac ex c̄ta sciencia ꞇ mero motu n̄ris p advisamentum ꞇ consensum Cancellarii ꞇ consilii Curie n̄rc Augmentacionū revencionū Corone

nre, dedim⁹ concessim⁹ ac p p̄sentes damus ꝛ concedim⁹ eidem Johi
quandam Annūatem sive Annualem pencōem quatuordecim libraƷ
sterlingoƷ ħend ꝛ annuatim pcipiend easdem quatuordecim libras
p̄fato Johi ꝛ Assign̄ suis a festo Annūciacōis ƀe Marie Virginis ultimo
p̄t̄ito ad t̄minū vite ip̄ius Johis vel quousq̄ idem Johes ad unū vel
plura beneficia eccliastica, sive aliam ꝑmocōem condignam, clari annui
valoris quatuordecim libraƷ aut ultra, p nos ꝑmotus fuit tam p
manus Thesaurarii Curie nr̄e p̄dc̄e p tempore existeñ de thesauro
nr̄o in manibƺ suis de revencoibƺ p̄dc̄is remanere contingeñ qᵐ p
manus Receptoꝛ pticulariū revencionū p̄dc̄aƷ de eisdem revencōibƺ,
ad festa Sc̄i Michis Archi ꝛ Annūciacōis ƀe Marie Virginis p equales
porcōes om̄o soluend Eo qd exp̄ssa mencio ꝛc̄. In cujus rei ꝛc̄.
Ricm Ryche.

T. apud Westm̄ Sc̄do die Julii A° xxviij° H. viij°.

XLI.

Ministers' Accounts: year ending Michaelmas, 29th Henry VIII (1537).

(Ministers' Accounts, 28-29 Henry VIII, No. 108.)

Comitatus Surr̄ { Compā omiū et singulorū ballivorum Firmariorum, ac omnium aliorum ministratorum domini Regis, nunc Henrici Octavi, de omnibus et singulis dominiis maneriis, villis, villatis, necnon omnimodis aliis possessionibus et heredit quibuscumque, nuper ad diversa Monasteria et Priorat̄ in Comitatu predicto dudum virtute et auctoritate Parliamenti suppressa et dissoluta spectañ sive quovismodo pertineñ in manibus dicti domini Regis modo existeñ, videlt a festo Sancti Michis Archi Anno Regni dicti domini Regis vicesimo octavo, usque idem festum Sancti Michis Archi ex tunc proximū sequeñ Anno Regni ejusdem Dn̄i Regis vicesimo nono, scilt p unū Annū integrum.

Terr. et possessiones nuper
priorat. de Tanryge pertinen.

Officiū Coll Comp̄us *Francisci Mores* ball ac Coll Reddus ibm p
Redd. tempus p̄d.

K

Arreragia. Nulla; sicut continet' in pede ultimi Compi Anni prox preceden.

Redd Assis cū Redd et firmᵃ in Tanryge.

Sed r̃ Compm de ij s. ij d. de Reddu Assis unius tenti et certarum terrarum ibm vocat Turneys Lande, q̃ Henricus Torner libe tenet sot ad festa Annunciacionis beate Marie Virginis et Sancti Michis Archi equalr, prout p quoddam Rentale inde factum et renovatum per Senescallum ibm vicesimo die Octobris Anno Regni Regis Henrici octavi vicesimo octavo, penes Auditorem remanen consimili modo apparet. Et de ij s. j d. ob, de Reddu Assis certarum terrarū vocat Harwarde Londe q̃ Robert Heyward libe tenet, sot ad ẽ t̃. Et de vi d. de redd assis certarum terrarum vocat Luxforde Lande q̃ Christoforus Luxford libe tenet, sot ad ẽ t̃. Et de xvj d. de reddu assis certarū terr vocat Hethe Londe q̃ Willmus Hethe libe tenet, sot ad ẽ t̃. Et de xx d. de reddu assis certarum terrarum voc Comporte Lande q̃ Johes Comport libe tenet, sot ad ẽ t̃. Et de xviij d. de reddu assis certarum terrarum voc Plawes tenement, q̃ Johes Plawe libe tenet, sot ad ẽ t̃. Et de ix d. de reddu assis certarum terr voc Standforde q̃ Edmundus Stanforde libe tenet, sot ad ẽ t̃. Et de ij s. de reddu certarum terrarum vocat Studmerhill in tenura Johis Squyer p Indenturam, sot ad ẽ t̃. Et de v s. iiij d. de reddu certarum terrarum vocat Dirgefelde in tenura Johis Holmann per Indenturam, sot ad ẽ t̃. Et de iiij s. de reddu xx acrarum terr nuncupatarū Le Olde Parke in tenura Johis Lyntonne p Indenturam, sot ad ẽ t̃. Et de vij s. de reddu certarum terrarum vocat Couny Pytches Downe Londe et Ovesnet [defaced] in tenura Willmi Dyxon p Indenturam, sot ad ẽ t̃. Et de xlv s. iiij d. de reddu certarum terrarum ibm vocatarū Lullinge et Goodweye Londe in tenura Johis Pope p Indent, sot ad ẽ t̃.

Smᵃ lxxiij s. viij d. ob.

Redd Assis cum Redd et Firma in Oxstedd.

Et de ij s. de reddu Assis exeun de uno crofto vocat Welbecke q̃ Moricius Welbeck libe tenet, sot ad ẽ t̃. Et de iij s. de reddu Assis exeun de terr voc Balle Londe q̃ Robertus Genys libe tenet, sot ad ẽ t̃. Et de iij s. iij d. de reddu assis exeun de terr voc le Londe q. Johes a Lee libe tenz, sot ad ẽ t̃. Et de viij d. de reddu assis exeun de uno tento cum gardino et una acra terr vocat Cowpers q̃ Henricus Cowper lib tenet, sot ad ẽ t̃. Et de xviij d. de reddu certarū terr vocat Crowhurst q̃ Henricus Cowp libe tenet, sot ad ẽ t̃. Et de ij s. vj d. de reddu assis certarū terraru vocatar Holme Lande q̃ Thomas Holmdenne libe tenet, sot ad ē t. Et de xij d. de reddu assis certarū terrarū vocat Cokes q̄ Riĉus Coke libe tenet, sot ad ē t. Et de xij d. de redd assis certarū terrarū vocat Alynslonde q̄ Thomas Aleyne lib tenet, sot ad ē t. Et de viij d. de reddu Assis certarū terrarū voĉ Brokyslonde q̄ Joħes Broke libe tenet, sot ad ē t. Et de ij s. vj d. de reddu assis certarū terr̄ voĉ Avys q̄ Witts Smythe libe tenet, sot ad ē t. Et de iij s. de reddu assis cert̄ terr̄ voĉ Pyrres q̄ Joħes Ownsted libe tenet, sot ad ē t. Et de xxxv s. viij d. de firma unius teñti et xiiij acr̄ terr̄ apud Barowe cum xiij acr̄ pastur̄ ibidem vocat Robyns Grove et Multrydenne sic dimiss Riĉo Holman p Indenturam, sot ad ē t. Et de xxviij s. de reddu unius teñti et certarū terrarū ibidem vocat Bakers dimiss Joħi Marten p Indenturam, sot ad ē t.

Sm^a iiij li. iiij s. ix d.

Redd div̄s teñt ad Holm̄ in Oxsted. — Et de xxx s. de reddū cert̄ terr̄ ibm vocat Prestfelde ad voluñ dimiss Joħi Loke, sot ad ē t. Et de vij s. de reddu unius teñti in quo Joħes Foster modo inhabitat, sot ad ē t. Et de xiij s. iiij d. de reddu unius teñti voĉ Phelipps apud Barowe in quo Wittmus Grene modo inħitat, sot ad eosdem term̄.

Sm^a l s. iiij d.

Redd assis cū redd et firm̄ in Godstone. — Et de xvj s. viij d. de reddu assis certarū terr̄ teñt et cotag̃ ibm p Wittm Barbour firmariū de Godstone virtute Indenture s; recept de diver̄s teñt ibm, sot ad eosdem terminos. Et de vj s. viij d. de reddu sive firma unius campi ibm vocat Priorsfelde dimiss Wittmo Harlyng p Indenturam, sot ad eosdem terminos.

Sm^a xxiij s. iiij d.

Firm^a cert̄ terr̄ in Chepstede voĉ Brownes. — Et de xv s. de firma cert̄ terr̄ ibidem vocat Brownes in tenura Riĉi Cadingtonne per Indenturam, sot ad eosdem terminos.

Sm^a xv s.

Redd assis in Edenbrydge in Com̄ Kanĉ. — Et de ij s. de reddu assis exeuñ de uno teñto ibm vocat Alchornes q̄ Andreus Cole libe tenet, sot ad eosdem terminos.

Sm^a ij s.

Redd assis in Chyddington in Com̄ Kanĉ. — Et de vij s. x d. de reddu assis ibm p anñ, so ad ē t.

Sm^a vij s. x d.

K 2

Redđ assis̃ in Longsutton in Com̃ South.	Et de xij s. de redđu assis̃ ib̃m exeuñ de cerĩ terr̃ voc̃ Chobhammes q̃ Thomas Byflete lib̃e tenet, sol ad ẽ t̃.

Sm^a xij s̃.

P̃quis̃ Cur̃.	De aliquo proficuo provenieñ de perquis̃ Cur̃ ib̃m hoc anno tent̃, non r̃ eoque nulla talia casualia hoc anno accidebant, per Sacramentum dc̃i Compt̃.

Sm^a null̃.

Vendic̃ bosc̃.	Nec r̃ de aliquo proficuo provenieñ de vendic̃ bosc̃ hoc anno, non eoque null̃ bosc̃ sive subbosc̃ venđ fuit infra dictum tẽpus, p sacr̃m sz.

Sm^a null̃.

Sm^a To^{lis} Offis xiij li. viij s. xj đ. ob̃.
de quibus,

Redđ Resolut̃.	Idem computat in Redđu annuatim Resoluto dño Borowgh exeuñ de terr̃ in Oxstede ad xxxvij s. iiij đ. p annũ. Et sic in allocatione h̃m̃oi pro uno anno integro finito ad festum Sc̃i Michis Archi dc̃o anno xxix^{no} xxxvij s̃. iiij đ. Et in Redđu annuatim resol̃ Nicholao Carewe militi pro terr̃ in Blechinglie p annũ xiiij s̃. Et in Redđu resoluto priori de Mertonne pro terris ibidem per annum iij s. iiij đ. Et in Redđu annuatim Resol̃ dño Regi pro terr̃ in [blank in Roll] p annũ xxxiiij s̃. v đ. ob̃ q^a. Et in redđu annuatim resoluto Abbati de Bello ad Maneriũ suum de Brodeham p annum xij đ.

Sm^a iiij li. x s̃. j đ. ob̃ q^a.

Procur̃ et Sinđ.	Et in denar̃ sol̃ Arch̃no Surr̃ pro procur̃ et sinodal̃ eccl̃ie de [blank in Roll] hoc anno ut in anno preceden̄ xvij s. vj đ.

Sm^a xvij s̃. vj đ.

Feoda et vađ.	Et in feodo dc̃i computan̄ ball̃ ac Coll̃ Redđ omniũ terr̃ et teñtorum dc̃i nup Prioratui p̃tinenciũ ex discrecione Com̃issioñ dñi Rp̃ hoc anno ut in preceden̄ xl s̃. Et in stipendio Cl̃ici Auditoris scriben̄ hunc comp̃m prout Cl̃icis Auditorum dñi Rp̃ ducatus sz Lancastr̃ alloc̃ consuevit. Et sic in allocacione ij s. Et in feodo Joh̃is Skynner Senescall̃ Cur̃ ib̃m, hoc anno ut in annis preceden̄ xiij s. iiij đ.

Sm^a lv s̃. iiij đ.

THE AUSTIN CANONS. 131

Expens̄ Et in denar̄ dc̄o computañ alloc̄ pro expens̄ Senescatt Cur̄,
Senesc̄ et aliorum officiariorum dñi Rᵽ ibidem existencium per dcm
Rentat ut pƷ bitt de pticul remaneñ xx s̃.
Smᵃ xx s̃.

Et in denar̄ p dc̄m Compu͞t libatᵽ Joñi Mores ⎫
Receptori dñi Regis Augmentacionū ⎪
Libacio   Revencionū corone ejusdem dñi Rᵽ in ⎪
denar̄.   Com̄ Surr̄ pred de exi͞t officii sui hujus ⎬ xlij s̃. xj d. ob qᵃ di.
anni debi͞t ad festum Sancti Micñis ⎪
Arcħi, dc̄o aᵒ xxix Rᵽ pred ut pƷ bitt mañ ejusd ⎪
receptor̄ signā. ⎭
Smᵃ xlij s. vj d. ob. q. di.

Smᵃ oĩm Alloc̄ et libac̄ ꝑd, xj ti. v s̃. xj^d. ob di qᵃ. Et
deƀt xlij s̃. xj d̄. ob qᵃ di. Qui exoñantʳ hic eoque Joñes
Reade eandem sum̄am de pte exi͞t premiss̄ debi͞t ad
festum sancti Micħis Archi Anno Regni Regis predc̄i
vicesimo nono, virtute et vigore trarum dñi Rᵽ patencium,
quarum da͞t est secundo die Januarii Anno Regni Regis
predc̄i xxix^{no} quarum quidem lr̄arum effec͞t in Comp̄o
Receptor̄ de eodem anno verbatim irrotut. Et c̃.
Quietus est.

Terr̄ dñicat. Comp̄us *Nich'i Carue* firmarii ibm p tempus predictum.

Arreragia. Nulla [Here occur some words erased at the time.]
Smᵃ nutt.

Firma. Sed r̃ Comp̄m de **xxv** ti. **vj** s̃. **viij** d̄. de firma terrarum.
Smᵃ xxv ti. vj s̃. viij d̄.

Smᵃ firme xxv ti. vj s̃. viij d̄. de quibus exoñatʳ hic de
xij ti. xiij s̃. iiij d̄. de ultima medietate hujus anni Eoq̷
predc̄us Joñes Reade eandem sm̄am recepit de firmar̄
ibidem, virtute et vigore ꝑdcarum trarum dñi Rᵽ patencium
ad festum Sancti Micħis Archi infra tempus hujus Comp̄i.
Et deƀt xij ti. xiij s̃. iiij d̄. Qui exoñantʳ hic eoq̷ oñantʳ
in Comp̄o Receptor̄ ibm de eodem anno. Et sic
eqƷ

Manerium de Rokesnest.   Compūs *Thome Bance* firm̄ ibm p tempus p̄d̄.

Arreragia.   Nulla [Here occur some words erased at the time.]

Sm^a nułł.

Firm^a Manerii.   Sed r̄ Compm̄ de ix łi. vj s̄. viij d̄. de reddu sive firma maṅii ibidem cum omnibus et singulis suis ptineñ vocat̄ Rokesnest unacū quad^am domo vocat̄ le Tyle howse in tenura Thome Bance, p Indenturam sigiłł Conveñ de Tanrege sigiłł, dat̄ ultimo die Octobr anno Regni Regis Henrici Octavi vicesimo sexto, ħendum, tenendum et gaudendum a festo Sancti Micħis Arcħi sequeñ datam ejusdem Indenture usq̨ ad fiñ xxj annorum, Reddendo inde annuatim ut supra ad festa Annūciac̄ beate Marie virginis et Sancti Micħis Arcħi ut p̄z Indenturam.

Sm^a ix łi. vj s̄. viij d̄.

Sm^a firme ix łi. vj s̄. viij d̄. de quibus exoñat^r hic de iiij łi. xiij s̄. iiij d̄. de ultima mediet̄ firme predc̄e Eoque predc̄us Joħes Reade eandem Summam recepit de firmario ibidem virtute et vigore predc̄arum łrarum dñi R_e patencium, ad festum Sancti Micħis Arcħi infra tempus hujus Compi. Et debt iiij łi. xiij s̄. iiij d̄. Qui exoñant^r hic Eoque oñantur in Compo Receptoris ibidem de eodem anno. Et sic

eqz.

Firm̄ de Sowthlonde.   Compūs *Georgii Topsell* firm̄ ibm p tēpus p̄d̄.

Arreragia.   Nulla, sicut p̄z in pede ultimi compi anni prox̄ preceden̄.

Sm^a nułł.

Firma.   Sed r̄ compm̄ de lxxvj s̄. viij d̄. de Reddu sive firma unius mesuagii sive teñti in Tanredge vocat̄ Sowthlond_e cum s̄ ptineñ in tenura dc̄i Computañ p Indenturam sigillo Conveñ de Tanridge sigiłł, dat̄ decimo sexto die Septembr̄ Anno Regni Regis Henrici octavi xv; ħendum tenendum et gaudendum omnia dc̄a premissa una cū firma quinq̨ vaccarū, ad terminū viginti iiij^{or} annorum, Reddendo inde annuatim ut supra ad festa Sancti Micħis Arcħi et Annunciacionis beate Marie Virginis ut p̄z Indenturam.

Sm^a lxxvj s̄. viij d̄.

Sm^a firme lxxvj s̄. viij d̄. de quibus exoñatur hic de xxxviij s̄. iiij d̄. Eoq̨ predc̄us Joħes Reade eandem

Smam recepit de firmar' ibm virtute predcarum trarum dñi Rp patenciū, ad festum Sci Michis Archi infra tempus hujus Compi. Et debt xxxviij s. iiij d. Qui exoñantur hic Eoq oñant' in Compo Receptor ibidem de eodem anno. Et sic

eq3.

Firma de Chamberlondes Downlandp et Scott^e Crofte.   Compus *Alicie Huntley* firm ibm p tempus βd.

Arreragia.   Nulla, sicut p3 in pede ultimi Compi anni prox preceden.

Sm^a nuɫɫ.

Firma.   Sed r̃ compm de 1 s̃. de Reddu sive firma certarū teri vocatarū Chamberlondp, Scott^e Croft, Myllfelde, Harteslande, et Downelondp, jaceñ in Tanridge predca, in tenura dci Computañ p Indent sigillo Conveñ de Tanridge sigiɫɫ, dat vicesimo die Marcij anno regni Regis Henrici octavi vicesimo primo; hendum tenendum et gaudendum ad finem et terminum xl annorū, Reddendo inde annuatim ut supra ad festa Annunciacionis beate Marie Virginis et Sancti Michis Archi ut p dcam Indenturam plenius p3.

Sm^a l s̃.

Sm^a firme l s̃. de quibus exoñat^r hic de xxv s̃. de ultima medietate hujus anni Eoq3 predcus Johes Reade eandem Sumam recepit de firmario ibm vigore predcarum trarum dci dñi Rp pateñ, ad festum Sancti Michis Archi infra tempus hujus compi. Et debt xxv s̃. Qui exoñant^r hic, Eoq oñant^r in Compo Receptoris ibidem de eodem anno. Et sic

eq3.

Tenementum vocat Botelers.   Compus *Ricⁱ Topsell* firmar ibm p tempus βdcm.

Arreragia.   Nulla [an erasure] p3 in pede ultimi Compi anni px preceden.

Sm^a nuɫɫ.

Firma.   Sed r̃ Compm de iiij ɫi. de reddu sive firma unius tenti vocat Botelers in pochia de Tanridge predca in tenura dci Computañ p Indenturam sigillo conveñ de Tanrige predca sigiɫɫ, dat vicēimo die Marcij Anno Regni Regis Henrici octavi xxj; hēndum, tenendum et gaudendum a festo Sancti Michis Archi q̄ erit in anno dn̄i M¹CCCCCxxxj^{mo} usq̝ ad terminū xxj annoȓ, Reddendo inde annuatim ut supra ad festa Annunciacōis beate Marie virginis et sancti Michis Archi.

Sm^a iiij li.

Sm^a firme iiij li. de quibus exonat^r hic, de xl s. pro ultima medietate hujus firme Eoq̝ dc̄us Johes Reade eandem sum̄am recepit de firmaȓ ib̄m virtuī dicī litteȓ dn̄i R̄ȩ ad dc̄m festum Sc̄i Michis Archi infra dc̄m tempus. Et debet xl s. Qui exon̄ant^r hic, eoq̝ on̄ant^r in comp̄o Recept ib̄m de eodem Anno

et eq3.

Firma de Thomlyns Land℮.   Comp̄us *Henrici Cowp̄* firm̄i ib̄m p tēp̄ p̄d.

Arreragia.   Nulla, sicut p3 in pede ultimi Comp̄i anni prox̄ preceden̄.
Sm^a null.

Firma.   Sed r̄ comp̄m de l s. de reddu sive firma unius tēnti et certarū terrarū vocaī Thomlyns Lande jaceñ infra pochiam de Oxstedd in tenura dc̄i Henrici Cowper sic sibi dimisś p̄ Indentē sigillo Conven̄ de Tanridge sigillaī, daī xxvj^{to} die Marcij anno Regni Regis Henrici Octavi xviij, hendum tenendum et gaudendum ad finem et terminū xxj annorum, Reddendo inde annuatim ut supra ad festa Annunciac̄ beate Marie et Sc̄i Michis Archi.

Sm^a l s.

Sm^a firme l s. de quibus exon̄atur hic de xxv s. de ultima medietate hujus anni Eoque dc̄us Johes Reade eandem. Sm̄am recepit virtute predc̄arum lr̄arum dn̄i R̄ȩ ad festū Sc̄i Michis Archi infra dc̄m tempus. Et deb̄t xxv s. Qui exon̄ant^r hic, eoq̝ on̄antur in Comp̄o Receptoris ib̄m de eodem anno. Et sic

eq3.

Duo tenementa in Oxstede.   Comp̄us *Thome Alyn* firm̄ ib̄m p temp⁹ p̄d.

Arreragia. Nulla, sicut continetur in pede ultimi Compi anni preced.
Sm̃ᵃ nult.

Firma. Sed r̃ Comp̃m de lxxvj s̃. viij d̃. de reddu sive firma ijʳᵘ tenementorum et certarum terrarum et clauš in tenura Thome Aleyne sic sibi dimišs p Indenturam sigillo Conveñ de Tanridge predc̃a sigill, dat̃ vicesimo sexto die Octobr̃ anno Regni Rp Henrici Octavi vicesimo septimo, h̃endum ad terminū xxx annoř, Reddendo inde ut supra ad festa Pasche et Sc̃i Mich̃is Arch̃i equatr.
Sm̃ᵃ lxxvj s̃. viij d̃.

Sm̃ᵃ firme lxxvj s̃. viij d̃. de quibus exoñatʳ hic de xxxviij s̃. iiij d̃. de ultima mediet̃ firme predc̃e eoq dc̃us Joh̃es Reade eandem sm̃am recepit de firmario ib̃m vigore pred̃ t̃rarum dñi Rp ad festum Sc̃i Mich̃is Arch̃i infra tempus hujus Comp̃i. Et deb̃t xxxviij s̃. iiij d̃. Qui exoñantʳ hic, Eoq oñantʳ in Comp̃o Receptoris ibidem de eodem anno.
Et eqз.

Dimid pars Rectoř de Godstone. Comp̃us *Rob̄ti Darby* firm̃i ib̃m p tempus predc̃m.

Arreragia. Nulla, sicut cont̃ in pede ultimi Comp̃i anni prox̃ precedeñ.
Sm̃ᵃ nult.

Firma. Sed r̃ Comp̃m de lxxj s̃. viij d̃. de firma dimidie ptp Rectorie de Godstone unacū decima pte omniū et singulorū grañ infra pochiam de Wolkhamstedd in tenura dc̃i Rob̃ti Darby per Indenturam sigillo Conveñ dc̃i nup Prioratt Sigill, dat̃ xijᵐᵒ die Augusti Anno Regni Regp Henrici Octavi xxijᵈᵒ, h̃endum ad terminū septem annorū, Reddendo inde p annū ut supᵃ ad festa Natat Dñi et Nativitatp Sancti Joh̃is Bap̃te equis porcioñ.
Sm̃ᵃ lxxj s̃. viij d̃. eł.

Sm̃ᵃ lxxj s̃. viii d̃. de quibus exoñatur hic de xxxv s̃. x d̃. de ultima medietate hujus anni, Eoq predc̃us Joh̃es Reade eandem sm̃am recepit de firmar̃ ibidem virtute predc̃arum t̃rarum dñi Rp ad festum Sc̃i Mich̃is Arch̃i infra tempus hujus Compī. Et debt xxxv s̃. x d̃. Qui exoñant^r hic, Eoque oñant^r in Compō Receptoř ibidem de eod anno.

Et eq₃.

Maneř de Godstone   Compūs *Willĩ Barbõ?* firmař ibm p temp^s p̃d.
als Blechinglye.

Arreragia.   Nulla sicut cont̃ in pede ultimi Compī anni px̃ preceden̄.

Sm^a null.

Firma.   Sed ř Compm̃ de iiij li. vj s̃. viij d̃. de firma mañii de Godstone cum omnibus terř tent̃is prat̃ et pastuř infra poch de Blechinglye in tenura predc̃i Willmi Barbour p Indentuř Sigillo Conven̄ dc̃i nup Priorat̃ sigill, dat̃ xxviij^{vo} die Junij Anno Regni Regis Henrici Octavi xiiij^{to}, hendum ad terminū xxxj^a annorū, Reddendo inde annuatim ut supra ad festa Sancti Michis Arch̃i et Annunciacionis beate Marie virginis equis porcionibus solvend ut in dc̃a Indentura plenius continetur.

Sm^a iiij^{li}. vj s̃. viij d̃.

Sm^a firme iiij li. vj s̃. viij d̃. de quibus exoñat^r hic de xliij s̃. iiij d̃. de ultima medietate hujus anni Eoq̃ dc̃us Jon̄es Reado eandem sm̃am recepit de firmario ibm virtute predc̃arum trarum dñi R̃p patencium ad festum Sc̃i Michis Arch̃i infra dictum tempus. Et debt xliij s̃. iiij d̃. Qui exoñant^r hic, Eoq̃ oñant^r in Compō Receptoris ibm de eodem anno.

Et eq₃.

Rectoria de   Compūs *Joh̃is Gaynsford* milite et Edwardi Lee Clici
Crowhurst.   firmař ibm p tempus predictum.

Arreragia.   Nulla, sicut continet^r in pede ultimi compī anni px̃ preceden̄.

Sm^a null.

Firma Rectoř.   Sed ř Compm̃ de liij s̃. iiij d̃. de Reddu sive firma Rectoř ibm cū omnibus suis ptlnen̄ in tenura dict̃ Computan̄ p Indentuř sigillo Conven̄ de Tanridge sigill, dat̃ xxj^{mo} die Septembris anno Regni Regis Henrici viij^{vi} octavo, hendum a dat̃ presenciū usq̃ ad finem et terminū vite natural predc̃i Joh̃is Gaynsforde;

Reddendo inde annuatim ut supra ad festa Natalis Dñi Annunciacionis beate Marie Virginis, Sancti Joħis Bapℸe et Sancti Michis Archi equatr.

Sm^a liij s̄. iiij d̄. ex̄.

Sm^a firme liij s̄. iiij d̄. de quibus exoñat^r hic de xxvj s̄. viij d̄. de ultim^a medieℸ hujus anni, Eoq, dc̄us Joħes Reade eandem sm̄am de firmař iℸm vigore βd̄ litteř dñi Rę ad dc̄m festum Sc̄i Michis Archi. Et deƀt xxvj s̄. viij d̄. Qui exoñant^r hic, Eoq, oñant^r in Comp̄o Recepℸ iℸm de eodem anno. Et sic

eq̄z.

Firma sit⁹ mañii in Hartfelde de Senty in Com̄ Sussex.

Comp̄us *Joh̄is Haywarde* firm̄ iℸm p tempˀ βd̄.

Arreragia. Nulla, sicut pz in pede ultimi Comp̄i anni prox̄ preceden̄.
Sm^a nult.

Firma. Sed ř Comp̄m de iiij li. de firma situs manerii de Sentie in pochia de Hertfelde in Com̄ Sussex̄ in tenura Joħis Heyward p Indenturam sigillo Conveñ de Tanridge sigilt, daℸ xxvij^{mo} die Februarii anno Regni Rę Henrici Octavi xij^{mo}; ħendum ad terminū lxj annorū, Reddendo inde ut supra ad festa Natat Dñi et Annūciac̄ois beate Marie Virginis equaltr.

Sm^a iiij li.

Sm^a firme iiij li. de quibus exoñat^r hic de xl s̄. de ultima medietate hujus firme, Eoq, predc̄us Joħes Reade eandem sum̄am recepit de firmař ibidem virtute predc̄arum trarum dñi Rę patenciū ad festum Sancti Michis Archi infra tempus hujus Comp̄i. Et deƀt xl s̄. Qui exoñant^r hic, Eoq, oñant^r in Comp̄o Receptoris iℸm de eodem anno.

Et eq̄z.

Westhall in Warlyngham.

Comp̄us *Willi Comporte* firmař iℸm p temp̄ βd̄.

Arreragia. Nulla, sicut conℸ in pede ultimi Comp̄i anni px̄ preceden̄.
Sm^a nult.

Firma. Sed r̄ Compm̄ de iiij li. xiij s̄. iiij d̄. de firma unius teñti cū omnibus terr̄ pratis pascuis et pastur̄, cū omnibus et singulis suis ptineñ in tenura Willmi Comporte p Indentur̄ sigillo Conveñ de Tanridge sigill, dat̄ [blank in Roll], hendum ad terminū xxvj annorum, Reddendo inde annuatim ut supra ad iiij^{or} anni terminos usual ut in dicta Indentura ad largum plenius continetur.

Sm^a iiij li xiij s̄. iiij d̄.

Sm^a firme iiij li. xiij s̄. iiij d̄. de quibus exoñat^r hic de xlvj s̄. viij d̄. de ultima medietate hujus firme, Eoq predc̄us Johes Reade eandem sm̄am recepit de firmar̄ ibm vigore predc̄arum lrarum dñi Rp̄ patenciū ad festum Sc̄i Mich Archi infra tempus hujus Compi. Et debt xlvj s̄. viij d̄. Qui exoñant^r hic eoq oñantur in Comp̄o Recept̄ ibm de eodem anno.

Et eq3.

INDEX.

Aaron, Elie : tenant, 38.

Abbeys in England : history of few yet written, 2.

Abbots, on Dissolution, appointed Bishops, Deans, or Canons, 89.

Absence : of Prior, 31, 66 ; of Canons only by licence and with companion, 17.

Accounts : rendered twice a year at least, 18, 68, 106 ; by Prior and Cellarer, 18 ; none rendered prior to 1308., 20 ; of kitchen expenses weekly, 21, 108 ; granges and animals, on oath, 21, 108.

Acquittance to Westhall Manor, 12.

Act of Parliament for Dissolution of Monasteries, 47, *n.*, 50 and *n.*

Adam : Prior, 1235., 10, 90, 102, *bis*, 108.

Adam of Salisbury, Monk of Winchester : a Commissioner for Visitation, 19, 107.

Aegstede (Oxted, or Okestede), William de : licence for grant to Priory, 12, 13.

Aegstede (Oxted, or Okestede), Roland de : owner of land, 12.

Alban, Thomas de St., Canon of Newark : appointed by the Bishop Prior of Tanridge, 2, 45, 112, 113, *bis*.

Alchornes : tenement in Edenbridge, 55, 128.

Aleyne, Thomas : lessee and freeholder in Oxted, 46, 55, 57, 128, 133, 134.

Alfrid Soxere : holding land and houses in Chepsted, 8, 101.

Alleyn, or Alyn, Bartholomew : a Canon, 41, 42.

Almoner, duties of, 72.

Alresford, William de, Notary Public : witness to Bishop's decree, 30, 118.

Altar of B. Mary : mentioned in 1262., 12.

Alyn, Thomas : see *Aleyne, Thomas.*

Alynslonde, 55.

Appendix of original documents, 97.

Appointment of Prior : by Chapter, 4 ; demission to Bishop, 4.

Archbishop : appeal by Archdeacon of Surrey against suspension, 35.

Archdeacon of Surrey: certificate of citation, 15, 27; induction of Prior, 25, 28; Commissioner for Visitation, 21, 109; procurations to, 51, 56, 129; excommunicate, 35, 124; Philip de Barton, 21, 109; William Inge, 35, 123.

Assheton, Nicholas, Justice of King's Common Bench: a sequestrator, 40, 124.

Auditor: of Duchy of Lancaster, 56, 129; salary of clerk of, 56, 129.

Augmentations: establishment of Court of, 47, *n.*; sale by order of, 50, 53; Kings Receiver, 56; granted pension to Prior, 48, 125.

Augustine, St., Canons Regular of the Order of: see *Canons Regular*.

Augustine the Great, St., Bishop of Hippo: institutor of Orders of Monks and Canons, 61.

Austin Canons: Canons Regular of the Order of St. Augustine, commonly so called, 3, 60.

Avys: land in Oxted, 55, 128.

Baigent, Mr. F. J.: all records from Diocesan Registry for this work supplied by him, 95.

Bailiff, accountant and collector, 56.

Bailiff of the House, 20.

Bakers: tenement and lands, 46, 55, 128.

Baldric: witness, 6, 100.

Ball's Londs, in Oxted, 54, 127.

Bance, Thomas: lessee of Rokesnest Manor, 46, 57, 131.

Banishment of Canon to another Priory, as a punishment, 23, 110.

Barbour, William: lessee of Godstone, &c., 45, 46, 55, 57, 128, 135.

Barnarde, John: Canon, President of Chapter on vacancy, 41, 42.

Barrow (Barowe, Le Barwe, or Borowghe), at Oxted: account of rents, 37, 38, 51, 56, 129; land called Robyn's Grove and Multrydene, 46, 128; land and tenement, 55, 128.

Barton, Master Philip de, Archdeacon of Surrey: Commissioner for Visitation, 21, 109.

Barwe, Le: see *Barrow*.

Battle Abbey: payment to, 51, 56, 129.

Battle, Abbot of: receipt for Oxsted, 37.

Beautre, John de, Notary Public: witness to Bishop's Decree, 30, 118.

Bederipe: part of tenure of land at Oxted, 38.

Beer made in 1308., 20.

Bells rung to assemble Chapter, 41.

Benedict XII, Pope: Constitutions for Regular Canons, 62.

Benedictine Houses numerous, 70.
Bermondsey: Curia Regis held at, 10, 102.
Berne, Richard at: tenant, 39.
Bersted, or Berstede, Walter de: Justice Itinerant, Sheriff of Kent, &c., 11 and *n.*, 103.
Berstede: see *Bursted.*
Bishop: interference in affairs, 22; appointing Prior by demission or on void election, 4, 28, 30; residence at Esher, 23, 24, 25, 30, 32, 39; Farnham, 19, 32, 33, 34; Merewell, 15, 16, 22, 42; Waltham, 32; Wolveseye, 40.
Bishops as visitors of monastic houses, 64.
Bittlesden Priory, Bucks: formulated confession, 89.
Blechyngle, or Blechinglegh, or Bletchingly: Hugh Heghstale, Rector, 40, 41, *n.*, 125; lands in, 45, 50, 56, 57, 129, 135; Garston in, 49.
Boke (or Broke): freeholder, 55, 128.
Bolle, John: witness, 7, 100.
Books given by Founder, 7, 101.
Borradaile, Rev. R. H.: occupier of present house on site, 78 and *n.*
Bostocke, Richard, of Tanridge: possessor of rentale, 38.
Botelers: tenement in Tanridge, 45, 57, 132.
Braces: tenement called, 39.
Breysted: see *Bursted.*
Brodeham Manor (belonging to Abbot of Battle), 56, 129.
Broke (or Boke), John: freeholder, 55, 128.
Brokyslonde, 55, 128.
Brome, Le: land in Chepsted, 8, 101.
Brownes: land at Chipsted, 46, 55, 128.
Bryan, Master Roger: Notary Public, 33, 121.
Bugles: tenement called, 39.
Bull given by Founder, 7, 101.
Burnard, Robert: witness, 8, 101.
Bursted: rents at, 38.
Bursted Manor, otherwise Oxsted: value, 39.
Business of Priory under seal and by common assent, 18.
Butcher, William: tenant, 39.
Byflete, Thomas: freeholder, 55, 129.

Cadingtonne, Richard: lessee, 46, 55, 128.
Cambridge, King's College: payment to, 53.
Canonical form of election of Prior, 15.

Canonical Hours observed, 79.

Canons Regular of the Order of St. Augustine, 1; called Austin Canons, 3, 60; established in 11th century, 62; title fixed 1139, 62; sometimes called Confraters, 2, 6; general nature of communities, 60; number of Canons various, 70; Rules, vide *Rules*; private life little known, 1, 59, 60; duties and austerities, 75, 79; dress, 74, 75, 76; tonsure, 76; chapters, 63, 64; occupations, 83, 84; legal business, 83; kept horses and servants, 63, *n.*, 71; hunting, 63, *n.*; portrait of mitred Prior, 70; sites selected for Priories, 76; early notices, 60; popular fallacies, 79; King Henry VIII and Cardinal Wolsey members of the Order, 65, 90; number of Priories at the Dissolution, 69.

Canterbury, Archbishop of: stopping at Priory, 13, 85; contribution towards war in France, 45.

Capital, carved: only fragment remaining, 77 and *n.*

Carbonell: tenement called, 39.

Cardinal Wolsey: Brother of the Order, 65; his titles, 66; his Rules for the Order, 66, 90.

Carewe, Nicholas, Knt.: Lord of Manor of Bletchinglegh, 51, 56, 129, 130.

Carne, Nicholas: lessee, 57.

Carshalton Church: clergy cited there, 14.

Carue, Nicholas: see *Carewe, Nicholas*.

Catalla, cattle, 12, *n.*

Catherine of Aragon, Queen: Sister of the Order, 65, 90.

Celebration of Divine Service daily, 3, 36.

Cellarer: as accountant, 18, 71; to render accounts twice a year, 18; account at Visitation, 19, 20, 107; accounts untrue, 20, 107; in fault, 22; imprisonment of defaulter, 79; deputy appointed 26, 114.

Chalice given by founder, 7, 101.

Chamberlain: duties of, 72.

Chamberlonds: land in Tanridge, 45, 57, 132.

Champyn, John: tenant, 39.

Chaplain, One of the Canons necessarily a, 3, 12; grant towards support, 36.

Chaplain, Henry, 6; of Crowhurste, 51.

Chaplain of Tanrigge, 51; of Farnham Church, 122; of Rigate (Ralph), 6, 100.

Chapter of the Order: General, 64; at Leicester, 65, 90; "*Quia propter*" Constitution, 41; attendance by proxy, 4.

Chapter, Grand: held twice a year, 18, 63; penalty ordered by, 69.
Chapter of Priory, 63; held daily, 68; assembled by bell, 41; Latin or French spoken in, 69; seal, 15, 42; Prior elected by, 4, 15; its president during vacancy of priorate, 4; correction of Canons, 21; Injunctions read in, 18.
Charitable object of the Foundation at Tanridge, 2, 6.
Charities of Monasteries, 73, 84.
Charles, Parson or Rector of Collesdon: manor leased to him by Priory, 12; co-adjutor of Prior, 26; having key of seal, 26; lessee of Westhall Manor, 30.
Charters granted to the Hospital, 5, 6, 7, 8.
Chase granted by Founder to Priory, 10, 102.
Chawre, Senior, Thomas: tenant, 38.
Chelesham, Reginald de: land held of him, 14.
Chelsham, Knight's fees at: inquisition respecting, 35.
Chepsted, or Chepestede: see *Chipsted*.
Chertsey Abbey: grant of Manor of Hamme by, 6, *n*.
Chipsted: gift of land in Ville of, to the Hospital, 8; receipts from, 38, 55, 128; land called Brownes, 46; grant at Dissolution, 50.
Chiveningge, Adam de: feoffor of land at Crowhurst, 14.
Chobhammes, lands at Long Sutton, 55, 129.
Chronicles of national and public events: kept only by Monasteries, 82, 83.
Church of Priory: Altar of St. Mary, 12, 103; church tower and cemetery granted at Dissolution, 49.
Church Service provided by Monasteries for the public, 85.
Chyddington, Kent (? Chydynstone, Sussex, which see), fee-farm rent, 55, 128.
Chydynstone, Chedingstone, or Chiddingstone, Sussex: receipts from, 37, 38, 50.
Cirencester, Prior of: mitred, 70.
Citation of opponents to election of Prior, 15, 27.
Citation of Prior: for non-residence, 31, 32, 119: to attend in Convocation, 41.
Clement VI, Pope: Constitutions for Regular Canons, 62.
Clere, High: Bishop at, in 1309., 23, 111.
Clerke, Laurence: tenant, 39.
Clochia: short cloak, 75 and *n*.
Cloisters of the Priory, supposed site of, 78.
Clothing of Canons: see *Rules*.
Co-adjutor of Prior appointed, 26, 29, 113, 117.

L

Cock and hen: in payment of rent, 38.
Coffin-lids remaining on the Priory grounds, 78.
Coke, Richard: freeholder, 55, 128.
Cokes land, in Oxted, 55, 128.
Colchester: judicial murder of Abbot, 88.
Cole, Andrew: tenant, 55, 128.
College: Priory sometimes so called, 3, 15.
Collesdon, Charles, Parson or Rector of: Manor leased to him, 12, 30; co-adjutor of Prior, 26, 113; had key of seal, 26.
Combers: tenement called, 39; land, 54, *n*.
Commissary of Bishop: giving directions, 26; in legal proceedings, 34.
Commission by Bishop for Visitation, 19, 21, 106.
Commissioners of King at Dissolution, 56, 58.
Compord, Henry: Receiver, 51.
Comport, John: tenant, 54, 127.
Comport's land in Tanridge, 127.
Comporte, William: lessee, 46, 58, 136, 137.
Compromissary appointment of Prior, 41, 42.
Concanons: see *Canons*.
Concord in Curia Regis, 9, 10, 11, 102, *bis*, 103.
Confession by Canons to Prior, 17, 105.
Confirmation of election of Prior, 34.
Confraters: members of Priory so called, 2, 6, 70.
Congé d'èslire, on election of Priors, 15, 27.
Conny Pytches: land leased, 46, 54, 127.
Constitutions: see *Rules*.
Convocation: ecclesiastical taxation through medium of, 85.
Convocation of Province of Canterbury: Prior of Tanridge summoned to, 46.
Convocation of Diocese: Prior summoned to, 4.
Corredy: nature of, 73, *n*.; granted by Prior, 43; form, 43, 83; rooms and provisions granted under, 43; penalty for default, 44; frequently granted improvidently, 43, 73 and *n*.
Court Rolls of Breysted, or Bersted, in Oxted, 44.
Coventry and Lychfeld, Walter, Bishop of: the King's Treasurer, 14, 104.
Cowper, Henry: freeholder, 55, 57; lessee of land in Oxted, 45, 127, 133.
Cowper, Richard: tenant, 39.
Cowpers: tenement, 55, 127.
Cows: lease of (with lands), 45.

Cromwell, Knt., Sir Thomas: guardian of Thomas Rede, minor, 52.
Crowhurst, Croweherst, or Craweburst: advowson granted to Priory, 14, 104; rectory leased by Priory, 45, 136; grant at Dissolution, 49, 50, 58; land there belonging to Priory, 14, 55.
Crowhurst, Chaplain of, 51.
Crowhurste, Junr., John: tenant, 39.
Crowhurste, Senr., John: tenant, 39.
Croydon: inquisition *post mortem*, held at, 35; *ad quod damnum*, 36.
Curia Regis: Concord in, 9, 10, 11, 102, *bis*, 103.
Curtains round bed forbidden to the Canons, 18, 105.

Daily performance of Divine Service in the Priory Church, 3, 36.
Dammartin family and pedigree, 5, 6, 7.
Dammartin, Odo de, son of William: Founder of the Priory, 5, 6, 7, 8, 10, 100, *bis*, 101, 102; witness to an endowment of Newark Priory, 5, *n*.
Dammartin, Odo, or Eudo, de, son of Odo: benefaction to the Hospital, 8, 10, 101, 102.
Dammartin, William de, father of Odo the Founder, 100.
Dammartin, William de, son of Founder: witness to Deed, *c.* 1200, 6, 100.
Dammartin, William de: witness to Deed, 13th cent., 8, 101.
Dammartin: village near Paris, 5, *n*.
Danmartin or Danmertin, Odo de: see *Dammartin*.
Danne, William: a Canon, 41, 42.
Darby, Robert: lessee of moiety of Godstone Rectory, 46, 57, 134.
Darssett, Master William, D.C.L.: Bishop's Chancellor, 40, 125.
Dates of years as in modern reckoning, 2; of foundation of Tanridge, 5.
Debts owing by Tanridge Priory in 1308., 20.
Deed of Endowment of Tanridge, earliest existing, 5.
Dene, Nicholas de la: witness, 7, 100.
Dene, Ralph: witness, 7 and *n*.
Denis, Priory of St., Hants: Prior of Tanridge translated to, 42.
Deprivation of Office of Prior for non-residence, 32, 120; of Cellarer, 22.
Despencer, Hugh le: inquisition on death of, 35; mesne lord, 36.
Divine Service daily, 3, 36.
Dirgefeld: land, 46, 54, 127.
Discords put an end to, 20.
Dissolution of the Priory: income at time, 4, 74; pension to last Prior, 125.

Doune, Henry atte: grant of land by, 26, 29, 117.
Door, outer: closed at due hours, 17.
Dormitory: curtains round beds in, forbidden, 18.
Downlonds, in Tanridge, 45, 46, 57, 127, 132.
Dyxon, William: lessee, 46, 54, 127.

Edenbridge: receipts from, 38, 55, 128.
Election and confirmation of Prior: licence to elect, 21; proceedings, 15, 41, 70; extreme care, 15; election made by Chapter, 15, 45; their proxy, 15, 27, 28, 34; citation of opponents, 15; adjournments, 15; election void for informality, 4, 16, 28, 37, 114; appointment demitted to Bishop, 30.
Eliotts: tenement, 39.
Elmeden, William: Canon, 41.
Elynbrigge, John: sequestrator, 40, 125.
Endowment of Tanridge: earliest existing Deed of, 5.
Enham, Master John de: Advocate in Winchester Consistory, 33.
Enham, Thomas de, Advocate in Winchester Consistory: witness, 121.
Eschaetor for Surrey: inquisition by, 25, 29, 117.
Esher, Essher, or Esshere: Bishop at, 23, 24, 25, 30, 32, 39, 106, 112, *bis*, 113, 117, 119, 124.
Eudo, or Odo de Dammartin, son of Founder, and benefactor, 8.
Excommunication of Archdeacon of Surrey, 35.
Exit without licence forbidden, 17.
Expenses of imprisoned Canon, 23.

Farnham: Bishop's residence at, 19, 32, 34, 107, 120, 123, 124.
Farnham Castle: Chapel of, 123.
Farnham Church: legal proceedings there, 33, 122.
Fasting, and as a penalty, 17, 79.
Fermery, Le: rooms within precincts, 43.
Fine for licence in mortmain, 14.
Food: according to means, 18; taken at meal times only, 18; not with external persons, 18, 106.
Forester, John: holder of tenements, 36; mesne lord, 36.
Forster, John: Prior, 1500., 42, 43, 44, 94.
Fortes: tenement, 38.
Foster, John: tenant, 55, 128.
Foundation at Tanridge for charitable objects, 3; by Odo de Dammartin, 5.
France: contribution of spiritualty towards war in, 45.

France, Mary, Queen of: Sister of the Order, 65, 90.
Fremyngham, John: Prior, 1441., 39, 40, 43, 93, 124.
French or Latin to be spoken in Chapter, 69, 82.
French, G. R.: Paper on Crowhurst Church, 58, *n*.
French, Richard: Prior, 1380., 37, 93.
Friars and Monks: distinction, 86; conduct of Friars conducing to he Dissolution, 86.

Gardyners: tenement, 39.
Garston (meadow), in Bersted, 44.
Garston (meadow), in Blechinglye, 49.
Gaynsford, or Gaynesford, John: lessee of Crowhurst Rectory, 45, 58 and *n.*, 135.
Gaynsford, William: sequestrator, 40, 125.
Geldeford or Guildford, Curia Regis held at, 103.
Genys, Robert: freeholder, 54, 127.
Ghost, Holy: Grace invoked at election of Prior, 41; Mass of Holy Ghost sung at election of Prior, 41.
Gifts of relics, chalice, and cattle, by Founder, 7.
Glastonbury: judicial murder of Abbot of, 88.
Gloucester, Lawrence de, Monk of St. Peter's, Professor of Sacred Theology: Commissioner for Visitation, 19, 22, 26, 107 *bis*, 108, 109, 113.
Godstone, otherwise Walkenestede: Manor (otherwise Blechinglye, sed?), 45, 49, 50, 135; land and tenements, 36, 46, 55, 128; perpetual vicar, 35; rectory, 46, 57, 134; grant at Dissolution, 49, 50.
Goodweye Londs: land, 46, 54, 127.
Gore, Le: lands, 38.
Gotham, John de: appointed deputy receiver, 109.
Graland: witness to Deed, *c*. 1200., 6, 100.
Graunesden, John: Prior, 1458., 43, 93.
Grava, Thomas de: solicitor, 9, 102.
Grene, William: tenant, 55, 128.
Grunvull, Master Peter de: Official of Bishop, 16.
Guildford, Curia Regis held at, 103.
Guldeford, Henry de: licence to grant advowson of Crowhurst, 14, 104.
Guyot de Provins: Satire on Monastic Houses, 60, *n*.

Hamme, Manor of, 6.
Hammes, William de: land charged with payments of money and shoes, 6 and *n.*, 100.

INDEX.

Hamond, John: Prior, 1458., 40, 43, 93; Canon, continuing a, 125.
Hanaper, Great and Small: fees, 51.
Hansard, John, Sub-Prior, afterwards Prior: elected Prior, 1323., 27; election void, but appointed by Bishop, 28, 115, 116; incompetent and interdicted, 4, 29, 30; resigned, 30, 118; lease granted by, 12.
Harlyng, William: lessee, 46, 55, 128.
Harteslonde, in Tanridge, 45, 57, 132.
Hartfelde: see *Hertfyld*.
Harward's lands: in Tanridge, 54, 127.
Haysant, Robert, Canon: a sequestrator on vacancy, 41, 125.
Haywarde, John: lessee of Manor of Sentie, 45, 58, 136.
Heghstale, Master Hugh: Rector of Blechyngle, a sequestrator on vacancy, 40, 41, *n.*, 125.
Heiden, or Heyden, Thomas de: Justice, 9 and *n.*, 102.
Hemington, Richard de: Justice Itinerant, 11 and *n.*, 103.
Henedene: payment to lord of, 38.
Henry: Chaplain, witness to Deed, 6, 100.
Henry de Pecham: Prior, 1323., 21, 22, 23, 24, 27, 91 (see further, *Pecham*).
Henry VIII, King: conduct undefended, 52, *n.*; Brother of Order of St. Augustine, 65, 90.
Herfeld, Surrey: accounts with, 38.
Heriot, relief and homage, 38.
Hertfyld, Hertsfelde, or Hartfelde, Sussex: receipts from, 38; Manor of Sentie in, 45, 49, 136; lands in, 50, 58.
Hethe, John at: tenant, 38.
Hethe, William: tenant, 38, 54, 127.
Hethe lands in Tanridge,
Heyward, Robert: tenant, 54, 127.
History: preservation solely through Monasteries, 82; materials for early printed histories obtained from them, 83.
Holm: tenements in Oxsted, 55.
Holman, John: lessee, 46, 54, 127.
Holman, Richard: lessee, 46, 55, 128.
Holmdenne, Thomas: freeholder, 55, 127.
Holmes Land, 55, 127.
Holodenlyn, or Holyndene: King Edward I at, 12; receipts from, 38.
Horses kept by Canons, 71.
Hospice: Foundation originally of that nature, 2.
Hospital of St. James, Tanregge: Priory first so called, 2, 6, 7, 8, 100, 101; objects, 2; soon became Priory, 3.

Hospitality of Monasteries, 80.
Hostellar: duties of, 72.
Howard, Sir Henry: former possessor of earliest deed, 5, *n.*
Howewots: tenement, 39, 54, *n.*
Humfrey: Prior, 1262., 11, 90.
Hunting by Canons forbidden, 63, *n.*, 67 and *n.*
Huntley, Alice: lessee of land in Tanridge, 45, 57, 132.

Imprisonment of a Canon, 23, 110, 111.
Income: in 1407–8., 37 ; Rentale, 37, 38, 39, 44 ; at Dissolution, 4.
Induction of Prior by Archdeacon, 25.
Infirm Brothers: care of, enjoined, 18.
Inge, Master William, Archdeacon of Surrey: excommunicate, 35, 123.
Injunctions by Bishop to Tanridge Priory, 17, 18, 19, 105 ; to be recited at intervals, 18, 21, 106 ; to Merton Priory, 64, *n.*
Innocent II, Pope: Order at Lateran Council, 1139., 62.
Inquisition: held by Eschaetor, 25, 117 ; *ad quod damnum*, 14, 16, 29 and *n.*, 36 ; *post mortem*, 13, 35, 122.
Instruments on election of Prior, 16.
Insula, William de: Justice Itinerant, 10, 102.

James, St., Hospital of, in Tanregge: Priory first so called, 2, 6.
John: name of many Priors, 43 ; Hansard, 1323., 12, 27, 92 ; de Merstham, 1341., 33, 34, 37, 93 ; Fremyngham, 1441., 39, 40, 43, 93 ; Hamond, 1458., 43, 93 ; Graunesden, 1458., 43, 93 ; Odierne, 1463., 40, 43, 94 ; Kyrton, 1469., 40, 43, 94 ; Forster, 1500, 42, 43, 44, 94 ; Lyngfeld, 1524., 42, 44, 48, 50, 95.
John, St., Widow of John de, 36.
John, St., William de: witness, 8.
Jury on inquisition relating to mortmain, 26, 29.

King: charge payable to, 56 ; his Receiver of Augmentations, 56.
Kingestun, William de: solicitor, 9, 102.
King's College, Cambridge: payment to, 53.
Kitchen expenses: account weekly, 21.
Kitchener: duties of, 72.
Kyrton, John: Prior, 1469., 40, 43, 94, 125.

Lancaster: fees of Auditor of Duchy, 56, 129.
Lathum, Walter: affirmation in suit in court, 39, 124.
Latin or French spoken in chapter, 69, 82.

Laundecote, Luke de: witness, 6, 100.
Lawrence of Gloucester, Monk of St. Peter's, Professor of Sacred Theology: Commissioner for Visitation, 19, 22, 26, 107, *bis*, 108, 109, 113.
Leases granted by the Priory, 45, 54, 56, 57; by Monasteries within year of Dissolution, 47; of cows (with land), 45.
Leatherhead: John May, Perpetual Vicar of, present at election of Prior, 42.
Ledered: see *Leatherhead*.
Lee, Edward (Clerk): lessee of Crowhurst Rectory, 45, 58, 135.
Lee, John a: freeholder, 55, 127.
Legal proceedings conducted with extreme care, 33.
Legate: contribution to war in France, 45; Cardinal Wolsey, 66.
Leicester: General Chapter at, 65.
Letters Testimonial granted to Canon, 39.
Leukenore, or Leuknore, Geoffrey de: Justice Itinerant, 11 and *n.*, 103.
Lexinton, Robert de; Justice, 9 and *n.*, 102.
Licence to Canons to elect Prior, 21; for absence from High Mass, 17; for exit from House by Prior only, 17; by Prior of Newark for Canon to be Prior of Tanridge, 30.
Literature, Preservation of, by Monasteries, 80.
Littilbyry, or Littlebere, Martin de: Justice Itinerant, 11 and *n.*, 103.
Loke, John: tenant, 55, 128.
London, Henry de, Rector of Withihame: witness, 30, 118.
Londs, Le: land in Oxted, 55, 127.
Long Sutton, Hants; receipts from, 38, 50, 55, 129; Manor Court, 55, 129.
Lowe, Master John, Professor of Civil Law: witness, 30, 118.
Lullinge: land, 46, 54, 127.
Luxford, Christopher: tenant, 54, 127.
Luxford's lands in Tanridge, 127.
Lychefeld: Walter, Bishop of Coventry and, 14.
Lymenesfeld: Walter de Merstham, Parson of, grantor of land to the Priory, 36.
Lyngfeld, John: Prior, 1524., 42, 44, 48, 50, 95, 125.
Lyntoune, or Lyntonne, John: lessee of land, 46, 54, 127.
Lysinae, John: tenant, 39.

Maldon Manor: grant to Walter de Merton, 82.
Marten, John: lessee, 46, 55, 128.

Martyrology: nature of, 83, *n.*; Bishop's Statutes enrolled in, 20, 83 and *n.*, 108.

Mass, High: by note, required by Rule, 17, 105; all Canons present, 17.

Mass of Name of Jesus: musical, 67.

Mass of Holy Ghost: sung during proceedings on election of Prior, 41.

Mass of St. Mary, by note, required by Rule, 17, 67, 105.

Mathew, Stephen: tenant, 39.

Mathewe, Edmund: tenant, 39.

May, Master John, Vicar of Ledered: present at election of Prior, 42.

Meals with unfit secular persons forbidden, 18.

Melwards, Walter: tenant, 38.

Merewell Manor (and Chapel): residence of Bishop of Winchester, 15, 16, 22, 42, 109.

Merstham, John de: Prior, 1341., 33, 34, 37, 93, 122, 123, 124.

Merstham, Walter de, Parson of Lymenesfeld: grantor of land to Priory, 36.

Merton College, Oxford: origin from grant by Merton Priory, 82.

Merton Priory: Cartulary, 5, *n.*; grant to Tanridge, 7, 8; friend to Walter de Merton, 81; extensive properties, 84, *n.*; charge payable to, 36, 51, 56, 129; grant of lease by, 38; Episcopal Injunctions to, 64, *n.*; Prior Walter, 1217., 7, 101; Prior Thomas de Wllst, witness, 7, 101.

Merton: Walter de, 81.

Mertonefeld: land leased from Merton Priory, 38.

Mertonmede: land leased from Merton Priory, 38.

Mille, Henry at; tenant, 38.

Ministers' Accounts, 45, 48, 53, 54, *n.*, 126.

Mitchell, Robert: Prior, 1470., 41 and *n.*, 42, 44, 94.

Mitred Priors, 70.

Monasteries and Monastic Orders in England: histories of few Monasteries written, 2; no history of Monastic Orders, 1; early establishment, 72; sites selected, 76 and *n.*; ecclesiastical provision for the public, 85; centres of civilization, 81; seat of learning, literature, and history, 80, 81; support of the necessitous, 73; heavily taxed by king and pope, 73, 85; restrictions on wealth, 72; frequently in need, and causes of their poverty, 74, 84; properties widely spread, 84; Dissolution, 45, 46, 72, 77; pretences for, 47; real occasion, 60; surrender enforced by violence, 88; judicial murder of Abbots not surrendering, 88.

Monastic life in England little known, 1, 59; popular fallacies, 79; few fixed Rules, otherwise self governing, 59; and see *Canons Regular* and *Rules*.

Monks and Friars distinguished, 86.

Mores, Francis, or John: King's Receiver of Augmentations for Surrey, 56, 126, 130.

Mortmain: Statutes, 72; inquisition relating to, 26, 29, 117; licence in, 13, 14, 104.

Moultredens (or Multrydene), land called, 39, 46, 55.

Mowherste, Richard: tenant, 39.

Muleton, Thomas de: Justice, 9 and *n*., 102.

Multrydene (or Moultredens): land in Barrow, 39, 46, 55, 128.

Myllfelde, in Tanridge, 45, 57, 132.

Nagham: Widow of John de St. John of, 36.

Newark Priory: endowment, 5, *n*.; cellarer of Tanridge imprisoned at, 22, 110, 111; cost repaid them, 23, 112; Bishop there, 21, 111; Canons becoming Priors of Tanridge, 24, 30, 118; licence given by Priory, 30, 112,

Northampton, Priory of St. Andrew: confession by monks of worldliness and misdeeds, 89.

Northampton, William: tenant, 39.

Norwich, Ralph of: Justice Itinerant, 10, 102.

Note, Mass by; 17, 67, 105.

Novatra, William de: witness to Deed, 8, 101.

Novices on the foundation, 69.

Number of Canons of the Priory always limited, 3, 41.

Obedience to Prior on his appointment ordered, 25.

Object (original) of the foundation, 2, 6.

Occupation of Canons: not at volition but as most useful, 18.

Ocreis: shoes, 75 and *n*.

Odierne, John: Prior, 1463., 40, 43, 94.

Odo (or Eudo) de Dammartin, Founder of the Priory, 5, 6, 7, 8.

Odo, son of Odo de Dammartin: grant to the Hospital, 8; grant of mast and chase, 10; his seal, 8.

Official of Bishop: Master Peter de Grunvull, 16.

Officers of Tanridge Priory, 71; see *Prior, Sub-prior, Cellarer, Precentor, Seneschal*.

Oisel, Gillebert and Richalda: litigants with Tanridge Hospital, 10, 102.

Okested, see *Oxted*.
Oksted, Roland de : grant to Priory, 104.
Oksted, William de: grant to Priory, 12, 13, 104.
Order to receive penitent Canon back, 24.
Ordinances made on Visitation, 1308., 17, 18, 19, 108.
Organ : playing by layman permitted in Priory Church, 68.
Oteweyes: tenement called, 39.
Othobon: Legate of Apostolic See, 17, 105.
Overy, Priory of St. Mary: Robert Mitchell, Prior of Tanridge, translated to, 41, *n*.
Ovesnet : land, 46, 54, 127.
Ownsted, John: freeholder, 55, 128.
Oxen given by Founder, 7, 101.
Oxted, Okested, Okestede, or Acgstede : land at, granted to Priory, 12, 104, 117; lease, 45, 46, 57, 133; Welbeck Croft, 54; Mortmain question, 26, 29; manor and court, 37, 38, 39, 44, 49, 50, 51, 55, 56, 129.

Pagan, Robert, son of : witness to Deed, 8, 101.
Pakke, John : tenant, 39.
Parke, Le Olde : land, 46, 54, 127.
Pastoral Visitation by Bishop, 16.
Patents granting properties at Dissolution, 51, 52, 73.
Patershill, or Pateshull, Martin de : Justice, 9 and *n*., 102.
Pawles : tenement called, 39.
Pecham, Brother Henry de: cellarer, 21, 109; deprived, 22, 109; banished and imprisoned, 22, 110, 111; forbidden to celebrate, 23; punishment mitigated, 23, 111; permitted to return, 24, 111; appointed Prior, 1323., 91 ; death, 27, 92.
Pecies : lands called, 38.
Peckham, Archbishop: Constitutions for Monastic Orders, 64.
Pedeleshurst, Walter de: Prior, 1306., 15, 16, 91.
Penalty for absence from High Mass without licence, 17.
Pende, John de la, Canon : witness at election of Prior, 16 ; appointed deputy-cellarer, 26, 114; as Proctor for Priory, 115.
Pendrell, Andrew : land owner, 35.
Pension to Prior at Dissolution, 48, 125.
Perefricht, Peter de : witness to Deed, 6, 100.
Peter's pence, 37.
Pevensey Castle, payment to Warden of, 38.
Phelipps, tenement at Barowe, 55, 128.

Philip de Wokyngham: Prior, 1335., 30, 92; and see *Wokyngham, Philip de.*
Picards: tenement called, 39.
Pictlake: meaning, 6, *n.*
Piers Plowman's Crede; reference to Monastic life, 60, *n.*, 67, *n.*
Pimpe, Ralph: witness to Deed, 6, 100.
Pip^r., Ralph de: witness to Deed, 8, 101.
Pire, William: tenant, 39.
Pire, William at: tenant, 38.
Pitanciar: officer of a Priory, 72.
Plawe, John: tenant, 54, 127.
Plawe's holding in Tanridge, 127
Players forbidden entrance to Priory, 68.
Playz, Hugh de: Justice Itinerant, 10, 102.
Pond at Warlingham illegally enclosed, 11.
Poor, The: relief by Monasteries, 73.
Pope, Collection for the, 37.
Pope, John: lessee, 46, 54, 127.
Precentor: duties, 72; head, during vacancy of priorate, 25, 27, 115, 116; Thomas de Woldham, 1306., 16.
Prestfelde: land in Oxted, 55, 128.
Pretences for dissolution of Monasteries, 47.
Prick-song in Choir forbidden, 67.
Prior: qualifications and duties, 18, 21, 70; see *Election*; in default of due election appointed by Bishop, 4, 16, 24, 28, 37, 114, 115; obedience to, 25; attending Convocation, 41, 46; two in England mitred, 70; power of correction, &c., 17, 21; care of seal of Priory, 26, but interdicted, 27; incompetence or desertion (only recorded faults), 4, 31, 33; co-adjutor appointed, 26; pension at Dissolution, 48, 125.
Prior of Reigate: commissioner for installation of Prior, 34.
Prior, Sub-: position and duties, 71; presided at election of Prior, 70; had key of Priory seal, 26; gave licence of exit, 17, 105; election, 17; afterwards Prior, 40.
Priories in England: history of very few yet written, 2; officers, see *Prior, Sub-prior, Almoner, Cellarer, Chamberlain, Gardener, Hostellar, Kitchener, Pitanciar, Porter, Precentor, Refectioner, Sacristan, Seneschal, Treasurer.*
Priors: Thomas, 1226., 9, 90, 102; Adam, 1235., 10, 90, 102, *bis*, 108; Humfrey, 1262., 11, 90, 103; Walter de Pedeleshurst, 1306., 15, 16, 91; Walter de Hetfeld, 1309., 91; Thomas de St. Alban,

INDEX. 155

1309., 24, 25, 91, 112, 113, *bis;* Henry de Pecham, 1323., 21, 22, 23, 24, 27, 91, 92, 109, 110, 111 (see *Pecham, Henry de*); John Hansard, 1323., 12, 27, 92, 114, 118, and see *Hansard, John*; Philip de Wokyngham, 1335., 30, 92, and see *Wokyngham, Philip de;* John de Merstham, 1341., 33, 34, 37, 93, 122; Richard French, 1380., 37, 93; William Sondercsh, 1404., 37, 93; John Fremyngham, 1441., 39, 40, 43, 93, 124; John Hamond, 1458., 43, 93; John Graunesden, 1458., 43, 93; John Odierne, 1463., 40, 43, 94; William West, 1464., 40, 94; John Kyrton, 1467., 40, 43, 94, 125; Robert, 1470., 94; William, 1470., 94; Robert Mitchell, 1495., 41 and *n.*, 42, 44, 94, 95; Robert Wodd, 1499., 42, 94; John Forster, 1500., 42, 43, 44, 94; John Lyngfeld, 1524., 42, 44, 48, 50, 95, 125.

Priors, on Dissolution; many appointed Bishops, Deans, or Canons, 89.
Priorsfelde, Godstone: field, 46, 55, 128.
Priory Church: see *Tanridge Priory.*
Priory of Tanridge, 1, 2; and see *Tanridge.*
Prison orders relating to a Canon, 23.
Proceedings at election of Prior, 41.
Proctor of Precentor and Canons, 27, 28, 34.
Property of the Priory, in 1200., 3, 100; in 1291., 13; value unknown to cellarer, 1308., 20; Tanridge, Crowhurst, and Godstone Churches, 49; Chelsham and Warlingham, 35; grant by Walter de Merstham, 36, 101; value of, in Tanridge and Wolkenstede, 36; at Dissolution, 3, 4, 48, 74; property of all dissolved Monasteries granted to the King, 47.
Proxy of Chapter, under Seal, 15.
Pyrres, land at Oxted, 55, 128.
Pytches, Conny: land, 46.

"Quia propter" Constitution of General Council, 41.

Ralph, Chaplain of Rigate: witness to Deed, 6, 100.
Ralph: Dean, 101.
Ralph, Parcarius: witness to Deed, 7, 100.
Reade, John: see *Rede.*
Reading: judicial murder of Abbot of, 88.
Recreation in moderation, 68.
Rede, Anthony: grantee in remainder, 51.
Rede, Henry: grantee in succession, 51.

Rede (or Reade), John: grantee of House and site at Dissolution, 49, 51, 52, 53, 56, 77, *n.*, 130, 131, 132, 133, 134, 135, 136, 137.
Rede, Thomas: grantee in remainder, 51, 52.
Rede, William, of Weybridge: father of grantee of House, 49, 51.
Redmigersh, John: holder of Knight's fees, 35.
Refectioner, duties of, 72.
Reforms needed from time to time, 65.
Reigate: Chaplain of (Ralph), 6, 100; Prior of, commissioner of Bishop, 34, 123; contribution towards war in France, 45; Robert Mitchell, Prior of Tanridge, translated to, 41, *n.*
Relics given by Founder, 7, 101.
Rentale in 15th century, 37, 38, 39, 44.
Richard French: Prior, 1380., 37, 93.
Richardson, John, of Diocese of Carlisle, Notary Public: present at election of Prior, 42.
Rigate, Ralph, chaplain of: witness to Deed, 6.
Robert: chaplain; witness to Deed, 7, 101.
Robert: Prior, 1499., 41, 94.
Robert Mitchell: Prior, 1470., 41 and *n.*, 42, 44, 94.
Robert Wodd, or Wode, Sir: Prior, 1499., 42, 94.
Robyn's Grove: land at Barrow, 46, 55, 128.
Rodondella: a cloke, 75 and *n.*
Rokesnest Manor, 46, 57, 131.
Rules of Order of Austin Canons: by St. Augustine the Great, 17; subsequent constitutions, 62; generally, 59, 60, 61; Wolsey's code, 65, 82, entered in Martyrology, 83; unity, and life in common, 61, 62; few fixed rules, otherwise each house self governing, 59; religious duties, 61, 64, *n.*; attendance at High Mass, 17; performance of Divine Service, 67; abstinence, 61; food only in refectory, 68; silence, 17, 68, 105; behaviour, 62; accounts kept and periodically rendered, 68; absence only by leave, 66, 105; recreation, 68; hunting forbidden, 63, *n.*, 67, *n.*; and sporting dogs or birds, 67; clothing, 18, 62, 63 and *n.*, 64, *n.*, 66, 67 and *n.*; tonsure, 67.
Rustynton, Sir Laurence de: co-adjutor of Prior, 29, 117.
Ryche, Richard: signing Order of Court of Augmentations, 48, 126.

Sacrilege: pretences for, 47.
Sacristan: duties of, 72.
St. John, William de: witness to Deed, 8, 101.
Sale by King: through Court of Augmentations, 50.

INDEX. 157

Salisbury, William of York, Bishop of: Justice Itinerant, 10 and *n*.

Sawnders: tenement called, 39.

Schire, Schyr, or Shyre, William de: Canon (of some other House), Bailiff: appointed receiver, 20, 22, 107, 108; cellarer, 22, 109; inspecting timber, 20.

Schirford, Simon de: preparing form of account, 20, 107.

Schools, Free: instituted by Monasteries, 82; only partially continued by name of Grammar Schools, 82.

Scolys, Master Roger: Notary Public, 33, 121.

Scotenenye, Robert, Canon: Proctor of Priory, 122.

Scott's Croft, in Tanridge, 45, 57, 132.

Seal of Chapter, 15.

Seal of Priory, 18, 42, 106; requisite for important matters, 18; kept under triple keys, 26, 114; use interdicted, 27.

Seneschal of the House, 68, 127; of Court, 56, 129; duties, 54, 71.

Seni, Benedick la: tenant, 38.

Sentie, or Seynt Tie, Manor in Hartfelde, Sussex: lease of, 45, 136; grant at Dissolution, 49, 52, 53, 58.

Sequestration: on vacancy, 40, 125; on account of dilapidations, 40, 74, 125.

Servants kept by Canons, 71.

Seynt Tie: vide *Sentie.*

Sheriff of County: payment for, 37.

Shoes, as part of rent-charge, 6.

Shortehal, Robert de: land-holder, 10, 102.

Shyre, William de: see *Schire, William de.*

Silence observed, according to Rules, 17, 105.

Singing: rules for, 67.

Site (see *Tanridge Priory*) granted at Dissolution to John Rede, 49.

Skynner, John: payment to, 51.

Skynner, John: Seneschall of Court, 56, 129.

Skynners: tenement called, 39.

Smythe, William: freeholder, 55, 128.

Smythes: tenement so called, 38.

Sonderesh, William: Prior, 1404., 37, 93.

Sondressche, Kent: accounts with, 38.

Sontynge, John de: Canon of Tanridge, 34, 122.

Sotulares: boots, 75 and *n.*

Souls of faithful departed, daily celebration for, 3.

Southwark, Bishop at, 114, 115, 116; and see *Suthewerke.*

Sow given by Founder, 7, 101.

Sowthelonds, or Sowthlonds, in Tanridge: lease of, 45; rent of, 57, 131.
Spiritualty: contribution to war expenses in France, 45.
Spoliation of Monastic Houses, 52.
Squyer, John: lessee of land, 46, 54, 127.
Standford, Edmund: tenant, 54, 127.
Standford's land, in Tanridge, 127.
Stanegrave, Robert de: feoffor of land at Crowhurst, 14.
Stangrave, Robert de: mesne lord of land, 36.
Stoket, John: tenant, 38.
Stonehurst, Robert: tenant, 39.
Strangave, Sir Robert de: Head of some other House, 20, 108.
Student sent to University, 69.
Studmerhill: land in Tanridge, 46, 54, 127.
Sub-Prior: see *Prior, Sub-*.
Suffolk, Charles, Duke of: Brother of the Order, 65, 90.
Suppression or dissolution of Monasteries, 45, 46, 87, *n*.
Surrender of Monasteries: enforced by violence, 88; Abbot of Reading judicially murdered for refusal, 88.
Surrender of Tanridge Priory: apparently 1536., 48.
Surrey, Archdeacon of: certifying due citation, 15; Commissioner for Visitation, 21, 109: to induct new Prior, 25, 115; procurations payable to, 51, 56, 129; excommunicate, 35, 124.
Surrey, Eschaetor for County of: holding Inquisition, 25, 29, 117; Receiver of Augmentations, 126, 130.
Suthewerke Conventual Church: proceedings there on election of Prior, 27, 101, 114, 115.
Sutton, Long, Hants: receipts from, 38, 50, 55, 129; Manor Court, 55, 129.

Talewrth, Adam and Peter de: witnesses to Deed, 8, 101.
Tandridge, modern spelling of *Tanridge*.
Tannerigge: see *Tanridge*.
Tanregge: see *Tanridge*.
Tanridge, spelt variously: Tandridge (modern), Tannerigge, Tanregge, Tanrigge, Tanrugge, Tanryg, Tenrugg.
Tanridge Church: belonging to Priory, 49, 50; Sir William, Chaplain, 34, 122; stipend, 51.
Tanridge Manor: early mention, 12, 44; annual payment to Priory, 122; at Dissolution, 49.
Tanridge Priory (and see *Priors* and *Canons*): history hitherto slight, 1; date of foundation, 5; Grant of Fraternity to, 36, 101; then

called Hospital of St. James, 2, 6, 100; called a Priory in 1226, 9; spoken of as a College, 3, 15; dedicated to St. James, 77 and n.; provision for Chaplain, 3, 12; chapel and altar of B. Virgin, 77; church, bell-tower, cemetry, and site, granted at Dissolution, 49, 77; site of cloisters, 78; ponds and vivaria, 49, 50, 76; small capital of pillar preserved, 77; engravings of, 1, 77; coffin-lids, 78; buildings utterly destroyed, 76; paving tiles, 77; leases granted, 45, 46, 47; whether surrendered, not known, 48; Archbishop of Canterbury there in 1296., 13; contribution towards wars in France, 45; dissolved in 1536., 48; property at Dissolution, 4, 74, 126.

Tanridge Priory: Canons bound by Rules of Order, 59, 60, 61; number always small, 3, 41, 70; directed to be kept up, 69; clothing according to Rule, and uniform, 18, 80, 105, and see *Rules*; all to be present at High Mass, 17; those in priest's orders to celebrate at appointed places, 17; one to be a chaplain, 3, 12; grant for chaplain, 36; to confess to prior, 17, and see *Chapter of Priory*; coffins, 78; charged with expenses of banished Canon, 23; corredy, as selected precedent, 83; Canons, 33, 34, and see *Priors* and *Officers;* church, bell-tower, and cemetry, granted at Dissolution, 49; Altar of B. Mary, 12.

Tanridge, Ville: mentioned at foundation of Priory, 2, 6; land, 9, 11, 13, 45, 102; granted to Priory, 36, 38; tenements called Botelers, Chamberlonds, Downlonds, Hartelonde, Myllfelde, Scott's Crofte, 45, 57; Studmerhill, 46.

Tanrigge: see *Tanridge.*
Tanrugge: see *Tanridge.*
Tanryg: see *Tanridge.*
Taxation: by Pope Nicholas IX, 13; towards wars in France, 45.
Techele: land so called, 38.
Te Deum laudamus: sung at election and confirmation of Prior, 34, 70, 123.
Tenrugg: see *Tanridge.*
Testimonial, Letters: granted to Canon, 39.
Thaleuurthe, or Talewrth, Peter de: witness to Deed, 6, 100.
Thomas: Prior, 1225., 9, 90, 102.
Thomas de St. Alban: Prior, 1309., 24, 25, 91.
Thomas de Wllst, Prior of Merton: witness to Deed, 7.
Thomlyn's Londs in Oxted: lease of, 45, 57, 133.
Timber: cut down only by assent of Chapter, 18, 106; by assent of Bishop's Commissioners, 20, 107.
Topsell, George: lessee, 45, 57, 131.

Topsell, Richard: lessee, 45, 132.
Torner, Henry: tenant, 54, 127.
Treasurer: duties of, 72.
Turbeville, Hamon de: witness to Deed, 6, 100.
Turneham, Ralph de: witness to Deed, 6, 100.
Turneys Lands, in Tanridge, 54, 127.
Tyccheseye, John de: taking part in election of Prior, 16.
Tyle House, Le: lease of, 57, 131.

Veni Creator Spiritus: sung at election of Prior, 41.
Vestments given by Founder, 7, 101.
Viâ compromissi: Prior appointed by, 41, 42.
Visitation of Monastic Houses, 64; of Tanridge Priory, by Bishop, 16, 31, 105, 118; ordinance thereon, 16; by Bishop's Commissioners, 19, 21, 26, 105, 109; by Vicar-General, 68.
Walkenestede, Walkamstede, Walkinsted, Wawensted, Wolkenstede, Wolkestede, or Wolkhamstedd, (otherwise Godstone): grants to Priory, 36, 46, 55; at Dissolution, 49, 50; Perpetual Vicar, 35, 123; tithes, 57, 134.
Walter, Prior of Merton: charter given by him and the Priory, 7, 101.
Walter de Hetfield: Prior, 1309., 91.
Walter de Pedeleshurst: Prior, 1306., 15, 16, 91.
Waltham, Bishop's, Hants: Bishop's residence, 32, 120.
Waltham, Essex: Prior of, mitred, 70.
Wambergh, Adam de: Official of Winchester and Commissary-General, 33, 118, 119, 122.
Warblington, Thomas de: litigant with Priory, 1262., 11, 103.
Warblynton, probably *Warlynham, Warlingham*.
Ware, Master John de: Advocate in Winchester Consistory, 33, 121.
Warin, son of Joel (or Fitz-Joel): Justice 1226., 9 and *n*., 102.
Warkyngton, probably *Warlynham, Warlingham*.
Warlingham, Warlynham, Warlinggeham: land given for endowment, 6, 13, 100; inquisition as to knight's fee, 35; pond enclosed by Priory, 11; Garston, 49.
Warlingham, Manor of Westhall: claim, 12; lands, 46, 136; inquisition, 26, 29; leased, 30.
Warlynham, John de, Senr. and Junr.: inq. *post mortem*, 35, 36, 122.
Warranty of land given for endowment, 6.
Washing by Canons, or men appointed, 66.
Water, Holy: received after compline, 68.

Watson, Simon, of Diocese of York, Notary Public: present at election of Prior, 42.
Wauton, John and Alice de: litigant with Hospital, 1226., 9, 102.
Wawensted (otherwise Godstone): grant at Dissolution, 49, 50.
Welbeck Croft: land in Oxted, 54, 127.
Welbeck, Maurice: freeholder, 54, 127.
West, William: Prior, 1464., 40, 94.
Westhall Manor, in Warlingham: claim in respect to, 12; leased to Rector of Collesdon, 30; lands in, 46, 136.
Westminster: Curia Regis held at, 9, 102; Patent dated at, 104; Order of Court of Augmentations dated at, 48, 126.
Weybridge: Rede family, of, 49.
Whynn, John: tenant, 38.
Wigram, Mr. Percy: possessor of still existing capital, 77, *n*.
Wilkin, Richard: tenant, 38.
Wilkin, Thomas: tenant, 38.
William, Chaplain: witness to Deed, *c.* 1220., 7, 101.
William, Sir: Chaplain of Tanridge Church, 34, 122.
William de Dammartin: father of Founder, 5, 6, 7.
William de Dammartin, son of Founder: witness to Deed, *c.* 1200., 6; witness to Deed 13th cent., 8.
William Sonderesh: Prior, 1404., 37, 93.
William West: Prior, 1464., 40, 94.
Wiltshire, William, Canon: Letters Testimonial granted to him by Bishop, 39, 124.
Winchester, Bishop of: Injunctions to Merton Priory, 64, *n.*; Injunctions to Tanridge Priory, 105, 108.
Winchester: Consistory held there, 19.
Withihame: Henry de London, Rector of, 30, 118.
Withyham Manor, Sussex, 38, 53.
Wlkest, Eustace de: witness to Deed 13th cent., 8, 101.
Wllst, Thomas de, Prior of Merton: witness to Deed *c.* 1220., 7, 101.
Wodd, or Wode, Sir Robert: Prior, 1499., 42, 94.
Wokyngham, Philip de, of Newark Priory: prudent and circumspect, 30, 118; appointed by Bishop to be Prior of Tanridge, 30, 92; commission to cite him, 118; citation, 119; deprived for desertion of duty, 4, 30, 31, 34, 120, 121, 123, 124.
Woldham, Thomas de, Canon: proxy for chapter on election of Prior, 1306., 15, 16.
Wolkenestede: } See *Walkenestede.*
Wolkhamstedd:

Wolsey, Cardinal: a Brother of the Order, 65, 90; his titles, 66; his Rules for the Order, 66, 82.

Wolveleye, John de: Commissary of Bishop, 33, 122, 123.

Wolveseye Palace, Bishop at, 40, 125.

Women: endowment warranted against claims by, 6; forbidden on premises, except in Church, 66; if suspected, converse with them forbidden, 18, 106.

Woods not to be cut without common assent, 18.

Worlingham: see *Warlynham*.

Wythyhamme, Sussex: payment to Court of, 38, 53.

Yard, Senr.: Richard a, *or* at; tenant, 38, 39.

York, William de: Justice Itinerant, 1235., 10 and *n*., 102.

www.ingramcontent.com/pod-product-compliance
Lightning Source LLC
Chambersburg PA
CBHW020304170426
43202CB00008B/487